Jo Wood

HEY JO

Jo Wood

HEY JO

A Rock and Roll Fairytale

HarperCollins*Publishers*

HarperCollins*Publishers*
77–85 Fulham Palace Road,
Hammersmith, London W6 8JB

www.harpercollins.co.uk

First published by HarperCollins*Publishers* 2013

2

A catalogue record of this book is
available from the British Library

HB ISBN 978-0-00-745846-2
TPB ISBN 978-0-00-745847-9

Printed and bound in Great Britain by
Clays Ltd, St Ives plc

MIX
Paper from
responsible sources
FSC www.fsc.org   FSC® C007454

FSC™ is a non-profit international organisation established to promote
the responsible management of the world's forests. Products carrying the
FSC label are independently certified to assure consumers that they come
from forests that are managed to meet the social, economic and
ecological needs of present and future generations,
and other controlled sources.

Find out more about HarperCollins and the environment at
www.harpercollins.co.uk/green

While every effort has been made to trace the owners of copyright material
reproduced herein and secure permissions, the publishers would like to
apologise for any omissions and will be pleased to incorporate missing
acknowledgements in any future edition of this book

For my children, Jamie, Leah, Ty and Jesse,
because I love them.

Acknowledgements

I have to thank Catherine Woods, who I thoroughly enjoyed writing this book with. To Carole Tonkinson, my editor, and all at HarperCollins for their hard work and patience. My agent, Eddie Bell, who got the ball rolling. Emily, for all her help and for being so wonderful. Amy, Trudi, Dolly and all in my office. Alan Dunn and my touring family. Lorraine, my long-time friend and her family, who I adore. My wonderful friends, Keith, Patti and the Richards gang, and Keith's manager, Jane Rose, who is my great friend. Dympna my oldest school friend. My mum and dad for my life. My grandchildren, my nephews and niece, my brothers and my sister, I love you all so much. To Fran, Meg, Kate and Mairead. To all my new friends, there are too many names to mention, you know who you are. Katy England for styling and to all those I have loved and laughed with. And finally to Ronnie, who was a major part of my life; I thank him from the bottom of my heart for my rock and roll fairy tale.

Prologue

Sunday, 26 August 2007
London

I was already awake, lying in bed, enjoying the last few moments of peace, when my alarm went off. I glanced over at Ronnie, but he didn't stir. It was midday, and I could see from the light pouring between the curtains in our bedroom that it was another beautiful English summer day.

I grabbed my robe and tiptoed downstairs to make myself a coffee. It was Sunday, and the house was completely quiet. I guessed Leah and her boyfriend, Jack, must still be upstairs in bed – and, looking out of the window, there seemed to be no sign of life from the little cottage in the garden where Tyrone was living.

As I waited for the machine to brew an espresso, I felt a little leap of happiness at being able to reach for *my* cup from *my* kitchen cupboard. It was so wonderful to be back in our own home in London after nearly two years on the road.

A Bigger Bang had lived up to its name: it had been the Stones' most epic tour yet. The boys had played China for the first time, and in Rio, an unbelievable one million people had come to watch their show on Copacabana beach. Keith had fallen out of a tree while we were on holiday in Fiji, scaring the hell out of us and leading to the cancellation of some dates while he recovered from brain surgery. But now here we were, back on home turf – and tonight was the very last show of the whole tour.

I had a quick shower and got dressed (black top, black mini-skirt, black tights and black Dior biker boots – colour is banned when you're working backstage) – then did my hair and put on loads of black kohl and mascara, the makeup essentials I've been wearing since my teens and could probably apply in my sleep. There was no time to make much of an effort with my appearance: I had to make sure everyone was ready to leave the house at 2 p.m. and get Ronnie to the venue in good time for the sound check two hours later.

By now the kids were stirring. Leah chatted to me in the kitchen while I made Ronnie's breakfast – a cup of tea, poached eggs and toast – then took it upstairs to him on a tray. He liked simple food, but never ate much. It would drive me crazy when I'd spent hours making an amazing meal and he ended up pushing it round the plate. Recently, Kate Moss joked to me that he was anorexic …

'Honey, time to wake up,' I said gently. 'I've brought up your breakfast.'

I got a sleepy grunt in return.

I heard the crunch of car wheels on gravel and looked out of the bedroom window to see a black Mercedes and a minivan pulling up outside the house. I waved to Gardie, Ronnie's Australian security guy, as he got out of the Merc. Show days in London were always madness because everyone, including friends, family and acquaintances, wanted to come to the gig. Today there would be Leah and Jack, Ty, Jamie and Jody, Jesse and Tilly *and* all the grandkids – hence the need for the van.

Hey Jo

As Ronnie showered and dressed, I packed his gig bag: a spare T-shirt for after the show, a towelling robe, extra backstage passes for any unexpected guests – all the essentials. For the past 20 years I'd worked as Ronnie's PA on all the Stones tours, so the only thing he had to worry about was getting up on stage and playing the guitar. The tours had got so huge, so spectacular, that they had to be run with military discipline. It was a far cry from when I had first hit the road with the Stones in the late seventies. The 1981 Tattoo You tour of the States had been particularly insane. Fuelled by coke and a virtual pharmacy of pills, we'd stayed up for days at a time, drinking and joking and having such a laugh. My motto was: 'If it isn't fun, it isn't worth doing.' I don't remember much of that tour, but we'd been so out of control that, when the time came for the boys to hit the road again (not until 1989: Mick and Keith fell out over Mick releasing his solo album), Mick had decided that we had to start being more professional.

'Ronnie needs a PA,' he'd said. 'You're with him on tour the whole time, Jo. You've got the job.'

'You mean I get paid for going on tour? Oh, yeah!'

'Yes, but you have to do your job properly,' said Mick, pointedly. 'No being late with the packing.'

I squirmed. During the Tattoo You tour we had fallen asleep following a three-day party. Security had burst into our hotel room just moments before we were due to leave for a gig to find the place trashed, with Ronnie and me passed out in the middle of it. That night the boys were three hours late and the audience were going wild by the time they finally made it on stage.

'Don't worry, Mick,' I said. 'You can trust me.'

From then on I was on the payroll – and was never late with the packing again.

I checked my watch: 1.55 p.m. Time to round up the troops. 'Come on, everyone, let's go – let's go! Have you all got your backstage passes?'

The kids and grandkids piled into the van, Ronnie and I climbed into the Merc with Gardie – and we were off. From our house in Kingston to the O2 arena it was far quicker to go by water rather than by road, so the cars dropped us at the pier in Putney where a boat was waiting.

It was a beautiful ride along the Thames and Ronnie was in a great mood. We chatted about the guests who were coming that night and the plans for the end-of-show party. As Ronnie had been touring for 30 years this was just another normal day's work for him, but he loved his job as much as ever. Getting up on that stage, doing what he did best, while night after night thousands of people screamed in adoration. Girls still threw themselves at him so blatantly that I sometimes felt I was in the way – especially now I was older. But in a few weeks' time we would be celebrating the thirtieth anniversary of our first date. We'd had our ups and downs, but we were still strong, and as we were coming to the end of a two-year slog we would finally have some time to ourselves to enjoy the rewards of all that hard work.

As we sped down the river, though, the sun sparkling on the water, I felt a twinge of sadness at the thought of it all coming to an end. I loved being on tour and would miss everyone hugely: not just the boys in the band, their wives and kids, but the backing musicians, roadies, security guys, office and tour staff, too. We had worked together for so long, we were like one big, crazy family.

The boat docked right next to the O2, where we jumped into waiting cars for the two-second drive inside the stadium. Being part of the Rolling Stones family is to live in a magical kingdom, where everything is taken care of and nothing is too much trouble. You're given the best tables in restaurants, you fly first class, you get the best limos to the best hotels – God forbid you should actually have to *walk* a few metres!

I went straight to Ronnie's dressing room, known as 'Recovery' on this tour, to drop off the gig bag, organize myself for the evening, and check that everything on his tour rider (an artist's list of backstage demands) was in the room. In the old days this would have meant loads of booze, but now that Ronnie tried to stay sober on tour it was bottles of Vitaminwater, a coffee machine and sometimes a plain chicken sandwich. I liked to make the room feel homely, so there would also be lilies, incense and scented candles.

While Ronnie hung out in Keith's dressing room (known as 'Camp X-ray'), I went off to talk to Isabol in Wardrobe and pick out Ronnie's clothes for the show. First, though, I stopped off to see Lisa Portman, who looked after Mick, to find out what colour he'd be wearing that night. If he was wearing red or blue, the rest of the boys couldn't wear red or blue. The only person who didn't comply with this was Keith. He would just pull stuff out at random and wear whatever he pleased.

Ronnie always wore the same shoes and skinny black jeans for shows, but I selected a couple of jackets and three tops for him to pick from that night, so he'd feel like he'd chosen his outfit. On the way back to the dressing room Caroline, the makeup artist, stuck her head out of the door.

'I need him at five fifteen today, Jo,' she said. 'Oh, and if you see Bobby Keys, will you send him over to me?'

'No problem.'

This was always my favourite time of the day on tour, when the excitement and energy were growing in the build-up to that night's show. I passed Mick in the corridor and said hi, then headed to the lounge. This was the hospitality room where all the guests and backing musicians would hang out in the run-up to the show. At the O2 the lounge took up a whole floor, as everyone had family and friends coming. Dinner was always set out during the sound check so it was ready to eat as soon as the doors opened at 6 p.m. Like a hotel buffet, there would always be loads of choice: salad, cheese, fish and chips, some sort of meat dish, a vegetarian option – and almost always an organic meal, too. I had first asked for this in the early nineties and the caterers had been brilliant at sourcing organic food wherever we had been in the world; in fact, there had been only a couple of places where they hadn't managed it. Sometimes I brought along organic produce from my own vegetable patch, too: on one tour I smuggled a whole suitcase of new potatoes to Paris, and backstage there was a huge bowl of them, dripping in butter, labelled, 'Jo's Organic Potatoes'. Every single one was eaten.

It was after the potato-smuggling incident that Keith said to me, 'The trouble with you, Josephine, is that you're addicted to organic food.'

I had to laugh. '*Addicted?* That's a bit rich coming from you, Keith!'

At eight thirty, with moments to go before show time, I headed down to the stage and positioned myself by the flight cases, the huge containers used to transport the band's kit around the world, so I'd be right there when Ronnie came on, in case he needed something. The roar of the crowd grew in anticipation and then – *POW!* Literally a bigger bang, as fireworks showered sparks all over the stage and the screens showed the Stones' tongue logo in the midst of a huge explosion. Then as the smell of smoke and hot lights filled the air, the lights came up and the opening guitar notes of 'Start Me Up' boomed out into the arena.

Wow. I never got tired of experiencing the first thrilling moments of a show.

I stayed by the amp for the first two songs and then, once I knew Ronnie was happy, it was back to the dressing room to lay out his robe and pack up the gig bag. I rarely watched a whole show, preferring to catch up with the rest of the crew, but I would always go back to my spot on the stage to watch Ronnie's solos and for the final few songs when they played all the classics: 'Paint It Black', 'Satisfaction', 'Brown Sugar' … The boys swapped it around every night so they never played the same set two shows in a row.

I went back to the lounge and found the logistics manager and Mick's PA, Alan Dunn, who was grabbing a bite to eat. I adored Alan; I'd known him for almost as long as I'd known Ronnie and we had a wonderful, flirty friendship. Years ago the Stones were working on an album in Montserrat and Alan – who didn't really drink – got so drunk downing B52 shots that he stripped naked and started chasing me around the garden waving his willy at me. No one blinked an eyelid, and in the end I had to lock myself in the bathroom to escape. I had so many funny times with Alan.

I'd never usually drink at a show, but tonight we had the end-of-tour party to look forward to after the gig, so I poured Alan and myself a small glass of wine each. We'd been chatting for a few minutes when I glanced at the set list. In a few minutes' time the boys would be playing 'Can't You Hear Me Knocking', with my favourite of Ronnie's solos. I said goodbye to Alan, promising to continue our chat at the party.

The song was just starting as I arrived back at my spot behind the amp on stage. It was a great show tonight – UK audiences were always loud and loyal, although they usually needed a bit of time to warm up. Typical British reserve, I guess. I could make out some of the fans' faces at the front of the crowd, but after the first few rows it seemed to be just an expanse of darkness, lit only by the flashes of cameras and phones. Standing on that stage listening to music that was so familiar to me, surrounded by people I'd known for years (not just the musicians, but all the roadies, riggers and tech guys behind the scenes, too), I truly felt like I was home.

Just to the side of where I was standing I could see Charlie Watts drumming away with fantastically precise rhythm. He caught me looking at him and pulled a face. I love Charlie; I could never tire of watching him play the drums. Darryl Jones on bass was standing just past him and then, bounding across the stage, shaking maracas, there was Mick. The guy is such a fantastic showman. I've never seen anyone else take an audience like he can and hold them in his hand for the entire show. I popped my head up a bit higher so I could see Keith, who was across on the other side. I've been lucky enough to meet some legends in my time – Bob Marley, Jerry Lee Lewis, Bill Clinton, Muhammad Ali, Madonna, Chuck Berry, Aretha Franklin, Marvin Gaye and, yes, of course, Mick Jagger, but Keith is the most extraordinary person, and one of my dearest friends.

Right at the front, Ronnie was getting stuck into his solo. *Oh, my honey!* Seeing him on stage still gave me goose-bumps. Whenever there had been hard times, whether it was his alcoholism, drugs or other women, it was in moments like this that all the bad stuff was forgotten. I was married to a creative genius, there was no doubt about it.

But as the roar of the audience drowned the last notes of the song, I was suddenly struck by the intense conviction that this was the last time I would be standing there, watching the Stones. It was almost like a premonition. *Make the most of this moment, Jo: you're never going to experience it again.* It hit me so unexpectedly, and with such force, that I was left quite emotional. *Where the hell did that come from? It must have been because it's the last show*, I thought. But, no, it was definitely more than end-of-tour blues. It was a feeling – a certainty – that everything was about to change; that my life would never be the same again.

If you had said to me at that moment that actually my premonition had been spot on and that I would never experience the thrill of touring with the Stones again, I probably wouldn't have been that surprised. I was in my early fifties; I was a granny. I had no regrets – after all, I'd been there, done that and got the T-shirt. Having clocked up 30 years on the road alongside the Rolling Stones, I'd *designed* the bloody T-shirt!

No, what would have shocked me – in fact, what would have absolutely devastated me – would have been to know that in less than a year's time I would have lost Ronnie. My world, my love, my everything.

1

'Ladies and gentlemen,' cried the circus ringmaster, 'the moment you've all been waiting for! Prepare to be amazed by the Fabulous Flying Josephine!'

I stood on my bed, waving at the crowd below, then took a deep breath and launched myself onto the trapeze. I flew through the air in a series of death-defying spins and landed gracefully on the ground as the audience went wild.

'Thank you, thank you!' I bowed, graciously acknowledging their cheers.

I picked up Bella, my favourite doll, who was that day playing the part of the ringmaster, and waved her arm at a couple of teddies.

'And now, bring on the clowns!'

I've always been a daydreamer. As a little girl I spent most of my time living in a fantasy world. I'd see something on TV or read a story and my imagination would run riot. As well as the circus phase, there was the time I saw a film about a little girl who wanted to be an actress and dreamt of 'seeing her name in lights'. From then on I was obsessed. *One day, my name will be in lights, too!* If *Britain's Got Talent* had existed I'm sure I'd have been first in line for the auditions. Seeing as I can't really sing and

– as viewers of the BBC's *Strictly Come Dancing* will vouch – have two left feet, I'm not sure what my talent would have been, but I doubt that would have stopped me having a go.

My mum did everything she could to feed and encourage my overactive imagination. I'd find tiny letters hidden about the house from Tinker Bell, postage-stamp-sized envelopes containing a note written in tiny fairy writing: 'Dearest Josephine, Mummy tells me you've been very helpful this week …' One day I came home from school to discover all 20 of my dolls lined up on the bed dressed in identical knitted jumpers and stretchy ski-pants. Mum must have been buzzing away on her sewing-machine for months, but to me it was as if it had happened in the wave of a magic wand. She had a real fairytale touch when I was growing up – and still does to this day.

Mum – Rachel Ursula Lundell – was born in 1934 in the heat and dust of South Africa's Eastern Cape, in a tiny village called Tsolo. My grandfather, George, was a Dutch builder, while his wife, Ellen, was the granddaughter of a woman of the Xhosa-speaking Pondo tribe. Ellen was the last of seven children and my mum, too, was the youngest of seven. According to folklore, the seventh daughter of a seventh daughter is capable of great magic, and Mum has always been convinced by her 'powers'. She will tell you about the time she cured the local butcher of his warts and healed her neighbour's eczema with just a touch. But whether or not Mum really does have supernatural powers, I definitely think there's something a little bit magical about the story of how this young African girl ended up travelling to the other side of the world and falling in love with my dad, who lived in leafy Surrey.

From a young age, Mum had a headstrong streak. She was sent to a convent boarding-school, where she got up to all sorts of naughtiness. She once broke into the convent pantry with her friend, Audrey, and the pair smuggled some sugar out in their bras. Weeks later, by the time the nuns broke up the racket, Mum and Audrey had turned professional, taking orders and selling the sugar to friends. Mum got 16 lashes with the *sjambok*, a heavy leather bullwhip. She's still got the scars, but she reckons it cured her sweet tooth for good.

When she was 12, a witch-doctor read her fortune and told her she would travel overseas, but it wasn't until she was 17 that something happened to seal the deal. By this time South Africa was in the grip of apartheid. The population was segregated by skin colour: black, white or – in Mum's case, as she was mixed-race – coloured. Shortly after leaving school she applied for a typist's job in a bakery where her brother, Desmond, was already working. The bakery woman couldn't have been nicer to the pretty, golden-haired girl with the Dior-style lace dress and quickly offered her the position, but just as they were walking to the door, Mum spotted Desmond and waved to him.

'Do you know that man?' the woman asked her.

'Yes, he's my brother,' said Mum.

The woman stared at her. 'I'm sorry,' she said quickly, 'but I can't give you the job.' She hadn't realized that Mum wasn't white.

In 1951 Rachel waved goodbye to Africa and went to England to stay with her sister, Joan, who was living in Surbiton with her English husband, a press photographer named Tony Booker, and got a secretarial job with the Milk Marketing Board. By now, she had grown into a very beautiful young woman – and had left a few broken hearts in South Africa. Shortly before leaving for England she had been working at her auntie's grocery in Umtata and one of the local lads would come by every week on the pretence of buying a few bits and pieces so he could stare at her. Then one day he handed her a love letter. 'Lots of garbage about how lovely I was,' is Mum's typically no-nonsense memory of it. It was a shame she didn't keep the letter as it was signed 'Nelson Mandela'.

A year after she'd arrived in England it was Mum's turn to fall madly in love. She was helping Joan in the garden when a friend of Tony's, Michael Karslake, stopped by. That evening, Michael – six foot two, with thick dark hair and a lovely smile, according to Mum – took her to the cinema. She can't remember which film was on because they snogged the whole way through it.

It was love at first sight for my dad, too. Born in 1932 in Surrey, Michael Howard Karslake was working as an architectural model-maker, after an apprenticeship at the London County Council's model-making department. He proved incredibly gifted at his chosen career. Nowadays, the intricate architectural models he built – ranging from the Thames Flood Barrier to a prototype helmet for racing driver Stirling Moss – would be created on a computer, but back then no project could do without the kind of skills he possessed.

Three years after that snogging session at the Surbiton Odeon, I came along, the first child of the newly wed Mr and Mrs Michael Karslake. (Scandalously newly wed, in fact: the ink had barely dried on my parents' marriage certificate when I was born just four months later, the surprise result of a romantic jaunt to Devon, with Dad on his Lambretta scooter and Mum in the sidecar, her pin-curled blonde hair wrapped in a silk scarf. I was a love child! I've been a bit of a romantic ever since …)

Our first home was 44 Vange Hill Drive, a redbrick council house in Vange on the outskirts of Basildon, with chickens in the garden and acres of climbable trees in the woodland just beyond the fence. Mum's African heritage didn't even register with me when I was a kid. Growing up she spoke English, Afrikaans and Xhosa, but I don't remember her having a strong accent (although she must have done, as I can hear the South African twang in her voice to this day) and, apart from being head-turningly beautiful, she didn't look very different from any of the other mums in our white, middle-class neighbourhood. In my mind, the only unusual thing about our family was the deerskin shield with crossed spears on the living-room wall, and the avocado tree that Mum was struggling to grow among the pansies in the herbaceous border.

It wasn't until her mother came to stay for the first time, when I was nine, that Mum's heritage really hit home. Granny Ellen was much darker-skinned than Mum and her manner was very African. I remember Mum putting on her favourite Miriam Makeba records and Granny would stomp around the kitchen, throwing her arms up and singing: 'Woo! Da-ba-da-ba-da-ba!' It was hysterical. And there was the sudden, amazed realization: 'Oh, my God, Mum's from *Africa*!'

I didn't get to visit my mother's homeland until years later, after Dad died in 1990. I was desperate to get away, and Ronnie suggested we go to Kenya. As soon as I stepped out of the plane, I was aware that I had some sort of connection to Africa, a bond I'd never felt with any other place. I fell in love, really. Many years later, I used Xhosa words, including *tula*, meaning 'quiet', and *langa*, for 'sunshine', as the names of the scents in my Jo Wood Everyday Organics range.

*   *   *

As a little girl, I was perfectly happy in my dream world, and didn't have that many friends; I still don't really. I'm actually very shy. I'm fine once I get to know you, but it takes me a bit of time to trust people; maybe that came from living with Ronnie for all those years. Even as an adult, if I was in a hotel and room service brought the wrong order, I'd always say, 'Oh, please don't worry, that'll be fine!' rather than make a fuss. It used to drive Ronnie mad.

Apart from my siblings – Paul came along when I was two, Vinnie when I was six, and then, when I was 10, my baby sister Lize – my main playmate when we lived in Basildon was a girl called Linda Wood. She was the daughter of Mum's best friend, Auntie Lily, and lived a few doors down. Linda was six months younger than me and quite spoilt. We used to play together with our dolls, but Linda had a *real* Sindy and a Barbie, whereas I just had Sindy's cheaper cousin, Tina. I wasn't a nasty child, but I suppose there was a bit of resentment there. On one particularly jealous day I made up a poem and chanted it to her in the garden: *Linda Wood, is no good, chop her up for firewood.* Linda had the last laugh, though. Years later, when I married Ronnie, she came to my wedding and was one of the first to congratulate me. 'So, Jo, now you're a Wood, too …' Talk about karma.

For the first years of my life, I was Mum's little shadow. I thought she was unbelievably glamorous, with her pencil skirts, stilettos and red lipstick. She loved clothes, and the house was always filled with pattern magazines from which she'd make the latest fashions on her sewing-machine. For a time she was an Avon lady and I would spend many happy hours playing with her makeup box, smelling the perfumes, patting the face powder so it puffed up in fragrant pink clouds and testing the lipsticks until I had tiger-stripes of Scarlet Lady and Passionate Plum up my arms. This girlie side of me frequently clashed with my inner tomboy. I loved climbing trees, so would go out looking immaculate and within minutes would have mud all over my skirt. There's a photo of me aged five dressed as the Christmas-tree fairy for a school play, an angelic little girl with white-blonde hair, a butter-wouldn't-melt smile, a sticky-out dress – and a pair of filthy plimsolls poking out of the bottom. To this day, that's me all over.

As I barely left her side, Mum roped me into helping with the chores so I learnt really young to clean and cook. One of my earliest memories is of perching on a stool at the kitchen table while Mum made chocolate fudge, testing whether it was cooked by dropping a little bit into a glass of water to see if it formed a ball. To me, it was like magic! When I was eight, Mum went to South Africa to visit relatives, and for the next six weeks I helped Dad run the house: ironing his shirts, cleaning the kitchen, caring for Paul and Vinnie. At that age, six weeks seems an eternity, but I remember Dad being so proud – and I loved playing the little housewife.

We were a very tight unit: just Mum, Dad and us kids. We didn't see much of our extended family, apart from summers spent at Auntie Mary's beachside house in Devon and occasional trips to see my paternal grandmother, Grandma Karslake, in Surbiton. She must have been only 37 when I was born (she had my dad ridiculously young, at something like 16) and with her pinky-mauve set hair and moles that sprouted wiry hairs, she always seemed such a jolly woman. One day I was sitting on her lap, playing with her necklace. 'Each bead is a different flavour,' she whispered, with a wink, blowing my five-year-old mind. I sneaked a lick when she wasn't looking.

But that's not to say the Karslakes lived a quiet, solitary life – quite the contrary. Every weekend our house was full of people, united by one all-consuming passion: Lambretta scooters. The soundtrack to my childhood is revving engines and the clatter of crash helmets, while the smell is petrol. If we didn't have a houseful of Lambretta fans at the weekend, we'd be heading off to a rally somewhere. Every summer we'd go to the Isle of Man for the famous TT motorbike races and watch Dad tear round and round the course for hours, thrilled by the noise, speed and smells.

A few years ago I fulfilled a lifetime's ambition by getting my car racing licence and zipping around the track at Silverstone in a Morgan turbo classic. In 2012, I went on a fantastic charity road trip with 55 remarkable women in a fleet of Maseratis, Ferraris, Rolls-Royces and Bentleys; my sister Lize and I were in my Mercedes AMG. The route took us from London to Monte Carlo, via Paris, Geneva and Milan, but my own adventure very nearly ended at Dover.

'Passport, please,' said the officer at the border.

Oh, God. I'd forgotten my passport. 'I've got my driving licence,' I said hopefully.

'You can't get into France without a passport,' he said.

Lize and I begged and pleaded with him and he must have taken pity on us because in the end he waved us through. 'I haven't seen you,' he said, with the ghost of a smile.

By the time Dad died he had built up a museum of at least a hundred scooters, every model Lambretta had ever made lovingly restored. He was such a craftsman. When I was eight he took me to the scrapyard where we found an old bike frame and parts. He took them back to his workshop, put them all together, renovated it to mint condition and – *ta-dah!* – I had a beautiful new bicycle with a basket on the front. I loved hanging out with him in his workshop, watching him make incredible models of new towns, marvelling at his steady hand as he painted tiny windows or the lines down the middle of the street. Sometimes he'd let me help, teaching me how to make bits of foam into trees and spray-paint them green.

If there was one cloud on the otherwise blissfully clear horizon of my childhood, it was school. I hated it with a passion, and would do anything I could to avoid it, until the magical day when I could finally escape at 16. The only reason I learnt to count was so that I could work out how many days I had to endure before I could leave. All that 'sit up straight, don't talk, learn this' just didn't sit with my dreamy, romantic nature. Even at my primary school, Swan Mead, I would often sneak home for beans on toast, with Mum as my willing accomplice: 'Don't worry, darling,' she would say. 'You can stay and have lunch at home.' Dad never found out because he was at work.

It was a good job he didn't: I don't think he'd have been pleased. Dad was in charge of learning – and he was quite the disciplinarian. I remember him shouting at me because I could not (or would not) understand how to tell the time. When I was struggling to learn my times-tables he wrote them out on rolls of wallpaper and stuck them all around my bedroom so when I lay in bed I could memorize them. I didn't. Maybe one of the reasons I rebelled against school was because he tried to push me so hard.

Dad and I had a wonderful relationship but, God, he was strict. I think that came from his father, who was extremely tough with him, and Dad's two years' national service with the RAF after leaving school. You crossed him at your peril. When I was seven I sneaked a tin of drinking chocolate out of the kitchen cupboard. Dad discovered me eating spoonfuls of it and I got the wooden spoon, seven strokes on my bum, as you always got the same number as your age. Another time, my brother Paul found a crowbar – he was a cheeky little boy and very funny, but always up to mischief. Well, I came round the corner to see him smashing it on the vicarage wall and freaked. 'Dad's going to kill us!' We all got the wooden spoon that time, even though I hadn't done anything. After another misdemeanour we had to choose our own stick from a tree and then he hit the back of our legs with it. It was absolutely terrifying, the prospect of knowing that this awful thing was about to happen to you – and there was no way you could get out of it.

We were all scared stiff of Dad, even the four-legged family members. I remember once he found Mum's cat eating food off the kitchen work surface. He picked Fusty up and threw him out of the window. That cat never went near him again. Dad was strict with us, but I learnt discipline, politeness and manners. I had the utmost respect for him.

*　*　*

I love animals but I'm not good at keeping pets. When I was little I had a rabbit called Snowy, but I soon got bored of taking care of him and forgot to feed him, so Dad told me he was giving him to the postman who lived down the road. 'Okay.' I shrugged. After a few days I started to miss Snowy and his soft white fur, so I trotted down the road and knocked on the door.

The postman's wife answered. 'Hello, Josephine.' She smiled at me kindly.

'I've come to see Snowy.'

She looked confused.

'My rabbit?' I said.

'Oh, yes. I'm afraid we've eaten him, dear.'

From then on I vowed never to have another pet. I wasn't going to go through that again.

*   *   *

Although they were always very sociable, my parents didn't really drink – apart from maybe a few at Christmas – and Dad never smoked. I remember watching *Ready, Steady, Go* on telly – I must have been about 10, and the Rolling Stones came on. Dad looked on disapprovingly. 'Disgusting lads.' He tutted into his tea. You can imagine how he felt when, years later, I brought one of those very same lads home to Sunday lunch – although by that time I'd caused him and Mum so many anxious, sleepless nights that my dating a rock star probably didn't seem so terrible, after all.

2

'Not far now, kids, just up this hill ...'

It was a few weeks before Christmas 1964 and we were crammed into the back of Dad's Singer Gazelle, with the little silver antelope that seemed poised to leap off the bonnet, on the way to see our new home. Dad and Mum were in the front (Lize was a large bump under her maternity dress), while Paul, Vinnie and I sat in the back, our excited chatter fogging up the car windows. We had only gone a few miles from our old house but, as the road twisted up through a dense green tunnel of trees, it seemed a world away from the suburban neatness of Vange.

A property developer Dad worked with had commissioned him to build a model for a development of six new homes in Benfleet on the site of the village's old vicarage. While Dad was going through the plans, which included a new home for the vicar, he noticed a large building at the back of the site – the old vicarage, which the developer was planning to pull down. Intrigued, Dad went to have a look at the place and immediately fell in love with it. Now he was taking the rest of us to see it.

We turned onto a muddy driveway, then the trees opened into a clearing and there it was. The Old Vicarage. I jumped out of the car, gasping with delight. The house looked like a miniature castle, with Gothic archways, church-style windows and a pointed red-tiled roof with high chimneys sticking up, like candles on a birthday cake. We heaved open the front door, and soon Paul and I were running from room to room, with Dad recording every shriek of excitement on his little 8mm cine camera. Inside, the house was a maze of small, oddly shaped rooms with stone fireplaces and wooden floors. It was cold and dark, the only light coming from bare bulbs that cast eerie shadows and revealed strange marks on the walls (we found out later that the vicar's son had played indoor football). After years of dreaming I was a princess in a fairytale, now I would live out that fantasy for real – and I certainly didn't care that my castle was more Brothers Grimm than Disney.

The house needed to be completely redecorated, but we moved in anyway and the renovations kept my parents occupied for the next few years. They were both pretty groovy and they kitted out the house with a mix of vintage finds and contemporary pieces: an antique refectory table and thrones with turned legs, a bright orange couch for the living room and a space-age copper lampshade on a coiled cable that I'd pull down over my head, like a spotlight, and belt out Hendrix's 'Hey Jo'. I got the interior design bug too, deciding on imitation bamboo-design wallpaper for my bedroom to make it look 'tropical'. Not exactly appropriate for an old stone vicarage in rural Essex, but I've never been one for sticking to the rules. My new home in Primrose Hill is decorated with vintage carpets, metallic skull-and-crossbones wallpaper, modern art and antique fringed lace shawls at the windows: I love the contrast and clash of styles, mixing the old and the new – my taste is very eclectic.

I would think of the Old Vicarage as home until my parents moved out 20 years later. It was a wonderful place. As its appearance suggested, it was alive with history, secrets and magic. The walls were built of stones from the ruins of Hadleigh Castle on the Essex marshes and were up to three feet thick in places. I remember exploring the attic one day, squeezing under the eaves to find a secret room in which there was a stack of great, thick Bibles and newspapers from the 1800s. There was even rumoured to be a body buried under the doorstep, which was a huge lump of grey rock that certainly had the look of a gravestone. I'm surprised we never ran into any ghosts.

The house was surrounded by ancient trees, with thick, low branches that looked like they'd been put there for the sole purpose of climbing. One evening shortly after we moved in, I remember scaling the huge conker tree (it would later become the focal point of my teenage love life) at the bottom of the drive and gazing out at the sunset over Canvey Island, marvelling at how beautiful it was and wondering what extraordinary adventure life had in store for me.

First, though, I had to get school out of the way. After screwing up the eleven plus at Lindisfarne College – I only wrote my name – I was sent to the local Catholic convent, St Bernard's, in the nearby suburb of Westcliff. I still hated school, but was fascinated by the nuns. What did their hair look like under their veils? What sort of *knickers* did they wear? One day, curiosity got the better of me: I scrambled up the high wall that surrounded their living quarters and peeked over to see their pantaloons hanging on the line in the yard, billowing voluminously in the breeze.

Although I had no interest in learning, I had a best friend at St Bernard's, Dympna O'Brien, who looked as Irish as she sounded, and shared my dreaminess and love of adventure. We used to get up to all sorts of mischief together. When an extension was being built onto the school, Dymps and I spent the whole term flirting with the builders. This was a strict Catholic convent, remember, with male visitors few and far between, so to have a load of fit young blokes to gawp at was the best. Every break-time it was the same: 'Ooh, let's go and see the builders.' We'd wave and they'd wink at us.

One day we decided to go up and talk to them properly, face to face. It must have taken weeks of planning. On the fateful day, we rolled our pleated navy skirts above our knees (it must have looked horrendous, great rolls of material stuffed around our waists), then sneaked up the stairs – out of bounds – and into the newly built corridor where the men were working away.

Dympna went boldly to the best-looking one. 'So,' she said, flicking her hair, 'd'you have a girlfriend or a wife?'

'Nah,' he said. 'But I do have a kid.'

Dymps and I looked at each other, wide-eyed in disbelief. How on earth had that happened? Not even married and he'd got a child! We didn't find out any more as, just then, Sister Mary caught us and put us in detention, but I remember being pretty shocked.

Mum and Dad had tried to teach me about the birds and bees when I was nine, but it had gone in one ear and out the other. It was around this time I went back to ask Mum for a recap: I needed to check out a rumour doing the rounds at school that you could get pregnant by kissing. This time I listened to every single detail. I went to school the next day and told Dympna the whole thing. 'I just can't imagine *doing* that with someone,' I said, shaking my head. 'Your wedding night must be *awful*!'

I loved Dymps – and we're still friends to this day – but, sadly, we weren't in the same class. I was in the stupid group. The only subjects I was any good at were art and cookery. (Ironic, really, as my least favourite teacher took us for Home Economics: a slim, grey-haired Welsh woman who was a non-nun or 'regular' – she once gave me the ruler for making faces at Margaret Kennedy because she smelt of wee.) The teachers kept sending home reports saying, 'Josephine doesn't apply herself,' and they were right. I just wasn't interested in learning. My parents were so worried that they took me to have an IQ test and were surprised to discover I was in the top 10 per cent in Essex. But while Dad was tearing his hair out at my lack of scholastic enthusiasm, it didn't worry me in the slightest.

I was barely twelve when my daydreams began to sharpen into a single focused ambition – and I certainly wouldn't need to know quadratic equations or the date of the battle of Hastings to achieve it …

It was the end of the 1960s and everywhere you looked – on magazine covers, newspapers and our little black-and-white telly – you saw a model called Twiggy. From the very first moment I saw that girl with Bambi eyes on the pages of *Jackie* magazine, I knew I wanted to be her. I thought she was *wonderful*. I started reading everything I could about her (this must have been after my reading had improved!) and it dawned on me that the skinny Cockney kid who had come from nowhere to become a huge star was really just like me. *Hey, Jo*, I thought, *you could do this, too!*

There was only one small thing standing between me and model superstardom. My face. I'd been an angelic-looking little girl, but since my second teeth had come through things had gone badly wrong. I was so conscious of my new, huge, gappy teeth that I wouldn't smile with my mouth open. Around the same time, Mum started cutting my fringe really short – 'so we won't have to do it very often'. Almost overnight I became this big-toothed, geeky-haired, skinny-legged kid. It was like the story of how the ugly duckling became a swan, but in reverse. All I needed was a pair of NHS glasses to complete the look.

I was 13, at the height of my Twiggy hero-worship, when my class was asked to write an essay with the title 'My Future Career'. With unprecedented enthusiasm, I wrote all about how I was going to be a top model and live in a flat in Knightsbridge, and how my brother Paul, a famous painter, would come to visit. The next day I came into class to find a group of girls reading my essay aloud in fits of laughter.

Determined to prove the bullies wrong, that weekend I holed myself up in our bathroom, propped a picture of Twiggy against the mirror and got to work with a black kohl pencil. As I had fair eyelashes and small eyes, it was quite a transformation. I got rid of the hated fringe by pushing it to the side and put on some lipstick. If I kept my mouth shut so you couldn't see The Teeth, I didn't look at all bad.

I walked into the kitchen where Mum was having tea with Auntie Lily, Linda's mum. I'll never forget the look on her face when she stopped mid-gossip to stare at me.

'Oh, my goodness, doesn't she look beautiful?' said Auntie Lily.

'She does,' smiled Mum. 'Just like Twiggy.'

Suddenly – miraculously – I could see I had potential. Now that the idea of becoming a model didn't seem quite so crazy, it occupied my every waking hour. I would stand in front of the mirror re-creating poses from magazines and daydream about being a model. It wasn't the money or fame that appealed: I just wanted to wear fabulous clothes, be in beautiful pictures and shimmy down a catwalk. Celebrity had a certain innocence back then.

I don't suppose my parents ever thought I'd really make it as a model. Mum was more up for it than Dad, though. When I first told him what I wanted to do with my life, he said that modelling was just another word for prostitution. I was confused. 'What's prostitution, Dad?' He shut up pretty quickly – but I didn't, and when Dad realized that this wasn't just a passing phase and that I really *did* have my heart set on the catwalk, he decided I should at least get some sort of qualification in it. To him, that made it more respectable. So, in the summer of my 14th year, my parents sent me – oh, joy! – on a course at the London Academy of Modelling.

The academy was on Old Bond Street and every morning I would get the train up to London by myself, feeling so glamorous and grown-up, striding through Mayfair like some groovy Biba girl. The tutors were former models and taught us etiquette, makeup skills and how to walk with stacks of books on our heads. Back then it was all about deportment – keeping your shoulders back and chin up – and nothing like the slouchy strut of today's models. There was no bitchiness or rivalry among the other girls on the course, just shared excitement at the whole magical experience. At the end of the two weeks we had our graduation show in which each girl walked the catwalk in three different outfits to be graded by the tutors. Mum made mine: an orange velvet dress with a fishnet skirt, a red bikini in terry towelling decorated with white daisies, and a green mini-dress that I teamed with a pair of Mary Quant green suede shoes that had square toes and little heels.

I was so nervous and excited, but as I sashayed along in my bikini, Mum's big African straw hat perched on my head, I remember feeling I had found my calling. Out of the 10 girls on the course I came second, behind a statuesque 17-year-old blonde whom I saw later in a few TV ads.

My blossoming in looks and confidence fortunately coincided with the realization that boys were rather interesting. As well as the school builders, Dympna and I had an ongoing flirtation with a cute lad called Andrew, who caught the same train to school as us in the morning. That ended abruptly after he showed us his willy. I was totally cool with willies because I had two brothers, but Dympna blanched at the sight of it. The rest of the day I'd catch her shuddering: 'Oh, it was horrible … *horrible* …'

Then there was the vicar's son, Michael, who had abandoned indoor football for other interests. He was a strange kid. The new vicarage overlooked our house and whenever he saw me come into my bedroom he'd hold up a sign saying, 'I LOVE YOU JO.' I would smile and wave, just to be polite, but then one day I saw him at the window with a telescope trained on my room. From then on, I kept my curtains closed.

My first 'official' boyfriend was Peter Beacroft, the son of one of our neighbours on Vicarage Hill. There was a little gang of us who would hang out 'down the circle', a patch of ground with the big conker tree around which the new houses had been built. I'd had a crush on Peter for ages, so I was giddy with excitement when he asked me on a date to the cinema. I spent ages getting dressed up in my green dress and shoes, but when he came to

pick me up at four o' clock (we had to go to the afternoon mati-
née, thanks to Dad's strict curfew) I just froze. I had no idea what
to say to him. It was never an issue when we were hanging out,
but this was A Date.

Things were slightly less awkward once we were sitting in the
cinema because we could focus on the film, until Peter lunged at
me for a kiss. I could feel the ice-cream I was holding dripping
down my hand and all I could think was, *What shall I do with the
ice-cream? I'm getting it on my dress! It's going everywhere!*

My first kiss, ruined by a 99.

I was Peter's girlfriend for the whole of the summer holidays.
It was a very innocent relationship: just a lot of snogging. With
Dad's iron-rod style of discipline, we didn't have a chance to get
up to much more. To stop us spending too long on the phone, he
had it mounted on the wall, complete with a coin slot that I had
to feed with shillings as we spoke or risk getting cut off in mid-
sentence. As was often the case, Mum sympathized and located
the key so that we could open the coin-box and recycle a single
shilling – a loophole that worked a treat until Dad got the phone
bill a few weeks later.

And then September came. Peter was leaving for boarding-
school and suddenly started badgering me to have sex with him
before he went. 'All my friends have done it,' he said, when
I refused. I went right off him.

A few weeks after Peter there was Paul Sidley, another of the
boys from the circle. He and I were great mates. He built a platform in the highest branches of the big conker tree and would
guide me all the way to the top. Then we would sit up there,
chatting and laughing, hidden from the world far below. He was
such a cool guy – and very cute. American, with blond hair,

freckles and gorgeous lips, like a teenage Steve McQueen. He was the first person I saw smoke grass. I remember him up that tree, furiously dragging away on this weedy little joint. I had the tiniest drag, but I don't remember it doing anything. Our romance fizzled out as quickly as that joint, but I have very fond memories of hiding in the branches with Paul.

* * *

'Hi, Tony, how are you?'

I was fifteen and a half, wearing my hottest hot-pants and clingiest top, leaning against the garden gate in what I hoped was a seductive fashion. *Oh, God, I fancy him so much …*

Tony Wilson was yet another of our neighbours on Vicarage Hill. He lived with his parents, but he was six years older than me and owned a super-cool boutique called the Ragged Priest in nearby Leigh-on-Sea. In other words, he was *way* out of my league. Tony had fair hair styled in a mullet, was fashionably skinny and always had the coolest gear.

I'd been trying desperately for ages to get him to notice me. Whenever he was outside his house, washing his Morris Minor – like he was today, in a pair of tight velvet flares – I'd be there, hovering around.

'All right, Jo?' He was polishing the bonnet, which was painted blue. *Like his eyes*, I thought dreamily.

And then something amazing happened.

'So, d'you fancy coming down the shop one day next week?' he asked. 'We've just got a new delivery in.'

I couldn't believe it. Was Tony flirting with me? 'Sure, yeah.' *Yes!*

Dymps and I popped down in our school uniform, skirts rolled up to our armpits. The shop was painted black inside, Faces was playing on the sound system and there were rails and rails of the most fab clothes. *Orange velvet bibbed hot-pants! A full-length Afghan coat!* I was in heaven. I don't really know which I fell in love with first – Tony or the Ragged Priest.

Not long after that, he invited me to his house while his parents were out and we ended up snogging on the living-room sofa. *Wow.* My first *proper* passionate kiss: the sort of kiss that convinces you it's LOVE.

Well, after that the nuns of St Bernard's didn't get a look-in. It was my last year of school and I was meant to be studying for my CSEs but I skipped classes whenever I could to join Tony on his trips to the wholesalers in London, with Mum hiding me behind the couch in the morning until Dad had gone to work so I could sneak out. I still had a 9 p.m. curfew to stick to, but Tony would take me out to dinner to these fabulous places. I remember my first ever night out in London, at a Polish restaurant called Borscht 'n' Tears in Beauchamp Place. I'd barely ever drunk alcohol, so I got paralytic on vodka. The next morning, Mum threw open my bedroom curtains and I felt like my head was actually exploding.

It was on a warm spring evening a couple of months after we started seeing each other that Tony took me on a walk up to the top of the hill above our houses. We ended up in this overgrown field, shaded by trees, and I remember looking out over the Thames estuary as the sun dipped below the horizon. Tony pulled me down into the grass and started snogging me – and the snogging started to get more intense. And then: 'I'll only put it in a bit, Jo, don't worry.' And that was how I ended up losing my virginity. I remember walking home on my own thinking, *Is that what all that fuss is about?* It wasn't that great *at all.*

Then one day my period was late. Worryingly late. By this time Tony had a little flat in Westcliff, so I went round to see him. 'Oh, Tony, I think I'm pregnant! What are we going to do? My dad's going to kill me!'

Tony was remarkably calm. 'Don't worry, Jo, we'll sort it out. This is what we're going to do …' He made me drink half a bottle of vodka and have a scalding hot bath. I got my period the day after.

Oh, how I adored Tony. My Ragged Priest! I was still at school, but now I had this super-cool boyfriend who owned a shop and introduced me to these amazing places. One day he took me to Biba in Kensington High Street and I felt like I'd just found Paradise.

Over the next few months my life changed to such an extent that – although I would never have imagined it possible – Tony's appeal faded into insignificance beside everything else that was going on. The extraordinary adventure that I'd suspected life had in store for me when I was sitting in the branches of the ancient conker tree? Buckle up, it was about to begin …

3

With trembling hands, I flicked through the pages of the *Daily Mirror* until I found what I was looking for: a photo of a young girl wearing a simple white dress and holding a daisy, her long blonde hair falling about her shoulders. She was smiling coyly at the camera. The picture filled a quarter of the page and was captioned: 'Jo Karslake, 15, from Benfleet in Essex'. I stared at the page in wonder. My dream had come true. I was a model.

My big break had come courtesy of an amateur photographer called Robert Hallmann, who had heard about my modelling ambition through a friend at the local photography shop in Benfleet and offered to take some pictures of me. I guess this sort of thing might sound alarm bells nowadays, but my parents knew Robert, so they were happy to let me have a go. I'd been going on about wanting to be a model for so long they must have thought, 'Well, let's see if she has what it takes.' I can remember the first set of photos I did with Robert, and we were both happy enough with the results to start working together regularly. Robert's talent, combined with my endless enthusiasm (and Mum's skill at re-creating the latest designer looks on her sewing-machine) proved a winning combination, and over the next few months we did loads of photos together around Essex. Me in a satin jumpsuit and knee-high boots posing in the ruins of Hadleigh Castle; me rocking hand-painted (by my brother Paul) flares outside a derelict farmhouse; me standing on a Canvey Island jetty, staring wistfully out to sea.

After the *Mirror* bought the daisy picture, Robert regularly sent photos to the paper, which ran shots of pretty (clothed) girls in the same way as the *Sun* now has Page Three. In another of Robert's photos that appeared, I'm wearing purple brocade hot-pants (made by Mum) and lilac boots, with the caption 'Miss Hot-pants!' You can imagine what a kick I got out of seeing my picture in print.

One day we got a call saying I had been selected as HMS *Caledonia*'s official mascot, and would I like to come up to the naval base in Scotland as their guest? Mum and I went up for the day, had tea with the captain, and then a photographer took some shots of me parading past a line of smiling sailors, who were all holding my picture. You can see from my face in the photos how much fun I was having, although I remember feeling very self-conscious as I was wearing tiny hot-pants and had a hole at the top of my tights that I was convinced everyone was staring at. Little things like that worry you when you're fifteen and a half.

Not long after my first appearance in the national press, a letter arrived addressed to 'Jo Karslake, Benfleet, Essex'. Dad was instantly suspicious and whipped it away before I could open it, but Mum gave me the gist later. Apparently it was from some bloke saying he wanted to take me 'into the hop fields and show you what *real* life is about'. As you can imagine, Dad freaked.

'We can't have this, Josephine. There's a load of strange men out there – and now they all know where you live!' He shook his head decisively. 'There's only one thing for it.'

I had a sudden dread that Dad was going to stop the modelling – but no: 'We'll have to change your name.'

Actually, that wasn't such a bad idea. Twiggy had upgraded from plain old Lesley Hornby and look where it had got her! I spent ages trying to think of something fabulous, but the best I could come up with was Goosey. Not brilliant. So in the end I stuck with Jo Howard, Howard being Dad's middle name. He was a bit happier after that.

*   *   *

The glorious day finally arrived: my last day at St Bernard's! I'd had 10 years of school and all I had to show for it was just three CSEs. I got a B+ in Art, much to Dad's disappointment, a B in Home Economics and a B in History. The rest? Forget it. But I was finally, amazingly, free, and without the restraints of school I could focus on my career.

The London Academy of Modelling had recommended an agency called Gavin Robinson, so armed with my new portfolio – a little folder I'd put together with my cuttings and Robert's pictures – Mum took me up to London for a meeting. At that time, Gavin Robinson ran one of the hottest agencies in London, so I was dizzy with excitement as we climbed the stairs at 30 Old Bond Street to his first-floor office. The girl at Reception directed us to a couch to wait and I sat, staring about me in wonder. The walls were covered with model head sheets, faces familiar to me from the pages of *Honey* and *19*; the phones rang non-stop; and every now and then some stunning girl would waft into the room, oozing confidence and sophistication. I wanted to be part of that world so, so badly.

We were shown into an office where Gavin was sitting behind a desk. He was very slim, trendy and had startlingly blond hair. 'Well, hell*oooo*, you must be Jo!' Gavin flung out his arms in welcome. 'Darling, come here and let me have a good look at you!'

I was stunned. I had never met a man like this before, and I couldn't work out why he was so flamboyant, so … *feminine*. It was fascinating.

Mum and I sat nervously opposite as Gavin flicked through my portfolio. I stared at him, trying to work out if he thought I had what it took. He had big, popping eyes that gave his face an appealingly impish air.

'Well, you'll need catwalk lessons, of course, and you absolutely *must* get those teeth fixed,' he said, as he peered at my photos.

'That's fine, no problem. I can do that.' Just then I'd have cut off my right arm if it had meant he would sign me.

Finally, Gavin put down the portfolio and beamed at me. 'Well, I think you're *fabulous*, darling. Just beautiful. And I'd love you to be one of my girls. You'll be the youngest on my books.'

The following week Gavin whisked me off to a posh dentist in Devonshire Place to have a brace fitted to fix the gap between my two front teeth; a gap that, ironically, is the height of fashion, these days. For the six weeks I wore it I spoke with a lisp. I remember going into the agency and muttering to the receptionist, 'Can I pleathe thpeak to Gavin?'

A willowy brunette standing nearby overheard me and gave a snort of laughter. 'If you want to be a model, *daaah*ling, you'd better learn to speak properly.'

I nearly died. I'd only just turned 16 and all the other models seemed so much older and more sophisticated. But Gavin kept telling me that he loved my sense of fun and freshness, and I trusted him completely. I adored him. He was warm, generous and hysterically funny. A few weeks after our first meeting we were in a taxi together when another car suddenly cut in front of us. Furious, our driver leant out of the window and shouted, 'Kiss my arse!'

Gavin sat forward and said, ever so smoothly, 'No thanks, darling, you might have dandruff.'

Once my teeth were fixed I had some pictures done for my model card. It was my first experience in a studio with a professional photographer. Robert Hallmann had been lovely, but he was a middle-aged-dad type. This guy – Richard Best – was in his early twenties, with long hair, jeans and a cool T-shirt. He was pretty hot, too. As I posed in a selection of home-made outfits, with Richard snapping away, I almost burst with happiness.

In September I started my go-sees, which are basically opportunities for models to meet potential clients. I was armed with my new card, featuring Richard's shots and the following blurb: 'Jo Howard. Height 5' 6, bust 33, waist 23, hips 35, inside leg 31, outside 40. Hair: blonde. Eyes: blue. Specialities: T, H, L, HR, S.' (I guess that last bit stood for Teeth, Hands, Legs, Hair and Shoes.) Go-sees were actually just a long, hard slog. I would spend all day travelling across London on a succession of buses and tubes, only for some magazine editor to take one look at me and say, 'Your hair's wrong. Next.' I'd often come out of those meetings close to tears. *Oh, God, my legs aren't long enough, my face is all weird, I'm never going to make it as a model …*

I can imagine how you might end up a blubbering wreck with an eating disorder. But I quickly came to accept that clients would be looking for specific things for each job, and if you weren't right for that one, you might be for the next. From then on, I enjoyed the go-sees. I loved meeting new people, having a chat and a giggle. And it was such a buzz being out in the world on my own. I'd go to the Wimpy Bar on Bond Street and have a lunch of ice-cream with chocolate sauce and nuts, just because I could.

I started working for all the teen magazines, especially *Jackie*. I'd usually get booked for the fun, playful shoots: roller-skating, jumping off walls – that sort of thing. I did a job with three other models for a German magazine in which we had to have a food fight. We turned up at the studio to find a huge table covered with cream cakes, buns and jellies. The other girls were a bit timid, but I really got stuck in.

My life became a dizzying succession of pinch-me moments. One of my earliest jobs was a TV commercial for Harp lager that was filmed up in the Lake District. The advert was set in ye olden days, with me acting the lowly wench opposite a handsome Scottish laird, played by this handsome hunk who was dating Charlotte Rampling at the time. There I was, clambering over the hills in a horrible brown outfit, while this famous actress's lover came striding over the fells towards me in a billowing kilt! I loved every second of it.

Considering how dramatically my life had changed in the space of a few weeks, it was little surprise that my romance with Tony fizzled out. My new world was so thrilling, so dazzling, that the Ragged Priest and its owner quickly lost their allure.

In September I was sent to Paris for a few days for the *prêt-a-porter* shows. I remember setting off with dreams of the Chanel catwalk, but the reality turned out to be altogether less glamorous. I stayed in a grotty little top-floor flat that reeked of drains and, despite countless go-sees, I didn't get a single job. Things looked up when one of the other models promised me a fabulous night out, but when I arrived at the restaurant I found her sitting with two much older men, all sweaty palms and leering eyes. Even at 16, it didn't take me long to work out that I'd been invited as dessert. After one clammy grope too many I made my excuses and fled.

I did manage to get to a couple of the shows in Paris and it was at one of them that I met a man called Peter Greene. I was talking to a couple of people when he came over to introduce himself. My memory is of a tall guy, with a brown beard, dressed in the latest trends – high platform shoes and tight flared jeans. He worked in the rag trade, he told us, and was in Paris on a buying trip. He was self-confident to the point of cockiness, but he was funny and flirty and had us all in fits of laughter. It was only a brief meeting, but when I turned to go he grabbed my hand.

'See you again, doll,' he said, almost as if it was a command.

I'd like that, I thought, with a smile.

*   *   *

'So, darling, how would you like to go to Acapulco?'

Gavin was smiling at me from the other side of his desk. It was November and I'd been working as a model for just a couple of months.

'Acapulco?' My eyes lit up. It sounded so glamorous. 'Oh, yes, please! Wow, Acapulco … Um, that's in France, right?'

Gavin laughed. 'Mexico, darling. There's a fashion show, all the big designers are showing, and I think you'd be perfect as one of the models. You fly out next week.'

I was unbelievably excited. There was quite a bit of hype around the show, too: the *Daily Mail* even ran a piece with the headline 'Our Girl in Acapulco!' next to my photo. For the 10-day trip I packed a tiny suitcase with just a bikini, a pair of shorts, two T-shirts and a beautiful dress Mum had made me: a backless halter-neck in blue voile with velvet trim. Apart from Paris, I'd never been abroad before. I didn't have a clue what I was letting myself in for.

I flew to Mexico with all the other models who were appearing in the show. To keep costs down, the plane went the longest way possible and the flight ended up taking 32 hours. Our first stop was Madrid, where we filled up with more models and their luggage until the plane was so overloaded that we hit the tops of the trees as we took off again. The girl next to me was screaming hysterically, but I was too excited – *We're going to Acapulco, baby!* – to notice that we were about to crash.

After Spain, we flew to Iceland. I'd taken my shoes off during the flight and my feet had swelled so much that I couldn't squeeze them back on again. I had to tiptoe barefoot through the thick snow to the terminal. Really, it's a wonder I made it to Mexico at all.

Finally, we began our descent into Acapulco. As the plane came in to land I had a tantalizing glimpse of blue sea, palm trees, golden sand – colours so vivid they almost stung my eyes. Then I stepped out of the plane and the heat hit me like a physical blow. *Bloody hell.* The warmest place I'd been before then was north Devon. I had no idea anywhere could even *get* this hot. In moments I was flushed, dripping sweat, and my hair had sprung into a ball of frizz.

I've always envied people who look effortlessly good on holiday – those lucky girls whose sleek hair goes sexily tousled and whose skin turns sun-kissed and golden. Me, I'm usually a mess for the first week. One of my defining memories of the Acapulco trip is sitting in my hotel room, staring at my reflection in horror, wondering what the hell I was going to do with my hair. I had no hairdryer, and nothing seemed to tame the frizz. I should just have given it a tousle and let it go wild, but I had never had to deal with that before.

Worse was to come. The day after we arrived I hit the beach in my bikini – and by the end of the day had burnt to a deep, angry pink. My hair had the texture of wire wool, my skin was red in parts, stark white in others: when it came to the fashion show, it's hardly surprising that I was given all the worst outfits. The one that sticks in my mind was a horrible cream calico dress that could have been a nun's nightie. In short, Our Girl in Acapulco was a great big Mexi-no.

I was one of the youngest models on the trip, but a girl called Stella – a chic 20-something with a penchant for turbans – took me under her wing. One night she invited me to a club and I jumped at the chance. Not only would I be able to give my new halter-neck dress an outing, but hopefully, in the dark, nobody would notice the sunburn and frizz.

My memories of the club are hazy: thumping music, semi-darkness, wild dancing and, above all, FUN! Stella and I got talking (or, rather, shouting) to a Spanish artist called Giorgio and his brother. Giorgio was in his thirties and dangerously hand-some. I think some coke was being handed around, although I hadn't a clue what it was. The room was unbelievably hot, so I downed whatever drink anyone put in my hand and just danced and whirled. *Wheeeee!* It was such a mad night.

At some point we left the club and my next memory is of climbing up a long flight of stairs with Stella, Giorgio and his brother to an apartment, or perhaps a hotel room. Then, to my horror, Stella and the brother started getting it on, noisily and energetically, leaving me alone with a clearly up-for-it Giorgio. Even though I was blind drunk, I started to panic. *Oh, God, he's not going to want to do that with me, is he?* I remember thinking I had to get back to the hotel, but I had no idea where we were. Thankfully, after a bit of a drunken fumble Giorgio fell asleep. I immediately gathered up my things and ran down the stairs into the street where I grabbed a taxi. I had no money, but the driver took pity on me and drove me back to the hotel.

A couple of days later, Giorgio turned up again, and I couldn't get rid of him after that. Wherever I went, he'd be hanging around: '*Hola*, Jo! You wanna come for lunch?' I suppose I was too young and naïve just to tell him to get lost, but by the end of the trip I was sitting on the back seat of the coach to go to the airport, waving to Giorgio as we pulled away from the hotel, feeling so relieved that I'd never have to see him again.

A couple of weeks after we got home, I was at the Old Vicarage helping Mum get lunch ready when there was a knock at the door. Dad answered it and came into the kitchen, a suspicious look on his face. 'Josephine, there's a man here who says he met you in Mexico.'

What the hell …?

I went out, and there were Giorgio and his brother.

'Hey, baby, we've come for a veeseet!'

That night they took my parents and me to Galadoro, an Italian restaurant in Hadleigh. They were very polite and we all had a pleasant evening, but at the end, Giorgio and his brother were sent packing for good.

* * *

Once I'd got back from Acapulco, it was as if someone had stamped on the accelerator: stuff started happening at breakneck speed. A few weeks before Christmas, the *Sun* asked me to be their Face of '72, a brilliant boost for my career that led to an appearance on the BBC's *Nationwide*. It was particularly special for me as Twiggy had been the Face of '66. A few weeks after that, following months of begging my parents to let me live in London, I finally waved goodbye to the Old Vicarage and moved into a flat off North End Road in Fulham, with an African model called Pegga. And just a few weeks after *that*, on my 17th birthday in March 1972, I got engaged to be married.

4

I can't remember where Peter Greene and I met again after that briefest of encounters in Paris. He was just one of those guys on the London scene who worked in fashion and hung out in the nightclub, Tramp. Peter was 28 and owned a very successful clothing business called She Type, which made cheap knock-offs of all the big designers' clothes. He was loud and Jewish and totally unlike anyone I'd ever met before.

We had our first date in February 1972. He took me out to dinner, then drove me home to Fulham in his Bentley. We snogged passionately in the car and then said our goodbyes, but as I walked up the path to my flat he wound down the window and called me back.

'Do you fancy coming on holiday, Jo?'

'Um … Yeah, I suppose so.' I know we'd only just met, but I was always up for an adventure.

'Great. I'll pick you up next Friday and we'll go to Tunisia. See ya, doll.'

And with that he spun the Bentley in a tight circle and sped off with a jaunty toot of the horn.

So, a week later I was sitting on a plane to Tunisia next to a guy I barely knew – and had only kissed a couple of times –

along with his mate, Tony Harley, and his wife, Maureen. I began to have serious doubts about the whole thing, especially when Peter nudged me midway through the flight and said, with a grin, 'We've got a double room.'

As it turned out, we had a fantastic week. We laughed and laughed. Peter had an endless lust for life and loved showing me new places and introducing me to a succession of fascinating people. By the end of the trip, while I'm not sure I was in love with him, I was certainly pretty smitten.

When we got back to London we went straight to his apartment in Baker Street and I fell for him even harder. The flat was the height of seventies cool, with thick cream shag-pile carpet on the floors, mirrored walls and a spiral staircase leading upstairs. Oh, it was all so fab! Peter had all the latest gadgets, including a big round TV and an eight-track stereo sound system. The guy clearly had style. From then on, I stayed at his apartment most nights.

Soon after we started dating, I took Peter home to the Old Vicarage to meet Mum and Dad: things were moving pretty fast between us. By now he had swapped his Bentley for a Ferrari. (Honestly, Peter changed his car more often than anyone else I knew: a black souped-up Mini with tinted windows one week, a red Jaguar E-type the next.) As we pulled up outside the house, Peter slammed on the brakes, sending a shower of gravel all over the flowerbeds. Not a great start.

'Promise me you'll be on your best behaviour,' I begged, for the umpteenth time, as we got out of the car.

'I promise, doll,' he said, dropping a kiss on my forehead. 'You worry too much.'

My parents hated him on sight, I could tell. He was too loud, too old (there was an 11-year age gap), too flash: everything they didn't want for their little girl. And any hope that Peter might charm them vanished for ever during lunch.

The conversation had turned to religion. I was instantly on edge: I wasn't sure if Mum, who was quite a strict Catholic, would have an issue with me dating someone Jewish.

'Well, of course you know Jo's Jewish,' Peter said.

Mum looked at me, then back to him, confused. 'No, I'm sorry, she isn't. Josephine went to a convent school.'

Peter grinned. 'She's Jewish by injection.'

Oh, God. Mum looked utterly horrified. I didn't dare risk a glance at Dad. But Peter just cracked up laughing, loving the reaction he'd caused.

Shortly after that disastrous Sunday, Mum phoned to try to talk some sense into me. 'You can't turn a sow's ear into a silk purse. And, believe me, Josephine, that man is a sow's ear.'

My reaction was typically teenage: 'But, Mum, I love him! You don't under*staaaaand*! Why can't you just be *happy* for *meeee*?'

In the end, we had to agree to disagree.

It was a few days before my 17th birthday, barely a month after I'd started dating Peter, that he gave me a diamond and sapphire engagement ring. There was no big proposal, certainly no getting down on one knee, he just handed it over: ''Ere you are, doll, this is for you. Now you can live with me, all right?'

I think he did it to keep my parents happy, making things legit between us. And Mum and Dad took the news of our impending nuptials pretty well in the circumstances. I think they must have assumed it was just some little madness that I was going through and that it was better to play along and keep quiet until I came to my senses. Mum even made me a stunning dress for the engagement party (also my 17th-birthday bash); a copy of one of

Marilyn Monroe's, it had a sheer black top with sequins covering my boobs and a full tulle skirt. As I glided around our fabulous apartment on the night of the party, pouring champagne for all the fabulous people who had come to celebrate my birthday, I felt like Marilyn herself.

In those early days, Peter and I had such fun. He was exciting and flamboyant, had money and the urge to spend it. I could go into his showroom and pick out whatever I wanted – it was around this time that I really started to get into designer clothes. We were out every night at the coolest places. We'd have dinner at San Lorenzo, then go on to Tramp or Monkberry's with his friends and their model girlfriends. Every year we would drive to the South of France with Peter's business partner, Steven, and his girlfriend, Jay, and his friend Harold Tillman and girlfriend Stephanie, with Stevie Wonder blasting on the eight-track. I loved the way he'd do these crazy, impetuous things without a second thought.

One day he came home with a St Bernard puppy he named Amyl – as in amyl nitrate, the chemical name for poppers. (Typical Peter humour.) Of course, Amyl quickly grew from a cute ickle bundle of fluff into a 200-pound dog. One day I came home to find that Amyl had pooed on the cream carpet and left poo pawprints all over the apartment. Trying not to heave, I rang Peter and told him to come home from work to clean it up. To his credit, he did.

A few months after our 'engagement', I fell pregnant. We weren't being that careful so it was hardly a surprise, but I was so young and naïve that it still came as quite a shock. Peter freaked out, so I had an abortion. He took me to a clinic in Harley Street and that was that. At the time, it didn't feel like such a big deal

– as terrible as that sounds now, it just seemed like a quick way out of a tricky situation. Besides, *I* didn't want to have a baby either. I was only 17 – and who'd want to book a model with a bump?

I was still working regularly and it was starting to cause problems in my relationship. Peter didn't like Gavin. There was an obvious conflict of interests: Gavin wanted me to work, Peter wanted me to play. I'd go out all night to Tramp, get completely pissed, then have to be up early the next morning for a shoot. Thankfully, I was young enough not to suffer from hideous hangovers. I was surviving on just a few hours' sleep a night. All those months of working hard and partying hard would prove brilliant training for what was to come later in my life …

* * *

In the April after my 18th birthday we went on holiday to Los Angeles. In typical style, Peter just turned round one day and said, 'I'm taking you to America, doll.' We went with Steven and Jay, Tony Bloomberg – a whole gang of us.

I fell in love with LA almost instantly. To this day, the smell of the place gets me every time: a heady blend of sunshine, hot tarmac and smog. We stayed at the Beverly Hilton and Peter rented a fantastic red Cadillac Eldorado with white leather seats. So cool! Our little posse went to all the trendy restaurants and clubs and hung out on the beach in Malibu. Then one day Peter suddenly said, 'Let's drive to Vegas.' So we did.

Las Vegas was still quite small in the early seventies, but even then it was such a mad place. I remember being particularly struck by the fact that every single car was a convertible. We stayed at Caesar's Palace, which was the most extravagant place I'd ever seen: huge fountains and marble columns, with all the female staff dressed in tiny little Caesar's Palace togas.

On our first night in Vegas we went to see one of Peter's friends who had a huge house there. The door opened – letting out a blast of icy air-conditioning – and there stood this guy with a moustache, permed Afro and white flared trousers with strawberries printed all over them. I stifled a giggle. It might have been the seventies, but if you're old enough for a moustache you're too old for strawberry-patterned trousers. Anyway, someone rolled a joint and we all sat in a circle, passing this thing around. It was the first time I'd smoked one properly and soon I was having the most terrible giggles over this guy's strawberry trousers. The more I smoked, the worse I got, and eventually Peter had to take me outside because I couldn't stop laughing. By now I was so stoned that when I stepped outside I thought I'd actually gone *inside*, because it was so hot in the garden and cold in the house. So there we were, clutching each other and giggling hysterically, when Peter looked at me and said, 'Let's get married.'

And right there, in the sweltering heat of a Las Vegas night, stoned out of my mind, it seemed like the most brilliant idea in the world. 'Yeah, come on, let's get married! *Woooo!*'

The next day I went out and bought a cream dress, Peter got the ring, we had a few drinks, and then we went to County Hall and tied the knot. As far as I remember, the groom was smiling proudly and the bride was giggling.

That night we went out to dinner with the gang, and during the meal Peter leant across and gave me a little white wrap of paper.

'Here you go, Mrs Greene, take this into the toilet.' He smiled. 'It's cocaine.'

I was pretty drunk by now. 'Ooh, great, I've heard about this stuff!'

Peter told me what to do with it so I dragged Jay off to the Ladies and did my first line of coke. I don't remember it having much of an effect, but I probably only did a tiny little bit.

That night Peter and I stayed in the honeymoon suite at Caesar's Palace. The next morning I woke up in that huge room, with its ridiculous circular bed and satin pillows, and stared at my finger. All I could think was: *Mum is going to kill me.*

It took me a couple of days to pluck up the courage to call home.

'Guess what, Mum! Peter and I got married!'

There was complete silence at the other end of the line.

'Mum? Are you there?'

After what seemed like hours, she finally spoke. 'That's like having my right arm cut off,' she said, quietly.

I'm sure my parents thought that Peter and I would never get married – and if we did, at least they'd have had a bit of notice about the wedding. Mum was devastated that she'd lost her daughter to someone like Peter. But from then on they just accepted I was married and made the best of the situation; there was nothing they could do about it, so there was no point in saying anything.

After we married I converted to Judaism to keep his parents happy. Peter was by no means religious: we celebrated the main Jewish holidays, like Yom Kippur and Passover, but he was pretty half-hearted about it. Yet I loved the Jewish culture, even enjoyed studying for my conversion, and I can still remember the Hebrew blessing over the bread. Peter's parents were also upset about our Las Vegas wedding, but for different reasons: they'd wanted us to have a big Jewish wedding. They were always lovely to me. 'A nice *shiksa* girl,' as his stepdad would say, with an affectionate smile.

* * *

Being married barely changed our relationship. I was only 18, remember, so the whole till-death-us-do-part thing didn't mean much to me. I certainly wasn't thinking seriously about my future, just having a wild, crazy time with my man.

The only place that things weren't particularly wild, however, was in bed. Perhaps the age gap was to blame, or maybe we just weren't that compatible, but while Peter was very affectionate, our sex life was never exactly dynamite. I hadn't had much experience so I guess I would just have accepted it as the way things were, but when I was on shoots with other models I began to be aware that everyone apart from me seemed to be swinging from the chandeliers and having multiple orgasms. I'd listen to my girlfriends saying, 'Oh, last night we made love for HOURS!' or 'He did this to me and then he did that to me and – oh, God! – it was just AMAZING!' And I was just sitting there thinking, *Well, I get it once a week if Arsenal's won.*

One day, after hearing yet another of my friends going on about a night of knee-trembling passion, I realized I needed to take matters into my own hands. It was time to call in reinforcements. I went into Ann Summers and came out with Spanish Fly drops and Long Stand cream. On the way home, I studied the instructions intently ('*Add three drops to a drink … Wash penis thoroughly then massage cream into penis …'*) and came up with a cunning plan.

A few hours later Peter came home from work. I put the kettle on as usual, but this time added a special ingredient to his PG Tips. *Drop-drop-drop.* 'Cup of tea, love?'

'Ah, thanks, doll.'

I watched him drink it all up.

'Shall I run you a bath?'

'Yeah, thanks, doll, that'd be great.'

I was sitting in bed with the Long Stand cream already on my hands when he climbed in. Before he could protest, I grabbed his willy and started rubbing the cream in.

'Oi, what are you doing?'

'It's fine, just some special cream. Just relax and enjoy it.'

'What? Leave it out, Jo …'

And with that Peter turned over, snapped the light off and went quiet. I don't suppose I can blame him – I had pretty much ambushed him. I lay there in the darkness, feeling stupid and frustrated. But about 20 minutes later, I heard Peter's muffled voice from the other side of the bed: 'It's working.'

I sat bolt upright. 'It is?' *Thank you, God!*

'Yeah,' said Peter. 'But because you're such a bloody mad woman I'm going to sleep.'

Even though we weren't having that much of it, sex was still happening, so I told Peter I needed contraception. He came home with some packets of pills and I started taking them, but they made me horribly bloated. In the end I went to the doctor, who told me they contained a dangerously high level of oestrogen and that I should never have been using them – so I just stopped. Then, in the first months of 1974, around the time of our first wedding anniversary, I discovered I was pregnant again – and as I was married there was no chance of an abortion this time. I was going to be a mum.

* * *

My bump was barely showing when one morning I woke to find Peter had thrown his arm across me in his sleep. His armpit was hovering somewhere near my face and the smell made me feel sick.

Oh, God, I thought. *I'm married to this man. I'm having his baby.* I quickly pushed his arm off me and he turned over, still fast asleep. I lay there feeling increasingly uneasy.

Okay, this is just because I'm pregnant. I still love him.

But it was like a switch had been flicked in my brain. My feelings for Peter seemed to change almost overnight. Perhaps it *was* the pregnancy hormones – or maybe it was because I'd finally started to admit the truth to myself. *I didn't really love Peter.* And now that that terrible thought had wormed its way into my mind, I didn't want the marriage, but what about our baby? I felt totally and utterly trapped – and there was nothing I could do about it.

5

Although he had been fairly indifferent about the pregnancy at first, Peter became increasingly excited about the idea of becoming a dad. He was in his early thirties by now, so I guess he felt ready for it. But as my due date approached, the less convinced I was by the path my life had taken. As I could no longer drink, our social life started to slow down (although I do remember going to Tramp with my huge bump clad in a fab silky patchwork dress from Antiquarius), and as I couldn't work, I spent a lot of time at the Old Vicarage with Mum. I tried to ignore my doubts about our marriage, blaming the negative feelings on the pregnancy, yet there was this constant nagging fear in the back of my mind that my career and my life were all but over. I was only 19.

It was a sunny September afternoon in 1974 when my contractions kicked in, then suddenly intensified. *Woooaaah.* I called Peter at work and shrieked, 'I'm having the baby!' He got a taxi home and took us both to Guy's Hospital. I'm actually pretty good at giving birth and went through labour drug-free with my other kids, but on that occasion I took everything the doctors could throw at me. The epidural only half worked, though, so on one side I was blissfully numb and on the other I could feel every gut-wrenching spasm. Peter stayed in the waiting room while I screeched and panted my way through the birth. While he was still excited by the idea of parenthood, he had a lot less stomach for the gory details.

At seven that evening Jameson Joseph Greene, a.k.a. Jamie, made his entrance into the world – and any doubts I had about being a mum simply vanished with one look at that gorgeous little screwed-up face. Oh, my little fella! It was all-consuming love at first sight. As I held him in my arms, I was overcome with happiness.

When we got home a few days later, Peter pretty much left me to get on with it. He was the opposite of a hands-on dad: a hands-off dad, so to speak. He never once changed one of Jamie's nappies, fed him or took him for a walk: that was all 'woman's work'. He just left me alone to do everything. Everything, that is, except Jamie's circumcision.

I tried everything I could to talk Peter out of getting it done. I was so upset at the thought of anyone hurting my precious little boy and just couldn't understand why Peter was suddenly playing the religion card. The guy had bacon on his bagels, for God's sake! But he was adamant. So when Jamie was a few days old, a rabbi came to our house (by this time we had moved to a terraced house in Shouldham Street, Marylebone) and performed the *bris*, while I sat in the bedroom crying my heart out. After it had been done, Peter's business partner, Steven, came into my room and held out a tissue with this little bit of stuff on it.

'How can you show me that?' I howled. 'OH, GOD!' It set me off sobbing all over again.

'It's all right, Jo,' smirked Steven. 'It's just smoked salmon.'

*　*　*

Luckily I took to being a mum, aided, no doubt, by all those years of helping to raise my brothers and sister. Jamie wasn't the easiest of babies, though. He was a beautiful little boy, but quite naughty and constantly demanding my attention – pretty much like he is now! I remember one particular night when he just wouldn't go to sleep. I'd fed him, winded him, changed him, checked his temperature, but he was still screaming. After hours of this, feeling utterly exhausted and with no idea what was wrong, I picked him up and shouted at him, 'Come on, Jamie, will you please just GO TO SLEEP!' Instantly, I felt terrible. *What is the matter with you, having a go at a little baby?* I never lost it with him again – and I never once smacked any of my children.

One of the things I enjoyed most about motherhood was breastfeeding. It was such an incredible, miraculous feeling, knowing you could sustain this little person. But Peter hated me doing it. If he came in after work and found me feeding Jamie, he'd say, 'Ugh! Don't do that in here, go to the bedroom.' After one too many times of being made to schlep upstairs to finish a feed, I expressed some breast milk and put it in Peter's tea. I watched him drink the whole cup.

'Did you enjoy that, Peter?'

'Yeah, it was all right.'

'Oh, I'm so pleased. 'Cos I put breast milk in it.'

His face was a picture. 'You didn't!'

I smiled. 'I did, actually.'

He wasn't at all happy, as you can imagine. I was, though. I thought it was hysterical.

We'd become more like flatmates than a married couple. While I'd hoped that having Jamie would bring us closer, it had the opposite effect. We weren't arguing, but we weren't really talking either. When Jamie was six months old I decided to start modelling again. I thought Peter would kick up a fuss, but he was fine with the idea so I hired a lovely Japanese au pair called Ushi and went back to work. I had left Gavin's while I was pregnant so I joined another agency, Gill-Raine. Coincidentally, the photographer who had been booked to take pictures for my new agency model card was none other than Richard Best, the guy who had taken those very first professional shots of me back when I was just starting at Gavin's.

The shoot took place on Primrose Hill. By this time Richard had become a good friend, but I'd always had a bit of a crush on him. Like most fashion photographers, he possessed great charm – and he laid it on thickly that afternoon.

'Oh, yeah, that's great, Jo, you look beautiful.' *Snap-snap-snap.* 'Just move your arm like that and turn your hip …' *Snap-snap* '… yeah, gorgeous …' *Snap-snap-snap.*

As I posed for him, I finally felt like I was getting my mojo back. I hadn't realized how out of touch I'd become with the old free-spirited, fun-loving Jo. And Richard was outrageously flirty during the shoot. It had been so long since I'd felt desirable – and desired – that it was a real kick that this hot guy clearly found me attractive.

When we'd finished work, Richard suggested we go back to his place 'for a celebratory glass of wine'. I knew Peter would still be at work and Jamie was happy with Ushi. So I went.

Richard lived nearby in a studio flat that was cluttered with camera equipment and rolls of paper. While I looked at his photos hanging on the walls, he got a bottle of white wine from the fridge and a couple of glasses and put the Steve Miller Band on the stereo. Then we sat down together on the sofa. It was late afternoon and the sun was filtering through the shutters at the window, casting bars of light on the wall behind us.

'To you, Jo,' he said, clinking his glass against mine. 'Just as gorgeous as ever.'

I smiled and took a sip. Richard was holding my gaze with those sexy brown eyes of his. I just knew something was about to happen. Suddenly he put his glass down, took mine from my hand, then leant over and started to kiss me. Softly at first, but then things got seriously wild and soon we were tearing off each other's clothes.

That was the day I had my first ever orgasm. I even remember the song that was playing at the time: 'The Joker' by Steve Miller Band. That was also the day that Richard and I started an affair. It was intense – just raw passion. The scales fell from my eyes and I finally knew what I'd been missing while I was married to Peter.

*   *   *

A month or so later I was over at Richard's flat when someone started banging at the door. A man's voice: 'Jo? Come out, I need to talk to you!'

Richard and I froze. 'It's Peter!' I mouthed at him, horrified.

'Jo?' Peter was still hammering on the door. 'Jo, I know you're in there!'

Eventually he gave up and went away, but it was a major wake-up call for me. I immediately called things off with Richard, but we parted as friends – and I couldn't be more grateful for what he did for me.

God, I felt guilty. The shock of my husband nearly catching me with another man jolted me into putting some effort into my marriage. For the next few weeks I tried to be the perfect wife: cooking Peter's favourite meals, being affectionate, keeping the house immaculate. I tried so hard to be good, really I did, but having Ushi to take care of Jamie and working in an industry that brought me into contact with so many handsome, charming men made it too easy to be bad. And while I never went looking for an affair, they seemed to keep finding me.

* * *

I met David on a shoot. He was an actor and model: blond, charismatic, kind of cool and very funny. We spent the shoot in fits of giggles, which made me realize how little Peter and I laughed any more. Afterwards, we went to the pub – and things progressed from there.

If anything, this was even more passionate than the affair with Richard had been. I was desperate for David and tried to see him whenever I could. I even faked a modelling job so I could go away with him to Brighton for a weekend. Things got very serious very quickly.

But as much as I was crazy about him, I knew we had no future. I was already married and the last thing I wanted was to get into another serious relationship. So I put my sensible hat on and called a halt to the affair, probably breaking poor David's heart.

Things between Peter and me were worse than ever. We were like a couple of OAPs: I'd cook dinner while Peter watched TV, and then we'd go to bed with barely a peck on the cheek. And the sex? Well, maybe it was because our relationship was so bad, but Peter wasn't interested.

Soon after David, it was another fashion photographer. His name was Eric Swayne and he was closer to my dad's age than mine – probably in his early forties. I was booked to do some test shots for a new magazine at his studio, which was below his split-level apartment on Thurloe Square in South Kensington.

The shoot was one of the sexiest I'd ever done: me in a silk kimono with nothing underneath, then in a little denim mini with braces. Eric had this sexy Cockney voice, and kept telling me how fabulous I was. He was very good-looking: dark, rugged, with a strong jaw. And when he suggested we should open a bottle of wine after the shoot … well, you can probably imagine what happened.

Eric might have been older than me, but he was so charismatic, so worldly. And he wanted to save me, which for a young girl in my miserable situation was a very attractive quality. I opened my heart to Eric and told him how unhappy I was, and he promised to be there for me. He told me, 'If you feel you can't take it any more and you need somewhere to stay, I'll take you in. I'll take you and your son.' He was truly my knight in shining armour.

A few days after Jamie's first birthday I was having lunch with my friend Samantha in Morton's Brasserie in Mayfair. Samantha used to date Richard Best but was now married to Adrian Lyne, who went on to direct the movie 9½ Weeks. We were sitting chatting – no doubt about my latest problems with Peter – when a smartly dressed woman came over to our table. 'I'm sorry to interrupt your lunch,' she said, in an American accent. 'But I need to do your numbers.'

She was looking directly at me, but I had no idea what she was talking about.

'I'm a numerologist,' she explained. 'There's something about you, my dear. I know it's none of my business, but I really think I might be able to help.'

With Samantha's encouragement, the woman sat down and I told her my date of birth and the other information she wanted. She scribbled a few notes, stared at her figures, then put her hand over mine. 'I hope you don't mind me saying this, but you are clearly a very unhappy young woman.' My eyes filled – she was spot-on. 'And if you don't sort out your current situation and follow your heart then you're going to be a very unhappy woman at forty.'

I looked at Samantha. 'You've got to leave, Jo,' she said. 'You've just got to.'

I knew she was right, but I was petrified. This was going to destroy Peter. But if I stayed in that relationship I'd just get more and more unhappy, and I didn't want Jamie to be brought up in that sort of toxic environment. And, of course, there was Eric on the horizon.

I'll take you and your son.

The next day I packed one small suitcase with a pair of my favourite shoes and all Jamie's stuff. I left a note for Peter: 'I'm so sorry, but I feel it's time for me to go. I'm fine, Jamie's with me, so please don't worry. I'm somewhere safe.' I phoned Eric and told him I was leaving Peter. He just said, 'Okay, darling, come on over.'

I lifted Jamie out of the cot. He gave one of his gorgeous smiles and I kissed him, breathing in that lovely baby smell. 'We're going on a little adventure, my darling,' I said softly. 'Just you and me.'

And then I picked up the suitcase and walked out of the door.

6

We'll get by
Oh, please, Jamie don't you cry
your mummy will get by
things will be hard
but I know you're a card
and we'll get by.

Oh, little one, you look so sad
things really aren't that bad
life is rough
but I know you are tough
and we'll get by.

Oh, Jamie, cheer up now
we've got through and how,
it's because I knew
it was all for you
and we got by.

*   *   *

It was around ten o' clock on the second night after my escape to Eric's when his front-door intercom buzzer sounded. He picked up the handset, listened, then turned to me.

'Now, Jo, don't panic, but Peter's here.'

Immediately, I panicked. 'Oh, God, what does he want? What am I going to do? Don't let him in!'

'He's the father of your child,' said Eric, calmly. 'We have to let him in.'

Moments later Peter burst into the room. He scowled at me. 'Where's Jamie?'

'In there,' I said. 'But he's asleep ...'

Peter shoved his way past me and went into the bedroom. A moment later he came back into the room carrying Jamie, who was by now awake and looking around him in a daze. Then he walked straight past us and out of the flat with my gorgeous boy in his arms. I went to chase after them, but Eric called me back.

'Don't stop him,' he said. 'You don't want Jamie to be in the middle of a scene.'

I cried my heart out. Eric was right, of course, as it would have been terrible for Jamie to see us fighting, but at the same time I knew that Peter had no idea how to look after our one-year-old son. He'd never changed a nappy, never prepared a bottle, never put him to bed. He didn't even know about Jamie's Night-night, the white cotton comforter that he never went anywhere without – except he just had, *because Peter had left it lying in his cot!* ('Night-night' was even Jamie's first word.) How on earth would he get to sleep without it? And where had Peter taken him? I had a sleepless night, imagining all these terrible scenarios, but early the next morning my mum called.

'Josephine, I've been sworn to secrecy, but I wanted to let you know that I have Jamie here with me.'

'Oh, thank God!'

'But you mustn't let Peter know I've told you.'

I agreed to play along – but really! As if my own mother wouldn't tell me that she'd got my child! So Jamie started his little life at the Old Vicarage – and within a few days I'd gone down to join him. It just wasn't going to work with Eric: as wonderful as he was, I was an emotional mess and I needed to be with Jamie.

Mum's attitude to me escaping my marriage was 'I told you so'. Dad was just pleased I wasn't with Peter any more. And they both adored Jamie.

After that, I barely saw Peter. One Friday evening, shortly after I'd moved down to the Old Vicarage, I'd been working in London but I was so broke I didn't have the train fare back to Essex. In desperation, I went and knocked on the door of our house.

'Hello, Jo.' If he was surprised to see me he didn't show it.

'I'm sorry, Peter, but is there any way you can lend me some money? Just five pounds for the train back to Essex? I haven't got a penny.'

'I won't give you the money,' he said, 'but I'll cash you a cheque.'

With no alternative, I wrote him a cheque for fifteen pounds, then watched him take a thick wad of notes from his pocket, slowly peel off three fivers and hand them over. I felt so humiliated and I guess I deserved it. But I vowed never to ask Peter for anything again. And I never did.

We divorced when I was 21. Peter remarried and had two beautiful daughters, Sophia and Lucy, who I am very close with. Years later he moved to Spain, where he lives to this day.

* * *

With my baby happily settled at the Old Vicarage, my priority was getting work. My parents couldn't afford to support Jamie and me and I had no savings because I had always given my earnings straight to Peter (and I clearly wasn't going to get a penny from him) so I had no choice. Plus, of course, I loved modelling. I was just lucky that Mum was still young – my sister Lize was 10 at the time – which meant she could easily take care of Jamie.

I started accepting every job (and party invitation) that came my way. I was only 20, remember, and determined to catch up on all the fun I'd missed while married to Peter. Two girlfriends above all helped me in this mission. The first was Lorraine Dellal – to this day my closest friend. She is the daughter of the flamboyant London property developer, Jack Dellal, known as 'Black Jack' for his love of gambling. I had first met her when I was still with Peter and she was about to marry a friend of his, a charming guy named David Morris. Now we reconnected, as Lorraine was in charge of booking the models at my agency.

My other partner in crime was a fellow model named Susan Harrison, whom I'd met at a fashion party. She had the most beautiful face, with wonderful lips, high cheekbones and a Romanesque nose, but an accent and down-to-earth attitude that were straight out of *Coronation Street*. Sue and I hit it off immediately. Her sister, Stephanie, had a house in Wandsworth but she was dating the motorbike champion, Barry Sheene, leaving the house empty, so Sue suggested that we rent it together. It was a perfect arrangement: we got the place cheap, as otherwise it would have been sitting vacant, and I could go down to the Old Vicarage at weekends for kisses and cuddles with Jamie. Life was about to get wild …

*   *   *

Sue and me. Double trouble. Sue was brunette, I was blonde, but we had our hair cut in the same long, shaggy style. I bought a little orange VW Beetle on hire purchase, the first car I owned, and we were out every night in it, zipping from Morton's to Monkberry's to a party at so-and-so's house. We'd only go out on dates if we could take each other so we knew we were protected. A message Sue left for me around this time is pretty typical: 'Arrived home to the phone already ringing again, some bloke from the States – friend of Clive's – wants to take us out. Can't handle all these bloody men …'

A few days after Christmas in 1976, Sue and I were at some party just off Hyde Park, chatting to Bryan Ferry – who by then was enjoying solo success after finding fame with Roxy Music – and *Monty Python*'s Eric Idle. It was getting late when Eric turned to us and said, 'Come on, girls, we're going back to Bryan's place. Why don't you come too?' Well, Sue was up for it, obviously, because she was seeing Bryan on the quiet, but I was thinking, *Sue's got Bryan – which means I'm going to have to do it with Eric! No bloody way …* So I told him it was late and we had to be going home, but Eric was so persistent that in the end I agreed we'd come, but that Sue and I would follow them in my Beetle as I didn't want to abandon it in town. We set off in convoy with

Bryan and Eric out in front. We were driving around Hyde Park Corner roundabout when suddenly I swerved off towards Knightsbridge at high speed – and the boys couldn't follow us because it was one-way. Sue and I were in hysterics all the way home. When we got back to Wandsworth, the phone was already ringing. It was Eric.

'What happened to you?'

'Oh, we just decided to come home,' I said. 'We're both tired and I've got to get up early tomorrow to see my parents before New Year's Eve. Sorry.'

'Come on, girls, come on over,' he said. 'There's no turkey left, but there's plenty of stuffing!'

*   *   *

We didn't do much in the way of drugs at this time. Partying was mostly about the booze, although if someone had some coke we might do the odd line. In those days it was so much purer that you didn't get wired or zombied-out, it just gave you a little boost of confidence. I never went completely mad – that came later. But one night I was in Monkberry's with Sue when our gay friend, Colin, called us over. He was holding out his hand and at first glance it seemed empty, but when I looked closer I saw this tiny little square, like a windowpane.

'It's acid.' He grinned. 'Want to try it?'

'Come off it, that tiny thing? That's not going to do anything!'

'Believe me,' said Colin. 'This stuff works.'

So Sue and I took it – and, WHOOSH, we were off!

My abiding memory of my first acid trip is lots and lots of laughter. After Monkberry's we piled into my Beetle (yes, I drove, can you believe it?) and ended up at a punk club where a bloke started chatting me up. He was coming on strong and, for a laugh, I told him, 'I won't have sex with you unless you do it with my friends Sue and Colin as well. We come as a package.' He must have been keen because he agreed on the spot. Then Colin piled in: 'We can't have sex with you before we check out the goods.' So that bloke came to the Ladies with us, dropped his trousers and showed us his willy. Well, that really set us off. Hysterical with laughter, we ran outside and got back into my car – but then the bloke appeared, trousers still round his ankles, and started banging on the window. As I tried to start the engine Colin locked the doors and eventually we drove away, screaming our heads off.

At some point we ended up at Colin's flat on Harley Street. We lay around for what seemed like hours, arguing over who was going to make a cup of tea, when suddenly the door flew open and a naked African guy was standing there holding a tray perfectly set with cups, saucers, teapot, sugar and a jug of milk. *Am I hallucinating?*

'Where did he come from?' said Sue.

Colin looked up. 'Umm … I think he might be a friend of mine.'

At that, the guy put down the tray and left the room.

At some point the next day – or possibly the day after that – Sue and I drove back to Wandsworth. This was where things got a bit scary. I remember sitting in the bedroom with Sue, staring at our reflections in the mirror, convinced we had thick white makeup all over our faces. We sat there, rubbing frantically at our cheeks, getting increasingly frantic; we had to talk ourselves through it so we didn't totally lose it. I hated that total loss of control so much – the feeling of being on a runaway train that you can't get off – that I never did acid again.

The last thing I remember is driving to the King's Road early in the morning with Sue and getting some T-shirts made that read, 'I love Ruby Morris.' This was in honour of a little acid poem we'd made up at some point during those crazy hours.

When you walk through the door, chuck,
Cup of tea and biscuit, luv,
Your pound's worth more at Ruby Morris.
Where else?

The 'chuck' bit came from Sue, because she was northern, the tea – well, you know about that part, we liked the name Ruby, and Morris came from David Morris, who was now Lorraine's husband. Sue had once had a bit of a fling with him. God, she was naughty.

Having said that, I wasn't exactly living like the Blessed Sister Josephine either. I had a succession of boyfriends. There was Richard North Lewis – still a friend – who worked for the company that produced model cards for the big agencies – probably because of the access it gave him to an endless stream of gorgeous girls. Women loved Richard: he was so utterly charming and good-looking, with big dark eyes and an infectious smile. He was incredibly naughty, and although I was his girlfriend for a while, I think I was probably just one of many.

Then I went out with Dodi Fayed. I had a mad crush on him. For our first date he took me to a private screening of a movie he had just produced. I must have been partied out, because the last thing I remember was fighting to keep my eyes open before falling asleep. Oops. Dodi and I saw each other for a few dates, nearly always at Tramp. I even went on a couple of dates with the footballer, George Best. He was pissed out of his brain both times I saw him. On our second and final date we were sitting in a bar when he turned to me and slurred, 'Marry me, Jo.' I just laughed. *You've got to be joking.*

After a while Sue and I had to move out of the house in Wandsworth and, soon after, Sue got engaged to the singer Lulu's brother, Billy Lawrie. Meanwhile, I moved to a flat in Fulham to house-sit for some friends and started seeing a guy called Flavio. He was Colombian, mad as a hatter and always had huge amounts of money and coke, although it didn't occur to me that he might be a major-league dealer, even when he announced one day that he was off to Bali for six weeks and was going to leave his 'stash' in my Fulham flat for safe-keeping. I watched as Flavio hid this catering-sized Maxwell House jar of coke in a recess in the chimney, out of my reach, 'so you won't be tempted, darling'.

Fool!

As soon as he'd left I was on the phone to my friend, Max. 'Flavio's left all his stash here, down the side of the chimney!'

'Right, I'm coming over,' he said.

We spent the whole of the next two days trying to reach that damn jar. We'd have a break for a bit, smoke a cigarette, then get back to the job. Eventually, using a tool fashioned from two bent coat-hangers, we managed to pull it out. We stood the jar on the table, then carefully unwrapped it, remembering how it was put together so Flavio wouldn't know we'd opened it. Take off the paper, peel off that bit – easy does it! – and finally we unscrewed the lid. It was crammed to the brim with the purest fluffy white Colombian coke. Carefully, I took out a scoop for me, a scoop for Max, we packed the jar back and then we were off. Tramp,

Monkberry's – we went crazy! A couple of days later we finished it, so we went and got some more. After a while we just attached a piece of string to the jar so we could pull it out whenever we wanted. For the next six weeks we were the most popular people in London, but suddenly Flavio was due to return and the jar was barely a quarter full. *Oh, God, what was he going to say?* I panicked, refilled the jar with flour, carefully wrapped it up and put it back in the chimney.

A couple of nights later I was in Tramp and one of the barmen told me there was a phone call for me.

'Hello?'

It was Max. 'Flavio's back!' he hissed. 'Why the hell did you put that flour in the jar? You've messed up his stash. He's looking for you, Jo!'

'Well, I thought if I mixed it up a bit he wouldn't be able to tell! Do you think—'

I didn't get any further. Just then there was a tap on my shoulder. I turned round and there was Flavio.

'Oh, heeeey, Flavio! It's so great to see you!'

He didn't look as if he felt the same. In fact, he looked a lot like a Colombian drugs baron who'd just found out he'd been robbed.

'You 'ave ruined my stash,' he said, quietly.

Fuuuuuck. 'I'm so sorry, Flavio, but, you know, you left me there with all that coke, it *was* a bit of a risk ...'

He was furious. But after he'd ranted for a bit, his anger faded and he was remarkably reasonable about the whole thing. He didn't kill me, after all.

And that was the last I saw of Flavio until a few months later, by which time he was still doling out the good stuff, but my life had changed again, this time beyond all recognition.

7

I looked at my reflection in the mirror and gave my hair a ruffle. *Not bad.* I was wearing a navy-blue dress with white flecks that used to belong to my granny (I've always been a vintage girl) with a tweed jacket and beige high-heeled boots. I loved the outfit, but I *really* didn't want to go out that night. I was, quite frankly, partied out. Giving myself a final once-over in the mirror, I tried a smile. *Come on, Jo, you might even enjoy yourself.*

It was 9 September 1977 and I'd had to move out of the flat in Fulham where I'd been house-sitting as the owners were returning, leaving me homeless. Although I had the option of going back to the Old Vicarage full-time, zipping back and forth to Benfleet in my Beetle was exhausting – and as much as I loved being with Jamie (who was about to turn three), I needed to be in London for work. At the time I was getting a lot of work, with Freemans and Grattan, the big mail-order fashion catalogues of the time, to give me a regular wage. More interesting jobs, when I was lucky enough to get them, included fashion shoots for *Jackie* and TV commercials. I yearned to be in front of the camera!

The solution to my housing crisis was, sadly, the indirect result of my friend Lorraine's marriage hitting bad times, with her and David deciding to spend time apart. Until I found something permanent, David said, I could stay in the guest room of their beautiful three-storey house off Kensington High Street. I gratefully accepted. Then, the day before I was due to move in, he called to say he was having a big party for Richard Jefferies and his new wife that night: would I like to come? I tried desperately to think of an excuse. After nearly two crazy years as a single girl about town, I'd been to so many parties I felt I'd met pretty much everyone in London, so I had no doubt it would be the same old faces, the same old chat. But David had been sweet enough to let me move in: I really had to make the effort.

So, my expectations were pretty low when I walked into the party that evening, but when I looked around the hall I was stunned. The place was packed with everyone I *didn't* know. All sorts of glamorous, exotic people – and I had no idea who most of them were! Perhaps it was going to be fun, after all.

I caught a glimpse of David, who waved and mouthed, 'Drinks in the kitchen!' so I made my way through the crowd, noting Rolling Stones bassist, Bill Wyman, deep in conversation with a leggy blonde. The booze was flowing and I grabbed a vodka and tonic. Reflected in the mirrored tiles above the sink, I saw a spiky-haired skinny guy standing directly behind me, pretending – and there's no polite way of putting this – to hump me. There he was, thrusting away, clearly thinking he was hysterical. *What an idiot.* But then he saw me watching him and shot me this cheeky smile and I couldn't help but return it. He was wearing a velvet jacket, a pair of gabardine trousers with strips of tapestry sewn down each side and Capezios – white dance shoes that were very popular at the time. I've always been a sucker for a good look and his was pure rock 'n' roll (although the tapestry trim on those trousers was *shocking*).

I knew who he was, of course – although probably only because I'd just seen Bill Wyman and made the connection – but I'd mixed with enough actors and musicians to be unimpressed by celebrity. I'd learnt that you should never take people at face value: you might meet a gardener who is fascinating and a rock star who turns out to be a complete dickhead. Besides, I wasn't the type to get fanatical about the Stones or any other band – and I certainly wasn't star-struck enough to flirt with him just because he was famous. You've got to remember that there wasn't anything like the cult of celebrity that exists today, when every girl seems to want to date a movie star or marry a footballer and the paparazzi stalk celebrities when they go out to get coffee. There just wasn't the interest. So I picked up my drink, still chuckling to myself, and slipped past him into the living room. A little while later, though, he came and found me again.

'Hi, I'm Ronnie Wood.'

'I'm Jo Howard,' I said. 'Nice to meet you.'

He had obviously been expecting me to scream or faint or something, because he reached behind him and pulled out a copy of the Stones album, *Black and Blue*. 'This is me,' said Ronnie, pointing himself out in the photo.

Oh, God, that's terrible, I thought. *He must think the world of himself.*

'So what do you do for a living, then?' he asked.

'I work in Woolworths,' I said. 'The main branch on Oxford Street.'

'Are you the manageress or something? In fashion?'

'Nah, I worked on records, but now I'm on the broken-biscuits counter.' This was where you could get a big bag of mixed broken biscuits for a few pennies. It was the first thing that sprang to mind because it was where Dad used to say I'd end up if I didn't work harder at school.

'You're having me on,' he said.

'I'm most certainly not,' I said, indignantly. I pulled out some pictures I had in my diary of a modelling trip I'd taken to LA and Vegas the month before. 'Look at this! Us girls were chosen out of all the Woolworths employees in England to represent the company in America.' I pointed at a couple of other people in the photo. 'This is the woman who organized the trip. And this is Mr Woolworth's son!' It was actually the photographer. 'We went round all the branches of Woolworths in California and met the staff. It was *so* exciting!'

Ronnie fell for every word of it, the twit. He kept going on about how he would never have thought such good-looking girls would be working at Woolies. After a few minutes of this, I made my excuses and went to get a refill, thinking that was the last of it – but once Ronnie had set his mind to something, he wasn't one to give up.

I was chatting to my friend, Gael, when he sidled up and said, 'Come with me, girls, I want to show you something.' He led us both upstairs to the bathroom and got out some coke.

'Ooh, great, thanks!'

After we'd had a line each we went to leave, but before I could follow Gael back downstairs he made a grab for me and tried to kiss me. I pushed him away, laughing. 'Oi, you're a fast mover, aren't you?' And with that I went back to join the party – and that was the last I saw of him.

I went to bed that night with a smile on my face, thinking about how I'd pulled a fast one on the Rolling Stone. He *was* cute, though …

The next day was moving day. I arrived back at the house in Kensington late that afternoon with all my bags. David opened the door.

'Hey, Jo,' he said, with a smile. 'There's someone here to see you. In the living room.'

I dumped my things, opened the door to the living room – and there, to my surprise, was Ronnie Wood, sitting with another guy, who, I later found out, was his chauffeur, Frank.

'You don't work in Woolworths,' he said.

'How do you know I don't?'

'Because I've just spent the last few hours sitting outside the staff entrance waiting for you.'

'Oh …'

Ronnie hung around for the rest of the afternoon. He was a skinny little thing, not my usual type at all, but he was very charming and had a mischievous sense of fun that I found really appealing. We giggled and flirted and by the end of the day, I was hoping I'd see him again soon.

Thankfully, I didn't have to wait long. A few days later David had another party at the house and Ronnie came along. This time he brought his wife. I knew about Krissy, with whom he had a young son, Jesse, but he insisted his marriage was all but over. They certainly didn't seem to be together.

Later that night when I was lying in bed, keen to get some sleep as I had work the next day, Ronnie suddenly appeared at my door. I didn't make much of a fuss. He closed it behind him and put a chair against it, a cheeky smile on his face.

'What are you doing that for?' I said.

'I don't want anyone else coming in.'

He came over and lay on the bed, but I wouldn't let him get under the covers or take off any of his clothes.

'Behave yourself,' I said, firmly. And he did – for a little while ...

The next morning I got ready and went downstairs, leaving Ronnie in bed, when David appeared out of the kitchen and started waving frantically at me.

'Sssh, Krissy's asleep on the couch!'

Krissy? As in Krissy Wood, Ronnie's wife? *You have got to be kidding.*

I went back upstairs and woke Ronnie. 'Did you know that your wife is asleep downstairs?'

'Oh, don't worry.' He yawned. 'I gave her a Quaalude sandwich. She'll be out for hours.'

*   *   *

Less than two weeks after our first meeting, Ronnie was scheduled to fly out to New York with the band to shoot the cover of *Rolling Stone* magazine and then on to Paris, where they would stay until Christmas, working on their new album. I knew I'd probably never see him again after that, so I wanted to spend every moment I could with him until he left. Thankfully, Ronnie felt the same way and for the next few days he took me everywhere with him, introducing me as Frank's girlfriend so that Krissy wouldn't get suspicious. There was a party at Eric Clapton's house, one at Jimmy Page's – he even invited me to a gathering at his huge Richmond home, The Wick. The 'chauffeur's girlfriend' line evidently wasn't that convincing, though, because it was at this party that Krissy – who hadn't put in an appearance all evening – summoned me to her bedroom. I knocked gingerly and then went in to find her sitting up in bed.

'Oh, *hiiii*,' she said, vaguely. 'I just want you to know I'm not in love with Ronnie.' She went on to tell me that they had nearly got divorced a few years back, but then her father had died and she was so devastated that they got back together again. 'I'm actually in love with Jimmy Page,' added Krissy. 'And I've lived for a year with him wearing just a sheet.'

'Um, okay. Thank you for telling me.'

After that bizarre encounter, I didn't feel too bad about the fact that I was falling for Ronnie. The more I saw of him, the more I fancied him. I used to analyse his face and think, *He's got little beady eyes, a big nose and no mouth, but put it all together and it just … works.* I thought he was unbelievably sexy – and that was before I even saw him play the guitar.

As his departure approached, things got even more intense between us. We were at a party in the country and I remember him sneaking through the fields at dead of night to this little cottage where I was staying. It was just madly, magically passionate.

And then the awful day came that Ronnie left for New York. We said our goodbyes, but there was no 'I'll miss you' or even 'See you again some time.' I resigned myself to the fact that our fling had been flung.

A few days after he had left I got home from work and, as I closed the front door, heard David call from the living room.

'Jo, quick, Ronnie's on the phone for you!'

Breaking into a delighted grin, I ran in and grabbed the receiver. 'Hey, how's New York?'

'Meet me in Paris, Jo!'

'What? In Paris? Where?'

'I'll be at a place called L'Hôtel.'

He gave me the address, but I didn't know much French and, besides, the line was so bad I could barely make out what he was saying.

'Okay, that's L'Hôtel on Friday. I'll be there, Ronnie. Can't wait.'

But he had already gone.

Once the initial buzz of euphoria had faded, it was replaced by an uneasy feeling that actually this was a really stupid idea. All I had was the name of a hotel and a vague date. I had no way of contacting him. Was I really going to blow a large chunk of my savings on a flight to Paris on the off-chance he might appear? After all, Ronnie wasn't exactly Mr Reliable … But I didn't have any jobs booked for the next few days – plus I was *desperate* to see Ronnie again – so, with the spirit of adventure that, over the years, had landed me in fun and trouble in equal measures, I decided to go for it.

On the Friday night I arrived at L'Hôtel at nine: I thought I'd get there later in the day to make sure Ronnie had already arrived. The hotel was tucked away a few streets from the Left Bank of the Seine on the rue des Beaux-Arts. From the outside, it looked like a grand private home, while inside it was like a magical cocoon, spinning dizzyingly upwards around a big circular lobby. This was seriously luxurious.

My heels click-clacked across the marble floor to the reception desk where I asked for Mr Wood. The guy flicked through the register.

'We 'ave no Monsieur Wood 'ere, mademoiselle.'

Shit. 'Are you sure? Mr Ronnie Wood. Could you check again, please?'

'I'm very sorry, but there is no one of that name staying with us.'

So, my worst fears had come true. The wanker had stood me up! I was stuck in Paris with no money and nowhere to stay. What the hell was I going to do now?

'Do you have any free rooms? I'm afraid I don't have a reservation.'

But the guy shook his head. 'I am sorry, mademoiselle, we are fully booked because of ze *pret-à-porter* shows.'

Now I *really* began to panic. I begged and pleaded, and I guess I must have looked really desperate because eventually the guy said there was a maid's room at the top of the hotel where I could stay. That night I lay in a tiny single bed in the smallest room I'd ever seen, feeling like an absolute idiot. I was exhausted, but couldn't get to sleep as I was planning how to sort out this mess the next morning. I must have dropped off at some point, though, because I remember waking up and seeing a dull grey light filtering through the crack in the curtains. I looked at my watch: 6 a.m. *Oh, God, this is awful.* I dropped my head back on the pillow and shut my eyes again. Suddenly the phone rang.

I leapt on it before it had a chance to ring twice.

''Allo, is that Mademoiselle Karslake?'

'Yes! I mean, *oui.*'

'Are you also known as Mademoiselle 'Oward?'

'I am.'

'Ah, we 'ave a Monsieur Wood down 'ere asking for you. Shall I send 'im up?'

Oui, oui, oui!

I was naked and looked a right state after my sleepless night, but I only had time to give my hair a quick brush and grab a sarong and tie it around me like a dress when there was a tap at the door. I opened it and there was Ronnie. I flew into his arms, all instantly forgiven.

'I'm so sorry,' he said, between kisses. 'Concorde blew an engine over Ireland so we had to land in Shannon, get a flight to London and then another one here.'

But I didn't care. *He hadn't stood me up after all!*

Someone shoved past us into the room. Without saying a word, or even looking at me, this dark-haired bloke sat down on the tiny square of carpet and started rummaging in what looked like a doctor's bag.

'Don't take any notice of Keith,' said Ronnie. 'It's been a long flight.'

I had seen Keith Richards once before, in Tramp when I was pregnant with Jamie. I had been sitting with Jan Gold, wife of the club's owner, Johnny, when she nudged me and said, 'Jo, look who's on that table.' And there he was: pale, scruffy, with black kohl smudged round his eyes. He looked high as a kite – and as if he'd rather be anywhere else than Tramp. *How cool*, I'd thought.

And now, here he was, sitting on the floor of my tiny hotel room. Keith reached into his bag and took out a silver spoon, a bottle of pills and a lighter. In a matter of seconds, he'd crushed some of the pills with a bit of water, cooked them up, then filled a syringe and stabbed it straight through his shirt. A moment's pause – then he looked up at me with a radiant smile. 'Hello, my dear. I've heard so much about you!'

8

The three of us spent the next three days cooped up in my broom-cupboard of a hotel room, drinking and taking drugs, only occasionally venturing out in Keith's Bentley to get a fix or a bite to eat. Food was not a priority: you don't have much of an appetite on coke. We'd go to these fabulously posh restaurants like La Coupole or Fouquet's and push sole Meunière around the plate. If we needed to sleep, Ronnie and I squeezed into the single bed and Keith slumped in the armchair, although sleeping wasn't much of a concern either. I was having the time of my life, getting high on coke and drunk on Southern Comfort and lemonade (I guess we needed the sugar), and I'm proud to say that I kept up with the boys all the way, matching them drink for drink, line for line. I can't even remember getting hangovers at the beginning. I must have built my system up by drinking every day, like an athlete in training for a marathon. Quite simply, I took to the rock 'n' roll lifestyle like I'd been born to it.

I adored Keith from the start – which was lucky, because he and Ronnie came as a pair. Keith and I have a special relationship to this day. One of the first things I loved about him most was his naughtiness. The three of us were dining in Fouquet's one night;

Keith loved the place, which I always found funny because he's such a rocker and Fouquet's is like somewhere you'd take your great-grandma: all white-coated waiters and starched linen napkins. Anyway, this old boy sitting a few tables from us at Fouquet's kept looking at Keith and, after dinner, he came up to our table and said, 'Monsieur Richards, may I please have your autograph?' We'd already noticed him – it was difficult not to, as he had a very large brown growth on his head. Keith took his piece of paper and wrote with a flourish: 'Where did you get that hat? Keith Richards.'

I was so shocked. 'Keith, you can't write that!'

'I just have, darling.'

As much as I loved hanging out with Keith, though, I only had eyes for Ronnie. I was besotted with the guy – and longing to have some time alone with him. We'd been in Paris for three nights and we *still* hadn't done it because of the ever-present Keith. We were lying cuddled up in bed together in the early hours one morning when I whispered to him, 'Don't you think this is all a bit, well, cramped?'

I thought Keith was asleep, but no. 'Quite right, Jo!' I heard from the foot of the bed. 'Why don't we move to my apartment?'

'What was that, Keith? You have a flat in Paris?' *So why the hell have we been squashed up in here?*

I got my answer later that day when we'd checked out of L'Hôtel and arrived at Keith's place. From the outside it looked amazing. It was on an upper floor of one of those elegant old buildings, fringed with little balconies, just behind the Tuileries Gardens. Inside, however, it was a pit. Dishes piled up in the sink. A white plastic couch, torn and filthy, like something you'd find poking out of a tip. His desk – Keith always has to have a huge desk, wherever he lives – was covered with papers and ashtrays filled with the remains of joints. But at least there was a bedroom with a double bed, which Keith very kindly said we could take. Quick as a flash, I turned over the sheets (I didn't hold out much hope of finding any clean ones), and Ronnie and I scrambled out of our clothes. Giddy with lust and desperate to get our hands on each other, we jumped onto the bed – and it collapsed beneath us with an almighty crash.

Keith appeared at the door to find us sprawled half-naked on the floor. 'Are you all right down there?'

'Yes! Sorry! All fine!'

While we were camping out at Keith's, I tried to clean the place up a bit without stepping on his toes. 'Keith, do you mind if I just wash the dishes?' Or 'Can I tidy the coffee table?' It also gave me something to do while the boys spent endless hours listening to music and playing their guitars.

My memories of those first days in Paris are a bit like my acid trip: the same crazy euphoria and laughter, but without the scary loss of control. Everything was new and exciting, passionate and rock 'n' roll. I was madly in love: with Paris, with fun and most of all with Ronnie. We were spending almost every waking hour with each other – and, thanks to all the high-grade cocaine, there were many, many of those. He was never one for grand declarations of love, but he showed it in other ways. One day he presented me with a gorgeous Yves St Laurent scarf decorated with butterflies, and when he sat and played the guitar or took out his pencils to sketch me, there was such passion in his creativity it left me breathless. Plus, of course, we were at it like rabbits …

After a few days *chez* Keith, Ronnie and I decamped to the new tower-block Novotel on the Left Bank. Shortly after we'd checked in, Ronnie announced, 'Right, now we're going visiting.' He led me into the hallway, went a few doors down and knocked. The door swung open to reveal a balding, bearded little cherub of a guy. 'Jo,' said Ronnie. 'Meet Chuch.'

Chuch's real name was Royden Walter Magee, though no one ever called him that. Detroit-born and fizzing with energy, he worked as Ronnie's roadie. It would be months before I saw what went into a Stones tour and the role of the hundreds of roadies who got the massive production from one city to the next, but Chuch was one of the select few who helped run things even when the band wasn't on the road. And for Ronnie – who had worked with him for years alongside Rod Stewart in Faces and would never have dreamt of joining the Stones without him – Chuch wasn't just the key guy: he was family.

Chuch and I hit it off immediately. He had such a great heart, the sort of guy who, after you'd worked hard and had a few beers, would get all emotional. 'Jo, *I love you, man*, you're my best buddy.' I became his assistant roadie – and over the years he would become one of my dearest friends.

Our stay at the Novotel lasted all of two days before Ronnie declared it 'soulless' and booked us into a hotel called the Château Frontenac just off the Champs-Élysées, which he promptly christened Château Front-and-Back. I turned our room there into a love-nest, draping scarves over lamps to soften the glare and lighting sticks of incense. So began a lifetime's habit of redecorating hotel rooms. On tour I would always take our own pillows and pillowcases, scented candles and framed photos of the kids to make wherever we were staying feel like home.

By the time I paid a brief visit back to the UK, after I'd been in Paris a couple of weeks, for a modelling job and, of course, to see Jamie, whom I missed like crazy (although he was having a lovely little life at the Old Vicarage), I felt completely settled in.

The Stones were in Paris to work on a new album, *Some Girls*, the first for Ronnie as a fully fledged member of the band he had joined, in the place of the departed Mick Taylor, some 18 months earlier. On the first studio day, Chuch and Ronnie were busy getting themselves ready to go while I sat on the bed watching them, wondering if I was expected to come along, too. Ronnie hadn't invited me – but then he hadn't said I shouldn't come, either. I suddenly felt weirdly shy. I hadn't met the other guys yet (Mick Jagger, drummer Charlie Watts and bass guitarist Bill Wyman) and wondered if they even knew about Ronnie's new girlfriend – if that was what I was. Luckily, Chuch must have sensed I was feeling like a bit of a spare part because as they were walking out of the door he called to me, 'Well, are you coming, Jo?'

'Um, will there be anywhere for me to sit?'

'Of course! Get your coat.'

'But what shall I do when we get there?'

He grinned. 'Just stick with me, kid.' So I did. In the early days in particular, Chuch proved a godsend. If there was anything I didn't know – about music, touring or just dealing with Ronnie – I'd ask Chuch.

The studio was nothing like I'd imagined. I'd thought it would be a cramped cupboard of a room, but it was huge – a soaring, cavernous space with high ceilings, little booths at the back and a large control room. Ronnie introduced me to Alan Dunn,

Mick's right-hand man, their engineer, Chris Kimsey, and then to the other guys from the band.

'So you're Broken Biscuit, then?' said Mick Jagger, in that familiar voice. From then on, that was what he called me. Never Jo. It was funny at first – not so much a year later when he was still doing it. Bill greeted me politely, while Charlie sort of shrugged me off.

Chuch showed me to a couch in the corner about 15 feet from where the boys were playing, and I sat there until gone five in the morning, greedily drinking in every moment of the whole magical experience.

As they were packing their things away, Charlie wandered over to me. 'You still 'ere, then?' he said. I didn't quite know how to react – but then he smiled and that was my introduction to his wonderfully dry sense of humour. I became good friends with Bill, too, and still am. But for me it was all about Ronnie and Keith, and it wasn't long before we'd become a tight-knit trio of studio musketeers.

From then on, the boys worked in the studio every day. Mick always wanted to get to work by early evening, but there was usually a dinner in town first and only afterwards did they go to the studio. They would often play on past dawn and into the following afternoon, sometimes even the next morning, depending on how many drugs had been consumed. At the end of the session we'd pile into Keith's Bentley, despite the hours of boozing, and he'd drive us to the hotel or we'd go back to his apartment and play dominoes. Keith would never let anyone go to bed until he had won. In the end I refused to play: 'You always have to bloody win, Keith, so what's the point?'

For me, the sessions were a real education. I loved seeing the

Mummy and daddy cutting their wedding cake, November 1954. They look so adorable.

The whole family outside the Old Vicarage when I was 16. This was taken by a photographer from the *Sun* newspaper when I was their 'Face of 72'. *From left to right*: Paul, dad (in his Beatnik era), Lize, mum, me, Vinnie.

Right: Me aged five with dad on one of his beloved Lambrettas. He gave me my own red Lambretta for my 21st birthday – and I still have it to this day.

Bottom left: This was taken in our garden in Basildon. I'm wearing a dress made for me by mum and a shower cap – I have no idea why!

Bottom right: Here I am as the Christmas Tree Fairy in my school play wearing my perfect tinsel-trimmed fairy dress and a pair of dirty plimsolls.

Above: Me and my siblings: Vinnie, Lize and Paul. I was 14 and at the height of my Twiggy obsession.

Left: So excited to be taking my first steps on the catwalk! This was during my graduation show at the London Academy of Modelling, wearing mum's African straw hat and a red towelling bikini she'd made for me.

My very first modelling shot, aged 15, taken by a friend of my dad who lived near us at the Old Vicarage. I love this picture as it reminds me of the excitement of growing up.

Hello Sailor… I was asked to be the mascot of HMS *Caledonian* after appearing in the *Daily Mirror*. You can just about see the hole in the top of my tights that I felt so conscious about!

My big break as the *Sun*'s 'Face of 72'. You can tell just by looking at me that I was in absolute heaven!

One of the many modelling cards from my career.

378
Jo Howard

Height 5'6½
Bust 33 Waist 23 Hips 34
Dress Size 8 - 10
Shoes 5 Gloves 6½
Inseam 32 Outside Leg 42
Hair Blonde Eyes Blue

Hauteur 1.69
Poitrine 84 Taille 58 Hanches 86
Confection 36 - 38
Chaussures 38 Gants 6½
Pantalon Int. 81 Ext. 107
Cheveux Blonds Yeux Bleus

Laraine Ashton-I.F.M.
01·629 3176

This is one of the photos taken by Eric Swayne around the time we started seeing each other, shortly before I left my first husband, Peter.

Mr and Mrs Green! The one and only photo from my first wedding in Las Vegas. Peter and I had just left County Hall where we tied the knot. God only knows why I'm holding a cuddly toy…

My gorgeous little fella, Jamie, at six months. Peter took this photo when we were living in Shouldham Street, Marylebone.

Striking my best rock
god pose with Ronnie's
guitar on one of the
early tours.

Peeping out at Ronnie
from between the flight
cases backstage. I always
loved being on the road
– we were like one
big family.

Under the stage during a
show in the early eighties.
Keith's standing above me
and Mick is walking away.

On the road – and in the air. On a private jet with Keith and Ronnie during one of
the Stones' tours. Keith has always been able to sleep in the weirdest positions…

Leah's first birthday party in Paris.

Alien invasion with Jamie and Keith's son, Marlon. Nassau, 1979.

Me and my little girl sunbathing in Mexico, where we had fled from our home in New York to escape the debt collectors.

Keith serenading Princess Leah!

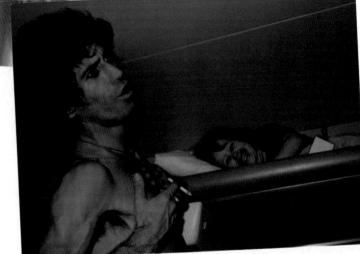

way the boys created music. At first it was just one long jamming session, but then gradually a song would take shape. I'd hear them say, 'Right, you come in on that bit, I'll play this riff,' and have no idea what they were on about. But as I was there night after night, I gradually started to understand how it worked, the way Ronnie would play a little bit that would then weave in with Keith. Nowadays when I listen to music I can hear all the different instruments and identify who's playing what bit – especially in the Stones – but that's only after years of experience.

While the boys worked, I'd drink, listen to the music, sketch and write in my diary. I made myself a den in a far corner of the room, using sound-buffering panels and a couple of big blankets draped over the top. Once that got broken down, I took over one of the booths and put up a sign saying, 'Josephine's Club. Members Only!' I had a little box for a table where I'd roll joints for Keith and put cushions on the floor for when Ronnie came in for a snog. This was also where I'd catch up on a bit of sleep at three in the morning if the boys were on a mad one. I woke up after one such nap at around 9 a.m., and as I lay there I noticed that it was eerily quiet. Sure enough, when I peeked out into the studio the band wasn't even there: in their place was an entire classical orchestra in full evening dress. I had to tiptoe out, muttering, '*Excusez-moi, excusez-moi,*' as I did the walk of shame between the strings and the woodwind. I eventually located the band in a smaller studio down the hallway. They all found it hilarious.

As the days went on, an assortment of people came and went from the studio: dealers and hangers-on. Apart from Jane Rose, the Stones' secretary, there weren't many other girls apart from me; the groupies came later, on the tours. But one day this stunningly tall blonde girl strode in. I recognized her instantly because I'd actually worked with her on a job about six months previously, a TV commercial for French perfume. When I had got to the studio, the director had given me the low-down: 'Jo, you're walking along the road with your boyfriend when this beautiful girl walks past. Your boyfriend looks at her longingly and you give his arm an annoyed tug, but she's wearing the perfume so she's irresistible!' *Great*, I thought. *I get to be the jilted chick.* Anyway, the irresistible perfume girl turned out to be Jerry Hall – who was at the time of the commercial was dating Bryan Ferry, my mate Sue's ex – and the guy playing my boyfriend was none other than Chris Jagger, Mick's brother. And now Jerry was dating Mick.

The weeks sped past and all of a sudden it was mid-December. Ronnie and I abruptly found ourselves at a crossroads. He was going home to spend Christmas with his family and I was going back to mine. No matter how often he told me his marriage was over, I could no longer ignore the fact that my man was married. We'd been living in this magical bubble in Paris, but real life was waiting for us to come home.

We had a very emotional night just before we left Paris. I was crazy in love with this guy – he had become my world – but he had a wife and a son, Jesse, who was barely a year old. I knew I wasn't prepared to be his bit on the side for ever; I couldn't do that to his family – or to my own. As we left each other at Heathrow airport I was crying and even Ronnie had tears in his eyes, but I knew I had to call a stop to what we had, at least to give him a chance to make things work with Krissy.

That afternoon I remember getting back to Sue's flat in Hammersmith, where I was staying before going to Essex for Christmas, and collapsing in tears.

'Oh, Sue, it's over!' I howled.

'It's probably for the best,' she said, gathering me up into a hug. 'You did the right thing.'

But I was inconsolable. 'Oh, God, I love him so much, I can't bear it …'

She tucked me into her spare bed and I tried to get some sleep, but it was pointless. As soon as I closed my eyes, all I could see was Ronnie's cheeky smile, and the tears started flowing all over again. I was a mess. The thought of not seeing him was so painful.

Then, at around 2 a.m., there was a loud banging at the front door. A pause, then it started up again. *What the hell?*

I heard Sue answer the door and muffled talking, then the sound of footsteps coming quickly along the corridor and finally the door to my room swinging open. Ronnie was silhouetted in the doorway.

'Jo, are you awake?'

He told me he had arrived at The Wick and had the most terrible argument with Krissy, then got back into the car and driven straight to me.

'I've done it, Jo,' he said. 'I've left my wife.'

9

That Christmas I spent a blissful few days with Jamie and my family at the Old Vicarage. I always loved seeing how settled Jamie was in the country with Mum (who at the time was only 43), Dad and my sister, who was only 10 years older than him. I remember watching him chasing the chickens around and giggling like a little loony. So, although it was always painful to leave him, I knew my baby couldn't have been happier. Then it was straight back to London and into the arms of my man. Now that we could be together officially, Ronnie and I were in giddy honeymoon mode – so we saw in the new year, 1978, by boarding a plane to the Bahamas with a Colombian drugs baron named Victor.

We had met the sharp-suited Victor back in Paris, where he'd been one of the small army of pharmaceutical Stones hangers-on, and he had invited us for a holiday at his rented place in Nassau: all expenses paid, luxury accommodation, the finest champagne and coke on tap. Ringo Starr was coming, too. But, as the saying goes, there's no such thing as a free lunch (or a free line) and in return for his largesse, Victor wanted Ronnie and Ringo to work on an album with him. Not that any of this was on my radar at the time: I was just thrilled at the prospect of a romantic holiday with my lover.

Things didn't start off too well. On the flight Victor was acting like a mad man as he was smoking 'dirty cigarettes' or DCs – little roll-ups containing smack – which he was intending to take in to the Bahamas. I didn't touch them, as they had the most revolting smell – if I think about it even now I gag – but Ronnie went into the bathroom for a sneaky puff. Shortly after he stumbled back to his seat, a flight attendant came over and crouched next to me.

'Excuse me,' she said to Ronnie, 'but I think your friend has left this in the toilet.'

She was holding out the bag of DCs. Ronnie must have got so stoned he'd left it in there.

'Oh, God, I'm sorry,' he said. 'Thank you ever so much. I'll get rid of them.'

She smiled warmly. 'Not to worry. Would you like another drink?'

Can you imagine that happening on a flight today?

As he was a drugs trafficker, I assumed that Victor would already have a plan in place to smuggle his stash through Customs, but as we started our descent he suddenly dumped the bag in my lap. It turned out that *I* was the plan.

'You are taking this in your bag,' he said.

'What? No way!'

But Ronnie thought it would be wiser to humour our host, so in the end we got a carton of duty-free cigarettes, removed all the cigarettes from the middle packet, stuffed Victor's stash in there, then carefully packed it up again to look like new.

Of course, when we got to Customs they immediately zeroed in on me; I must have been giving off guilty vibes. As they went through my bag, I offered up a silent prayer of thanks that we hadn't hidden the stash in there. Then the inspector held up the duty-free bag containing the carton of cigarettes. 'Is this yours?' he asked me.

'No,' I said, pointing at Victor. 'They're his!' I was damned if I was going to risk life in prison for him.

As Victor scowled at me, the inspector took out one packet and carefully checked inside, but to everyone's immense relief it wasn't the doctored one and we were finally waved through.

The house in Nassau, which Victor had rented from a music-industry friend, was like something out of a Bond movie, with huge picture windows looking out over a white-sand beach and a dazzling turquoise strip of sea. It was surrounded by a handful of guest villas, a huge pool, and boasted its own recording-studio complex. As Victor gave us the guided tour, I finally began to relax after the stresses of the journey and felt ready for some fun – and it looked like the party had already started in the living room, where a group of people were scattered around, drinking and chatting. In my jet-lagged haze, I thought one of the guys looked vaguely familiar. I looked a bit closer. *It couldn't be …* Oh, shit – it was. My old friend, Flavio, whom I hadn't seen since I'd stolen thousands of pounds' worth of his cocaine, then ruined the rest with self-raising Homepride. Great, so that was two pissed-off drug dealers I was now sharing a holiday home with …

Thankfully, however, Flavio was happy to forgive and forget the flour incident and, despite the bumpy start, it turned out to be a wild couple of weeks. We'd get out of bed as the sun went down and the boys would play music. I don't recall Victor's album ever getting made – I think he just wanted the kudos of getting a Rolling Stone and a Beatle into the studio together – and soon after our holiday he was packed off to jail for many, many years, busted by his own dad who had never approved of his son's career path.

On one of our last days in Nassau, Ronnie and I were sunbathing on the beach (it must have been one of the very rare occasions we were awake before sunset) when I glanced at him and saw the sun shining through his nose. I hadn't noticed it before, but there was a huge hole in his septum. He could have put a finger up each nostril and touched them together.

Ronnie, bless him, got all worried about it. The drugs had eaten through the cartilage, he explained. 'Do you still love me now you know?'

I showered him with kisses. 'Of course I do, silly!'

Truth be told, I loved him more and more each day. I had fallen hard – we both had. So, when our holiday came to an end and Ronnie had to head back to Paris to finish work on *Some Girls*, there was no question that I would go with him – and I arranged for Mum and Jamie to come to stay with us days after we got there.

We moved into an apartment in a handsome grey-stone building near the river that we nicknamed Complaining Mansions: the people downstairs were always grumbling about our noise. (I guess we *were* keeping pretty antisocial hours.) Now that we were staying in a proper apartment, rather than a hotel, I could throw myself into creating a home. Ronnie loved games, so we went out and got an elaborate model racing circuit, on which he, Keith and assorted other visitors would spend hours when they weren't making music. And although food still featured low on the list of everyone's priorities, I loved cooking huge, homely meals for whoever dropped by. Soon after we moved into Complaining Mansions, I whipped up a big Old Vicarage-style roast for 16, including Keith, Jane Rose, Mick and Jerry, Charlie and Chuch. Another night George Benson turned up; I remember being proud that he had seconds of my spaghetti Bolognese.

I spent many happy hours wandering around the local food markets, although the language barrier occasionally proved problematic. I had assumed my French would pick up during this time in Paris, but whenever I was out with Ronnie and Keith everyone just spoke English to them. It was my first taste of the crazy attention the Stones attracted wherever we went in the world. Everyone just *loved* those boys. It was only when I was out on my own that the locals suddenly didn't know a single word of English. Anyway, on one of my early solo outings, I found a stall selling a stunning selection of wild mushrooms. With a smile, I pointed to the ones I wanted.

'*Combien, mademoiselle?*' asked the stallholder.

I had no idea about weights, but the prices seemed to be in kilos, so I just said, '*Un kilo.*' The guy started shovelling them into a huge bag, more and more, while I stood there desperately trying to work out how to tell him to stop. Have you any idea how many wild mushrooms it takes to make a kilo? A hell of a lot, as it turned out. When he eventually handed over the bulging sack, I was too embarrassed to do anything but pay up. For the next week we ate mushroom soup, stuffed mushrooms, mushroom omelette and mushroom fricassee.

Settled in Paris with my man I was deliriously happy, but one thing would have made my life complete: Jamie. Keith had been joined in Paris by Marlon, his eight-year-old son with Anita Pallenberg. Marlon was a great kid, full of fun and cheekiness, and I love him. While the Stones were in the studio I'd take him roller-skating in the park, then bring him back to Complaining Mansions for bangers and mash. But hanging out with Marlon made me miss my own boy even more. I was in the midst of legal wrangles with Peter over custody, and until those were resolved, I couldn't take Jamie out of the UK full-time. An entry in my diary from this time reads: '30 January 1978. Slept all day, woke at 8 p.m. Called Mum and talked to my little fella. Jamie said he "wished I'd come out of the telephone"! Missing him LOTS.'

In early February I went back to the Old Vicarage and returned to Paris with Jamie, Mum and my now teenage sister, Lize. Jamie had never been on a plane before, and as we climbed he turned to me, eyes wide, and said, 'Mummy, why have the clouds fallen down?'

By now I had taken Ronnie to the Old Vicarage, and while he had been his usual charming self, I knew my parents were very concerned that their daughter was shacked up with one of the very same 'disgusting lads' that Dad had banned from our TV all those years earlier. But Ronnie was on his best behaviour and we had a wonderful week. It felt as if my life was coming together. It also made me think that once the album was finished – and the custody issues with my ex had been resolved – I could start planning for a future in which I could make a real home with the two people who mattered to me most: Jamie, my little baby; and Ronnie, whom I had dubbed, only half jokingly, in my diary, 'my big baby'.

* * *

We had been back in Paris just a month when I first started to feel ill. Until recently I'd had no problem keeping up with the boys and happily indulging in whatever was on offer. Now, even getting out of bed was a struggle. At first I thought that all the partying must have caught up with me, but when I started experiencing the familiar waves of queasiness I realized it wasn't a hangover: it was morning sickness.

I don't know why it came as such a surprise to me, really. Ronnie and I hadn't been at all careful – quite the opposite. It just hadn't occurred to me that I might fall pregnant: I was too drunk, too high, having too much fun even to think about it. But now here I was – and my feelings about it were strongly mixed. On the one hand the thought of having a child with Ronnie, whom I was so madly in love with, seemed wonderfully romantic, but how on earth would a baby fit into our lives? We were about as far from a conventional domestic set-up as you could get.

I was scheduled to go back to the UK for the weekend to see Jamie, so I decided I would break the news to Ronnie just before I left. I was terrified. We'd only been together for a few months and, besides, he was a rock 'n' roller! I'd probably be abandoned with a squealing kid and leaky boobs while he went off with a younger model. The thought sent my already volatile emotions into overdrive.

We were sitting on the sofa having a final cuddle before my cab to the airport arrived when I finally plucked up the courage to tell him.

Just as I feared, he didn't look too happy. 'You're *what?*'

'I'm pregnant,' I said. 'I don't want this to upset our relationship.'

But Ronnie just sat staring into space, looking like – well, like he'd just been told his relatively new girlfriend was up the duff.

'It's okay, you don't have to say anything now,' I went on, helplessly. 'Take the weekend to think about it. We'll talk when I get back.'

After a few moments, Ronnie looked at me. 'I don't have to think about it, Jo.'

I tried desperately to read his expression. 'You don't?'

He pulled me into his arms, a huge smile across his face. 'We're having our baby.'

* * *

On our final night in Paris, we had a huge party at Complaining Mansions to celebrate my 23rd birthday. It was a punk-themed party and I wore shiny plastic trousers and an artfully ripped T-shirt. I had designed the invitations: 'You are invited to bang your head on the wall, pass out and throw up!' Luckily no one seemed to notice that any throwing up I did was not related to over-indulgence …

The next day we were booked on a flight to London, then straight on to Los Angeles, where Ronnie was setting up a base in preparation for the boys' tour of the States later in the year. As usual with Ronnie, there hadn't been much discussion about our plans, no heartfelt declaration along the lines of 'Come and live with me in America, my darling!' It was just sort of assumed that I would be going with him.

As we boarded the plane I felt a shiver of delight at turning *left* into the first-class cabin – something I would never take for granted over subsequent years. I had come from quite a modest background so I never lost my appreciation of all the lovely things money brought with it. We had flown first class to Nassau a few months before, when I had loved the luxury and the feeling of being someone quite important, but this time it was different. This wasn't just the start of a holiday: I was on the way to America to build a home and a family with Ronnie. As I settled into the plush leather seat and sensed the first flutterings of our baby inside me, it felt like the beginning of the rest of our lives.

10

Our first home in LA was on Forest Knoll Drive, a minute from Sunset Boulevard in the car. The house was pure Hollywood. You walked through the front door to be met by the sight of a huge swimming-pool and a huge open-plan space. All the rooms were on one level, with a vast living area complete with an enormous central fireplace around which the bedrooms were arranged. It was a party house, through and through – in fact, before we moved in it had been used primarily for shooting porn films – so our little rock 'n' roll family fitted right in. Keith adopted one of the spare bedrooms as his own, closely followed by Ronnie's old Faces keyboard player, Ian 'Mac' McLagan, in another, and we were off!

Even though I was pregnant I still tried to keep the same hours as the boys, but obviously was not matching their levels of consumption. I hope it goes without saying that I never did drugs when I was pregnant. My diary entry for 11 April 1978 reads: 'Got up at 6 p.m. and cooked roast dinner for breakfast.' There were some wild nights. Dealers would be coming and going at all hours, including one girl, Cathy Smith, who virtually moved in for a time. I remember her and Keith having a massive row that only ended when Keith pulled out his gun, put it to her head and said, 'I'll give you forty-five reasons to get out of this house now.' She left – and if I had known then what she would end up doing later I would never, ever have let her in my house in the first place.

I'd have a sip of a drink just to feel like I was still part of the gang, but being straight while everyone else was drunk or high wasn't easy. Throw my raging hormones into the mix and it's no surprise that Ronnie and I had our first proper argument at Forest Knoll. I can't remember what it was about, but I remember being so upset that I decided to get back at Ronnie by making him think I'd run away. It was the early hours of the morning when I got my passport, climbed out of our bedroom window and scrambled up onto the roof to hide. *I'll show him*, I thought, furiously. I was quite comfortable at first, but as the sun came up on another glorious LA morning, my little rooftop hideout got hotter and hotter. The heat was soon unbearable, but the thought of Ronnie rushing around downstairs, frantic with worry, desperately phoning everyone we knew trying to find out where I had gone, made me stick with it. Then suddenly Ronnie's head popped up by the edge of the roof. 'You might need this,' he said, holding out a glass of water.

He had known I was up there the whole bloody time.

I was more deeply in love with Ronnie than ever, but was full of hormone-fuelled insecurities about our relationship. I poured out my feelings in my diary and in poems. Ronnie actually used one of my poems as inspiration for his song 'Lost And Lonely' on his 1979 solo album *Gimme Some Neck*.

Hey Jo

Lost and Lonely
I'm lost and I'm lonely
And looking for you
Out of my mind
Coz it's you I can't find
Pouring rain
Hearts in pain
Never again.

Humble and helpless
Looking hard for your love
If there could be a next time
I promise I'll stand by you
Wastin' away
Nothin' to say
Forgive me for today.

Next to you
Helping you through
I'm still hanging in there
I'm a true fine woman
You're a certain one of a kind
If you left me now
I'd only go crazy.

Only the blind can tell
I'm looking for you
Can anyone else see I've been waiting
Only from heartache can we live to learn
We should be together again.

Ronnie wanted to keep the pregnancy secret as he was in the middle of divorce negotiations with Krissy and didn't need to muddy the waters, so I hid my blossoming bump in dungarees and baggy jumpers (fortunately the height of fashion at the time) and I don't think anyone guessed. Mick clearly didn't. In those early days, he would try it on with me as soon as Ronnie had left the room.

'Come on, Jo,' he'd say.

'You should be so fucking lucky, Mick,' I said. 'In your *wildest* dreams.'

I never fancied Mick and, besides, I only had eyes for my Ronnie; there was nobody else in the world for me. I can honestly say I didn't fancy anyone else for 30 years.

In late May, when I was about five months pregnant, we took off for Woodstock, in upstate New York, and the countryside studio where the Stones were rehearsing for the summer tour. Keith had decided to come off heroin ahead of the tour and a scheduled court appearance in Toronto following a drugs bust there the year before. By then Ronnie had told the boys I was pregnant. The three of us shared a little house near the rehearsal-room complex and Jane Rose cared for Keith as he went cold turkey, which seemed to be like the worst flu you could ever imagine. She saw him through it, staying in his room as he went through the DTs with the help of a little black box that gave a painless zap of electricity to get the endorphins flowing. Keith still carried on with the coke and hash, but heroin's different. It's a physical addiction, rather than a mental one, like coke. It takes a matter of minutes to get hooked and then your body starts to crave it – and Keith had been on smack for 10 years, so you can imagine how hard those weeks were for him.

I stayed well away from heroin and am so relieved I never got into it, but I did try it once by accident. In the eighties, Ronnie and I were so skint for a time that a dealer used to give us all the empty plastic bags the coke had come in so that he could scrape them for a line. One day he got a new batch and Ronnie gave me the first line. I snorted it, then immediately gagged.

'Christ, what is that stuff?' It had tasted revolting.

Ronnie tested it to find out what it was (you just burn a little and smell it) and pulled a face. 'Oops, sorry, baby,' he said. 'I've just given you a line of smack.'

That night, I remember trying to write a message in the front of a book I was sending as a birthday gift to my friend, Wendy Worth: 'Dear Wendy, Happy Birthday. Lots of love, Jo.' But I was so out of it that it took me all night long to do it. I tore out page after page of the book, trying to write just those few words. Then, at seven in the morning, I started to be violently ill. I threw up and threw up and threw up. It was a horrible experience. Not just the sickness, but the total loss of control. Never again ...

After a week or so in Woodstock, Keith started to come round and then he just blossomed, becoming even funnier and more entertaining than ever. With his appetite returning, he got stuck into his favourite meals: shepherd's pie, roast lamb, sausages and mash – any combination of meat and potatoes. The next thing he wanted was some female attention. Things with Anita Pallenberg had really run their course, so I called my agency to see if anyone was around and it turned out that this fabulous Swedish model called Lil Wenglas Green was in New York. Lil was great – very blonde, very beautiful and a real laugh. Keith arranged a helicopter for me (my first helicopter ride!) and I went to New York to pick her up. And, just like that, she and Keith got on like a house on fire and were together for a couple of years.

It was a nice little set-up in Woodstock. I was beginning to need lots of sleep because I was getting bigger so I'd go off for naps. The weeks flew by and suddenly it was June, and we were off to Florida for the first night of the Some Girls tour.

11

It was the sound of the crowd that really got me. That unbelievable primal roar, so loud you can feel it vibrating through you. And the fans at the front, their faces twisted into what looked like screams of agony, almost as if they were in pain or pleading for their lives, climbing over one another in a desperate attempt to get an inch closer to their idols. To have tens of thousands of people screaming, crying, desperate for *you* – it's really not in the least surprising that rock stars have big egos. The whole experience was utterly overwhelming. As I stood at the back of the stage in Florida, watching the Stones perform live for the first time, I felt totally in awe of the boys for inspiring such a mind-blowing reaction. Even experiencing it from where I had positioned myself, half-hidden behind an amp, the adrenalin rush was better than the hit of any drug I'd ever tried.

Though Ronnie hadn't been with the Stones for long, and this was his second tour with them, I'd never been on tour with anyone; it was an incredible first taste of something that would eventually become a major part of my life. In later years the tours would become slick, professional operations, involving an organizational cast of thousands and years on the road. Things were on a far smaller scale when I first joined the team, although the key players were the same – and for me the main man was always Chuch. Ronnie was too preoccupied with his perfor- mance to worry about what I was up to, so Chuch showed me where to stand so I could be discreet and not get in anyone's way. As ever, he was my saving grace. I was devastated when he passed away in 2002.

Then there was Johnny Starbuck, another of the key roadies who remains a close friend to this day. His real name was Gary Howard, but he changed it because he'd always loved the name Johnny; one day he noticed a sign for 'Starbuck Street' and it all fell into place. As roadies had such a physical job they weren't usually that fussed about their appearance, but Johnny looked as cool as his name suggests. He was a handsome guy and was always sharp in a spotless T-shirt and a pair of tight jeans. We used to flirt like crazy.

While the boys got ready to go on stage I'd try to make myself useful; I watched Chuch string the guitars, ran errands and made the drinks. The last thing I wanted was to feel I was in the way: I wanted to be a cog in this incredible machine, however minor. But, really, what could I do? I couldn't sing, I didn't know how to play a musical instrument (Ronnie often tried to teach me 'Maggie May' on the guitar but I'd have forgotten it all the next morning) and I wasn't strong enough to lug boxes.

What I did know, however, was clothes. At this time the styl- ing for the tours was a bit haphazard. The boys, with the excep- tion of Mick, just used to pull out stuff from their closets – and Ronnie had some pretty dodgy stuff lurking in his. (Remember those tapestry-trimmed gabardine flares he was wearing when we first met? Well, turned out he had six or seven pairs.) Gradually I started to take more of an interest in his styling.

Ronnie and Keith were into wearing women's clothes at the time, so one day I put Ronnie into my pink velvet Fiorucci jeans with a Victorian white blouse and a waistcoat. He loved the outfit so much he wore it for the *Miss You* video. It would be another 10 years before I was officially on the Stones' payroll, but in those early days it was my way of making a contribution.

Keith has described the Stones on tour as a 'pirate nation' and he's spot-on. In the early days especially, you'd get this bunch of crazy characters, a mix of oddballs, outlaws and scoundrels, who would join the band on the road. One of the most infamous of these reprobates was Freddie Sessler, whom I met for the first time on the Some Girls tour.

Ronnie and I were settling into our hotel room in Florida when he told me we were going visiting. He led the way down the corridor, my little bump and I trotting behind, and banged on a neighbouring door. A moment later it swung open to reveal a dumpy little dude. He had straggly grey hair combed over an expanse of bald patch, a huge nose and a tiny willy. He was standing there buck-naked.

'Hi there, I'm Jo!' I said brightly, deliberately looking beyond him to avoid the sight of his willy and coming face to face with a naked girl lying on the bed. 'Oh … hi to you, too!'

He handed Ronnie a big bag of powder. 'Here's da coke,' he said. 'I'll catch you later,' and he slammed the door. A moment later I heard a burst of girlish giggles from inside.

And that was my introduction to the legendary Freddie Sessler.

Freddie was a Holocaust survivor from Poland and had been around the Stones for years. He was one of Keith's closest friends: his Man Friday and go-to guy for drugs. And on later tours, when I wasn't pregnant, I was to fully indulge in all of Freddie's wares. Freddie would always have jars and jars of the pharmaceutical cocaine known as Merck. It was totally different from the coke that came out of Colombia, so beautifully smooth you could stay up for days on it without feeling wired. It makes me feel stoned just thinking about it. He had pills, too, endless rainbow-coloured handfuls of little red barbiturates called Seconal; half-red, half-turquoise pills called Turanol; and yellow Percodan, an opiate like morphine. I was never that into pills, but Freddie would always want you to take them. He would shove them into my mouth, and though I'd try to hide them under my tongue to spit out when he wasn't looking (a trick I learnt from Ronnie), if I wasn't quick enough they'd start to dissolve. The taste was so nasty, unimaginably bitter. And then there was this spray-can of stuff that Freddie used to waft around – you'd inhale the fumes and go into orbit. WHEEEEEE! It was the maddest stuff. At one point I started to worry about what it was doing to my brain. I stayed up many, many nights on a cocktail of Seconal, Turanol and vodka – it's a wonder I'm still alive, really.

Keith adored Freddie like a second dad, but Mick couldn't stand him and was always slagging him off, which made it difficult to know how you should feel about him. I was always a bit scared of him, as he was such a dark character. And he could be obnoxious. 'This is my son Larry,' he would say. 'He's the victim of a burst rubber.' Charming, eh? And Keith would tell a story about how one of Freddie's wives (he'd somehow had many) had once caught him with another woman. Despite being mid-shag he point-blank denied it. 'Well, who are you gonna believe?' he said to her. 'Me or your own eyes?'

Yet, as old and ugly as he was, Freddie would always get these gorgeous girls. He'd sit backstage and say, 'I vant a groupie, I vant a vodka and I vant a line!' I gather the levels of debauchery on the Some Girls tour were pretty tame compared to earlier ones, but for a tour virgin like myself it all seemed pretty wild – and Freddie was usually mixed up in the middle of it, surrounded by half-naked girls.

One day on tour, as Freddie slobbered over yet another pretty teenager, I asked Keith what these girls saw in him.

'Well, what do you think, Jo?'

'It must be the coke.'

Keith shook his head.

'Well, perhaps they're trying to get in with you through him.'

'Don't you get it, Jo?'

'No, I really don't.' Freddie's charms were totally lost on me.

Keith grinned and started waggling his tongue.

'Oh, no!' I gasped. 'No, not that. You have got to be kidding!'

But Keith just laughed. 'What can I say? Apparently he gives the best head.'

Freddie died a few years ago but near the end of his life, when he was well into his seventies, he came over to our house for dinner with the family. That night I saw a very different side of him. Maybe it was because he knew he was dying, but for the first time ever he seemed to show a genuine affection for me. Who knows? Perhaps the silly old sod had been quietly keeping an eye out for me for years. At the end of the night he took my hands and said, 'Jo, you've been the best thing for Ronnie. You're such a good woman.' I was stunned, as he'd never said anything like that to me before.

In fact, in the early days, it had seemed like Freddie had done everything he could to screw up my relationship with Ronnie. On that first tour we were hanging out in the hotel after a gig when Freddie appeared with this perky blonde girl, a waitress, who zeroed straight in on Ronnie. It was clear that they already knew each other – in fact, I quickly worked out that he had shagged her the last time the band was in the States. So there I was, heavily pregnant and seething with jealousy, as this girl drooled all over my man. He was clearly enjoying the attention – and Freddie was *loving* the fact that I was getting so upset about it. *Fucking Freddie*, I seethed silently. *I bet you set this up deliberately.* I tried taking Ronnie aside to tell him how upset I was getting, but he refused to understand.

'She's just my mate!' he said. 'I used to go out with her and I don't any more. What's the problem?'

In the end I stormed back to our room, hoping Ronnie would follow, but the minutes ticked past and I realized he wasn't going to come. As I sobbed into my pillow, it occurred to me that I had two options: I could lie there feeling sorry for myself while Miss Texas wiggled her boobies at my bloke, or I could redo my makeup, slip into something a bit more sexy (well, as sexy as a maternity smock could be) and go back down there with a big smile on my face to remind Ronnie of what he'd got. In the end I took the second option. I strode back into the room, plonked myself down next to the waitress and started chatting to her. With us two girls getting along like old friends, Freddie got bored, wandered off, and soon Ronnie muttered to me, 'Get rid of her, will you?' My man and I went up to bed alone.

I learnt a very important lesson that night. Groupies were one of the inevitable downsides of life as a rock-star's girlfriend, like hangovers and jetlag. No matter how much fuss I made or how upset I got, those girls weren't going to go away. From then on, my way of dealing with them was always to make friends with them. 'Hi, I'm Jo, Ronnie's girlfriend, what's your name?' It always seemed to defuse the situation. And if that failed, I'd make them really strong drinks until they were so pissed, they'd do something stupid and Ronnie would tell them to leave. I'm not saying I wasn't jealous – far from it. It turned my guts to see other women all over my man. Another night on that tour, I was watching Ronnie from the side of the stage and during his solo I saw him cross the stage to where two pretty girls were screaming and I thought, *I bet I see you two in our hotel room later.* Sure enough, when we got back there they were, giggling away.

But, thankfully, it was Mick whom most of the girls were after. He'd see one he liked in the audience, give security a nod and they'd take her back to the hotel. It became a bit of a game to me, scanning the front rows and trying to pinpoint the girl who'd take Mick's fancy that night.

I used to turn a blind eye to these goings-on, because I adored being on tour and I knew if I made a fuss I wouldn't be allowed on the next one. The other wives and girlfriends would put in occasional appearances: Jerry would come and go, Shirley Watts was more into her dressage horses than life on the road, and Bill Wyman's wife, Astrid, would come to the bigger shows until they split up, after which Bill just had woman after woman after woman. But me? I was there all the time.

We toured America from early June till the end of July. What really blew me away were the stadium concerts: places like John F. Kennedy Stadium in Philadelphia, the Municipal Stadium in Cleveland, Soldier Field in Chicago and, most impressive of all, the Superdome in New Orleans, which at the time broke records as the biggest indoor concert ever. We're talking tens of thousands of people – 80 thousand in New Orleans and an incredible 90 thousand crammed into the stadium in Philly.

The last dates of the tour were back in California. By now I was seven months pregnant and I remember everyone joking that I was going to have the baby at the side of the stage. When the tour reached Los Angeles, Dad came out to visit and brought Jamie, then four, with him. I was a bit worried as to how Dad'd take to the rock 'n' roll lifestyle but on the night of the show I spotted him in the front row, arms in the air, dancing along with Mick, wearing a huge smile. I hadn't even known my dad could move like that! And I was so proud to show Jamie his new step-dad playing in front of thousands. He just loved it.

Dad got on with Keith especially well: Keith was fascinated by Dad's Lambretta collection and model-making and in return Dad was intrigued by Keith's intellect. Meanwhile, I was struggling with the late nights and would often fall asleep while the party raged on around me. One night Ronnie was drunk and started having a go at me over something. He was just being a bit obnoxious and dismissive, but I was so exhausted and hormonal that I flew into a rage and tried to hit him.

'Okay, Jo, I think it's time for you to go home,' he said – and the next morning I was put on a flight back to LA.

In all honesty I was pretty relieved to get home. The boys only had a couple of dates left of the tour – and, besides, my nesting instinct had seriously kicked in. But I wasn't content with going to buy a crib or painting the nursery. *Oh, no.* I might have been just weeks away from giving birth, but from the moment I got back to Forest Knoll Drive I threw myself into looking for a whole new home.

12

22 August. Went to see house in Mandeville Canyon today. It's really nice. Think we might get it.

Within a month, amazingly, we had moved into the home of my dreams. If the place on Forest Knoll Drive had been built for partying, this was most definitely somewhere for raising a family. Situated in Mandeville Canyon in Brentwood, it was like a house from a child's picture book, with an apple-green wooden exterior, white window-frames and a veranda that ran all the way round. In the garden there was a guest cottage and a swimming-pool, which (as the house once belonged to the famous swimmer and movie starlet, Esther Williams) must have seen some wild pool parties over the years.

There was another really great thing about the Mandeville Canyon house. When Ronnie and I went to look round we got chatting to the housekeeper, a tall, elegant woman called Jaye, who agreed to stay on when we moved in. She would work for us for many years – and then for Mick and Keith's families, too – and within just a few months felt like one of the family.

We moved into Mandeville Canyon at the start of September and I got straight down to work, painting and wallpapering, not just the new baby's nursery but a racing-car-themed bedroom for Jamie, too. I was still battling Peter's efforts to keep me from bringing him out to live with us in LA, but I wanted to be sure there was a bedroom for him when we did. I'm sure even Peter recognized that our son needed to be with his mother, but that didn't stop him doing everything he could to block it happening. Thankfully, Jamie was safely cocooned at the Old Vicarage throughout, but it meant that until everything was resolved, he could come to the States only for brief visits. 'Thank you, Peter, for being so fucking difficult,' I wrote in my diary, following a particularly tense conversation with the lawyers after he had announced he wanted Ronnie to pay for six flights a year so that he could visit his son. 'Your true colours shine through!' I added: 'Ronnie makes up for everything, though.'

If I'd hoped for a few weeks of quiet nesting to prepare for the baby's arrival, however, I was to be disappointed. Ronnie had started work on his solo album, *Gimme Some Neck*, so no sooner was he back from tour than the house was crammed with musicians and roadies again. Keith moved into our guest cottage while Mac and Chuch took the guest rooms. I'd cook huge meals for them and the guys would stay up all night, smoking, drinking and making music. It was pointless me going to bed early (even more so asking them to keep the noise down), so most of the time I just stayed up with them.

I'd always loved listening to music, but since I'd been with Ronnie I'd become immersed in it like never before. If there weren't people sitting around jamming, there would be music on the stereo. I was exposed to all sorts of genres I'd never heard before; I fell in love with reggae, in particular. But where you or I might enjoy a song, then move happily on to the next, the boys would become fixated on a particular track and play it endlessly. Ronnie – and even more so, Keith – would listen intently to the same song over and over and over again. While I found it fascinating that they could listen to it so many times, it sometimes became a little tedious on the 18th airing. One time Keith played a country song called 'Apartment Number Nine' constantly for weeks, maybe months, so he could perfect every note. Every word of that song embedded itself in my brain. And there was no way you could just get up and change the music. So many times we'd be sitting in a hotel room on tour, or even at home, and some loony who hadn't been hanging out with us before would get up to put a different song on and Keith would go mental: '*Don't touch the fucking music!*' It was non-negotiable: this was their music and that was all there was to it. In the end, I found ways to get the boys to change the music without asking them. I might say, 'Ooh, Keith, I just love that song by Gregory Isaacs – you haven't got it, have you?'

And he'd go: 'Oh, yeah, I'll find it for you, darling.'

On the rare occasions that I'd put headphones on to listen to other music, theirs was so loud I couldn't actually hear it – and there was no point in asking them if they could turn it down a bit. The volume level was another non-negotiable. It's a wonder I can still hear, really.

As well as rehearsing at home, Ronnie also rented a house down the road on Mulholland Drive to use as a recording studio, a fabulously tacky place that was built to look like a medieval castle. Like Forest Knoll, this place was once used as a set for porn films. (Either there were a lot of blue movies made in LA at

the time or we were using particularly dodgy estate agents.)
I spent a lot of time there hanging out with the boys and one
night was so tired that I went to a bedroom they were using as
the bass amp room and fell asleep. I woke with a jolt about eight
hours later to the deafening thump of bass coming from the
amps. I stormed downstairs in a haze.

'I can't believe you started playing bass!' I said to Ronnie. 'You
knew I was asleep in there!'

'Jo, we've been playing bass for the last eight hours.' He smiled.

I must have been so exhausted I'd just slept right through it.

One night my frayed nerves suddenly snapped. I'd cooked
another mammoth meat-and-potato-fest for the boys and had
gone upstairs to try and sleep, a pillow clamped over my head to
block out the noise, when I became aware of the stench of burning fat. I'd got off lightly with morning sickness during the pregnancy, but the one thing I couldn't cope with was the smell of
burning fat. I went downstairs to find Keith cooking a huge pan
of bacon and eggs. *What the hell?* I'd spent hours making dinner
and cleaning up – and now the kitchen was covered with grease
and dirty dishes again! I don't lose my temper very often, but
this was too much. I grabbed a bottle of perfume and started
spraying it round the kitchen and all over Keith's food like a
woman possessed.

'What the fuck are you doing?' he said, calmly.

'What the fuck am *I* doing?' I said, my voice a squeak of rage.
'I'm about to give birth and you're frying fucking bacon and the
smell is making me retch and *I can't stand it!*'

And with that I stormed upstairs in tears. Ronnie came up to
find out what was wrong. My little outburst was so out of character, I think everyone was a bit stunned.

I must have fallen asleep, because the next thing I remember is looking at the clock in the darkness. It was 3 a.m. I lay there, just listening. *Something's not right ...* And then it dawned on me: the house was totally, blissfully silent. I crept downstairs and there wasn't a soul there. The kitchen was spotless. And on the side, there was a note from Keith. Beneath a little doodle of some fried eggs, my lovely Keith had written: 'I'm sorry about tonight, darling. I won't come back until after you've done your birthing.'

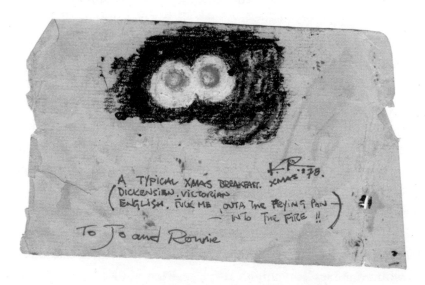

Another doodle of fried eggs by Keith,
similar to the one he left me.

Shortly before my due date, my friend Wendy Stark threw me a baby shower, with champagne, tea and cakes, and invited a whole bunch of girls, including Jerry Hall, who was living in LA with Mick; Rod Stewart's wife, Alana; and Wendy Worth, who was dating a guy called Peter Asher from the duo Peter and Gordon, whom she later married. I wore a pair of lilac silk dungarees that just fitted over my little fat tummy and got a heap of wonderful gifts. But the best present of all arrived a few days later: my darling Jamie, along with Mum and Lize, who had all come for a month's stay. On their first night I cooked a big roast dinner for family and friends, feeling overjoyed to have my loved ones together. My only concern was Keith. Now, Keith consumed drugs like everyone else had cake. Just before I served the roast, I took him to one side and said, 'Keith, my mum's never seen cocaine before. Can you please not do it in front of her?'

'Don't worry, darling,' he said, with a wolfish grin. 'I'll break her in gently ...'

Feeling far from reassured I started to dish out the roast lamb, but by the time everyone had finished their plates (and had had seconds) I'd started to relax. The boys were behaving impeccably and Mum was clearly charmed. I had got up from the table to tidy the dirty dishes away, thrilled at how well the evening was going, when suddenly Keith declared, 'And now for dessert!' With that, he pulled out a big bag of coke and slammed it on the table.

Without waiting to see Mum's reaction, I just picked up a pile of plates and walked straight into the kitchen. Moments later, she followed me in. 'Josephine, do you realize what Keith is doing in there?' she said.

'Yes, Mum, but he's been doing it for years.' I sighed. 'I can't stop him. It's just his way of life.'

Mum's face was a picture of total disapproval. 'Does Ronnie do cocaine as well?'

At that moment a little white lie – well, actually, an *enormous* white lie – seemed like a good idea.

'No, of course he doesn't!'

'Are you sure?'

'Yes, absolutely,' I said, and hoped that Ronnie would be a bit more discreet than Keith.

But, three days later, after Keith and Ronnie had been up for 72 hours and counting, Mum cornered me again.

'I know Ronnie takes cocaine,' she said to me.

'Really? How?'

'Because he's been walking around with a straw behind his ear since we got here.'

The next few weeks were, as Keith put it, a real 'breaking-in' for Mum, who until this point had had little experience of drugs beyond Silk Cut and a small sherry at Christmas. A few days later she was sunbathing by the pool when Keith sauntered over, smoking a great big joint. Mum started laying into him about how bad it was and why he shouldn't be touching 'that stuff'.

'Come on, darling,' he said, 'just have a puff. You might like it.'

Keith handed the joint to Mum, who took it between her thumb and forefinger and flung it into the pool. I'm sure Keith had decked people for less but, to his credit, he just sat back and proceeded to roll two more joints.

'Here you go, Rachel,' he said. 'Here's one for me to smoke and one for you to throw in the pool.'

*   *   *

Like most nights, on 21 September an informal party was in full swing downstairs and I was dozing in bed when, at around

9 p.m., the contractions started to kick in. With a few drinks inside him, Ronnie was fussing around like an old woman, asking if he should time how far apart the contractions were, and I remember getting quite annoyed with him. 'For God's sake, just go away,' I said. 'I'll tell you if they speed up.'

I must have fallen asleep as the next thing I remember was waking up with a doctor standing over me. He had a very nice face. 'Come on, Jo, it's time to go to hospital,' he said, with a smile.

That's the really scary moment, isn't it? When you know it's started, that there's no way back, and the next few hours are going to involve a hell of a lot of blood, sweat and tears. But *so* exciting as well, because at the end of it, if all goes well, you're going to meet this wonderful little person.

Ronnie, Mum and the very nice doctor helped me downstairs and Ronnie drove me and him in his green Mercedes up Sunset Boulevard to the big Cedars Sinai medical complex. In the end it was an easy birth – well, as easy as these things get. Ronnie was with me in the delivery room and took pictures of the whole thing. It was certainly worth documenting: at 1.55 a.m. on 22 September our beautiful little girl entered the world, all 7 pounds 3 ounces, and 21 inches of her. We named her Leah after Ronnie's mum, Mercy Leah, and Michelle after Michael, my dad. As I cradled my daughter, I was wheeled into the recovery room where not only Ronnie was waiting but Keith too, the pair of them having dodged hospital regulations by dressing up in full doctor's scrubs and telling the head nurse they were *both* the father. My dear friend, Chuch, was there too, and from the Jack Daniel's fumes on their breath it was obvious that they had all been celebrating.

Later that day we went home. There's a picture of Johnny Starbuck pushing me out of hospital in a wheelchair – how cool is that? Getting a Stones roadie to shift you to the car. My tummy looks so flat in that photo I don't even look like I'd had a baby, which – as you can imagine – I was pretty pleased about.

Ronnie was overcome with emotion and pride when he phoned his mum and dad and proclaimed the arrival of 'the first girl in whole generations of Woods'! He seemed just as smitten as I was as he cradled Leah in his arms or sketched her while she slept in her crib, her little fat fists clenching in her sleep. I'd come to realize that, although he wasn't great with words, when Ronnie picked up his sketchbook and pencil that was his way of showing love.

Unfortunately, he had to take off for New York when Leah was just 10 days old because the Stones had been booked to appear on *Saturday Night Live*. The timing wasn't great, as I was laid up with a fever after getting the most awful bout of mastitis while breastfeeding. I remember watching the boys on TV and feeling really sorry for myself: there was I, stuck in bed with a raging temperature and burning boobs, while they got to hang out with John Belushi! I was so jealous – although John and I would later become very special friends.

Of course, I was already a mother when Ronnie had met me, but now that we had a baby in the house – and hopefully Jamie moving in before long as well – I was far more focused on that side of things, and my life became even more of a balancing act. On one hand there was family, on the other rock 'n' roll – and for the next 30 years, I would constantly juggle the demands of both. Yet despite my best efforts, the two frequently collided, like when Keith and Mum almost came to blows over the blow.

Shortly after Leah's birth a famous French actress, who lived nearby with her musician boyfriend, came to meet the new arrival. Let's call them Brigitte and Steve. I was breastfeeding Leah as we chatted away (I was probably moaning to her about the mastitis) when Brigitte suddenly changed the subject.

''Ey, Jo,' she said. 'You know me and Stevie are 'aving an affair with that Oriental girl, China?'

'Yes, Brigitte.'

'*Weeeeeell …*' she said, as Leah chugged away contentedly at my boob, 'China is so tiny I 'ave to bend over double to lick her pussy. Me and Stevie were thinking it would be better to get somebody more your size.'

To be honest, I was never into girls anyway, but at that particular moment, still achy from giving birth, with swollen boobs and a sore back, I really couldn't have been less up for it. 'Um, thanks for asking, Brigitte, but that's not my thing.' I shrugged. 'I'm just into the old knobber.'

And with that we went back to talking about fashion or the weather, as if all she had asked was whether I fancied joining her and her bloke for a cup of tea.

*   *   *

Eventually Mum, Lize and Jamie went back to the UK. Saying goodbye to Jamie was the hardest it had ever been and I was absolutely determined that this time would be the last. Peter was still fighting over the divorce and even Ronnie's lawyer said that we should agree just to get things moving. If I had actually believed Peter's argument – that he needed money so he could come out to LA several times each year to see Jamie – I would have done. But I knew he wasn't short of a bob or two and, more importantly, I was pretty sure he had no intention of staying connected with his son. I dug in my heels and said we'd see him in court back in the UK, where I intended to fight for full custody of Jamie.

At the same time Keith was preparing for his own day in court in Toronto. He and the rest of the band had convinced themselves that he was going to get a jail sentence, so we were thrilled when we got the phone call saying he had got off. The only condition was that the Stones do a free concert in Toronto to benefit the blind.

That day, as Ronnie and I were cuddling in bed, with Leah's crib alongside, we got our first taste of another staple of LA life: the brushfire. As the flames started tearing down Mandeville Canyon and the alarm was raised along the road, I raced around the house, convinced it was going to burn down, trying to work out what we should take with us. In the end we bundled into the jeep with Leah and her things, a couple of changes of clothes, a few of my favourite photos and Ronnie's sketches, and fled the scene to a luxurious hotel called L'Ermitage, in Beverly Hills. The house was fine, but we had a few days' second honeymoon before returning home.

We headed to London in the middle of December for the court showdown with Peter. I was nervous, but set on doing whatever was necessary to get Jamie back with me and had this whole little speech prepared. I needn't have worried, though. Peter – true to form – didn't even show up on the day, and the judge awarded me full custody of our son.

That Christmas we stayed in festive luxury at the Ritz in London, a blissfully happy ending to the most incredible year of my life. It had been barely twelve months since I'd got together with Ronnie, but we already had our beautiful daughter and now, finally, Jamie would be able to live with us as well.

I had my private worries, though. As much as I adored Ronnie – and I did, more than ever – I struggled with jealousy over the way girls threw themselves at him, and with the frustration I so often felt over how closed he could be. On the night before we left LA for London, I poured out my fears in a raw, rambling note in my diary.

> Thursday, 14 December 1978
> *It's only been a year and a third and it's hard*
> *for me to believe when I look around our house*
> *– it still doesn't seem that I should say our*
> *house, our bed, I always feel I should say his.*
> *I feel a great unsureness that he'll leave me, yet*
> *deep down I know that we belong together, it's*
> *like it's so perfect it's quite unreal, but I just*
> *take it all and without a thought of what it's*
> *like looking from the outside. Why? I know*
> *I am totally body and mind in love with*
> *Ronnie. But he's really a stranger – yet it's so*
> *right, like we've never been without each other.*
> *One thing I fear though: me, the way my heart*
> *races when I realize all the other women that*
> *want him, rich, beauty, fame, evil, but I've got*
> *to share that with him, cos I know he's proud of*
> *himself for going where he's gone and did it on*
> *his own … Why has this happened to me?*

Ronnie obviously read it, because on the opposite page he wrote a response:

Here's why, my beautiful Joey ... If you let it
(and we do) – time fits certain things together
and, if something is natural, unashamed, rock
steady and POWERFUL, then time and fate
will lock these elements together – FOREVER.
Knowing that it has bonded a perfect
relationship, capable of withstanding the
hardest forces of evil – out to try to destroy this
bond that you and I, and our children have ...
then it can move on to try to end problems that
really need solving in one way or another, that
are only too real in this hard world where
nobody and nothing really gives a shit! We have
a precious BOND – one which I would never,
NEVER let come to an end – cos I LOVE YA
and everything about you – and never
underestimate yourself, just because I have
achieved things that may be evident in material
things – people trying to build your ego and
saying, 'You're really great, man!' and 'yes, yes
yes' – well let me tell you that none of those
gangs of people even exist! AS LONG AS
THERE'S JUST ONE OF YOU AROUND! MY
BABY XXXX

I could have wept with happiness when I read that note. Ronnie was right: our relationship *was* perfect. And I felt that even more strongly as we gathered at the Ritz, both sides of our extended family together, on Christmas Day. Later that evening, drunk and happy, Ronnie did a little sketch in my diary: him, me, Jamie, Leah in her cot, a Christmas tree and a turkey. It was his way of telling me that we were a rock-solid little team.

That night I slept wrapped in his arms, totally content, blissfully loved-up and so excited about what the new year would bring. We had already planned to spend the first weeks of 1979 in Nassau and I couldn't wait to hit the beach with my babies. My future seemed as cloudless as a brilliant blue Bahamas sky.

I didn't have the slightest clue that in a few months' time, dark clouds would have blotted out the sun and our lives would have spiralled dangerously out of control …

13

The year 1979 started out really well. With the kids in tow, Ronnie and I flew back to Nassau where the Stones had rented a big house by the sea. While the boys were in the studio working on the album that would become *Emotional Rescue*, I'd play with the kids on the beach: Jamie, now a headstrong four-year-old, Keith's son Marlon and, of course, chubby little Leah, who napped happily in a sun-shaded stroller. I was still breastfeeding and taking care of the kids so I didn't see much of Ronnie, but I'd leave him little love notes to find when he got back from the studio in the early hours. It was such a great holiday for me and the kids.

Although I had the responsibility of kids, in my early years with Ronnie we seemed to spend a lot of time just goofing around. One evening, the guys were all having a big meeting in the living room – all the boys were there, as well as Jane Rose, Alan Dunn and Prince Rupert Löwenstein, who ran the Stones' financial affairs. I walked past the door and, instead of the usual music chat, heard them talking about aliens, debating whether UFOs actually existed. It sounded like things were getting pretty intense, too. I went into the kitchen where Marlon and Jamie were having a pre-bedtime snack and asked, 'How do you fancy getting dressed up, boys?'

Trying to keep them quiet, I wrapped silver foil around our arms and legs, made antennae out of wire coat-hangers and covered our bodies in bin bags. The final touch was drinking-chocolate powder rubbed over our teeth to make them black. Then the three of us walked jerkily into the living room, me at the front, followed by Marlon and then Jamie. '*Coooome aloooong, chiiiiildren*,' I said, in my best alien voice. As we paraded across the room, everyone in there fell totally silent and just stared, open-mouthed. I'm not sure what had been smoked that night, but for a moment they looked almost scared. I hadn't been prepared for that sort of reaction, and when we got back to the kitchen, I turned to the kids and said, 'Oh, God, what have we done?'

Moments later Jane burst in, doubled over with laughter. 'You gave us all such a fright!' she said, whipping out her camera to prove once and for all that aliens really did exist.

I've always been something of a fancy-dress connoisseur. I would have made an excellent *Blue Peter* presenter. On tour there would be nights when everyone would be sitting round, listening to music and getting stoned, and I'd end up creating these bizarre costumes out of whatever I could find in the hotel room. One night I transformed myself into Ronnie's then manager, a big guy called Jason Cooper, by slicing an empty body-lotion bottle in half to make a huge nose, then cutting the bristles off a hairbrush and sticking them onto gaffer tape for a beard. A hat to cover my hair and a pillow up my top and – 'Hi, I'm Jason Cooper.' Another time, Keith told me he'd give me a hundred dollars or a gram of coke if I could go back to my room and return dressed as a schoolgirl in 20 minutes. When I came back in full costume, he said, 'All right, do you want the money or the coke?'

'I'll take fifty dollars and half a gram, please!'

When we returned to LA from Nassau, I made the decision to stop breastfeeding. My relationship with Ronnie had its roots in partying – drinking, smoking joints, doing coke – and I was desperate to be back rocking with him. I'd had the odd drink while Leah was tiny, but I felt terribly guilty because whenever I did the poor little mite always got a runny tummy so usually I stayed on the wagon. But now she was four months old and we were about to go off on tour again – not with the Stones this time, but with the New Barbarians, a band Ronnie had formed with his best music buddies, including Keith, Mac and the Stones' sax player, Bobby Keys. As they rehearsed at our place, playing the material from Ronnie's new solo album, I felt very much part of it from the start. I even designed the official tour T-shirt.

The New Barbarians got off to an ideal start – opening for the two Rolling Stones concerts in aid of the blind in Toronto that had been part of the court deal on Keith's drug charge. Their warm-up man on the first night was none other than John Belushi and the pair of us hit it off instantly. While the boys were on stage, we spent the night being really silly and joking around.

When the tour stopped in New York a few days later, we went round to John's house after the gig. He was running around me like a puppy. 'Is everything all right, Jo? Can I get you anything? Do you need another drink?' It was blindingly obvious that he fancied me – and I'm sorry to say I made the most of it.

'John,' I'd say, 'I'm feeling a bit cold.' He'd run off and turn on the heating.

'Sorry, I'm a little too hot now!' He'd jump up to open a window.

Over the next few years, John would be a regular visitor at our LA home. One day, while Ronnie was in the studio, he took me to the Playboy Mansion. There I was, surrounded by all these chicks in tiny little dresses with great big boobs and blonde hair. Ronnie was so furious when he found out; it's one of the only times I remember him being jealous. But John made no attempt to hide the fact he had a crush on me. The phone would go in the night and it would be John.

'Jo, guess what I'm doing?'

'I don't know, John.'

'I'm playing with myself while I'm speaking to you.'

'JOHN!'

Then one night we were all hanging out together – Ronnie had passed out on the couch – when John suddenly asked me to run away with him. 'Please, Jo, I love you,' he said earnestly, while Ronnie snored a few feet away.

'I can't run away with you! I've got a boyfriend!'

'Please, just say you'll think about it,' he said.

'No, John, I think it's better that we just stay as friends, okay?'

*   *   *

The New Barbarians were on the road for two wild weeks, and from what I can remember – not much, if I'm honest – the tour was a brilliant success. Even the fact that Ronnie had funded it out of future proceeds from the solo album (and ended up in debt to his record label) didn't take the shine off the satisfaction I knew he felt at how well everything had come together.

And now that I was free to party with the guys again I went absolutely ballistic. Ronnie chartered a plane and we partied our way across the States. There's a photo of me dressed up as a sexy soldier in a peaked cap and miniskirt, marching along waving a bottle of Jack Daniel's, leading Ronnie, Keith and Lil across the tarmac from our jet. I went crazy on that tour – up all night every night, as high as a kite on coke and adrenalin – and the madness continued when we got back to LA. I had always been a proficient partier, but now I went *hardcore* – quite literally. Chuch had a team of roadies who prided themselves on being able to stay up all night, take drugs and still do their jobs the next day, and they called their gang Hardcore. One morning, after we'd had another wild night's partying, those boys were all crashed out on my sofas. While I collected all the dirty glasses and emptied the overflowing ashtrays, it suddenly occurred to me that, as I was the only one who was still awake, I was probably the most hardcore of the lot.

Later that day, I cornered Chuch.

'Chuch, I think I should be in Hardcore,' I said. 'You should really make me the only female honorary member.'

'Okay,' he said, with a smile. 'If you go round and ask all the guys in Hardcore, we'll see what we can do.'

Over the next few weeks I went round and got everyone's approval, and from that day on I was officially Hardcore.

*　　*　　*

Our lives were one long party. At times, Ronnie and I would wake up around 2 p.m. and have a bit of breakfast, usually yogurt with honey, often followed by a line of coke. I'd spend the rest of the afternoon running errands, doing household chores and hanging out with the kids. When the sun went down I'd have my first drink and more lines, and then we would be up all night partying. Ronnie loved having people around, so there would always be a houseful – friends, dealers, musicians, actors. I suppose the only time the two of us spent together alone and sober was when we were asleep, but it didn't matter – we were crazy for each other! The pair of us barely argued, and the sex was fantastic. Sure, Ronnie could be annoying when he was drunk, but I was drunk, too, so it didn't matter.

And the harder I partied, the thinner I got. I started to lose interest in food; there were days I'd wake up shaking because I hadn't eaten anything for so long. But I didn't care: I was *skinny*! I'd always struggled to lose weight, but now I was so tiny that I could fit into kids' clothes. At my thinnest I was seven stone and comfortably fitting a size 24 waist jean. It wasn't until I saw a video of myself on a trampoline in our garden at Mandeville Canyon that I realized quite how thin I'd got. I remember staring at this scrawny, stick-limbed figure in a black leotard, miniskirt and pink shiny leggings with a big bow in her hair, crazily jumping around, still wearing her high heels, and thinking, *Oh, my God, it's Olive Oyl!*

Looking back, I have no idea how I managed to make that lifestyle work, but there were always home-cooked meals on the table, the house was tidy and my kids were secure and happy. Like many working mothers, I became adept at juggling – it was just that, rather than working in an office, my job was partying. My brother Paul, then 21, was staying with us to help out, plus, of course, I had the wonderful Jaye, who had quickly been promoted from housekeeper to nanny to both. Meanwhile, I had enrolled Jamie in the local nursery school, where Rod Stewart and Alana were sending their daughter, Kimberley. During the hours I spent with the kids, we had something resembling a really normal home life. And it *was* normal to us. I'm sure our lifestyle would have raised a few eyebrows, but we were living in this wonderful, crazy bubble, and we didn't really concern ourselves with what was going on outside.

In September the band returned to Paris to continue work on the album they'd started in Nassau. We rented a lovely apartment on avenue Victor Hugo and it felt great to be back where it had all begun for Ronnie and me. His mum came to visit – the first time she had ever left England – and they drank every pub in Paris out of Guinness. We had a beautiful first-birthday party for Leah in France, followed with a stop in England before we headed back home to LA. And that was when our perfect little bubble suddenly burst.

14

It started with a knock on the front door one Thursday night. Ronnie went to answer it and came back into the living room with Bobby Keys, the Stones' sax player. I always loved seeing Bobby – I still do today. He was born on exactly the same day as Keith – 18 December 1945 – and, although one of them is from Dartford and the other the heart of Texas, the pair of them are as close as twins. Bobby is brilliant company and, in those days, totally wild, even by Ronnie and Keith's high standards. Bobby would snort, sniff or smoke whatever you put in front of him, then just keep going until he fell over. It's a wonder they got him on stage; in fact, many times it was hit and miss. On one occasion on tour the roadies had to break into Bobby's hotel room just before he was due on with the band and found him lying on the floor, passed out in a pile of sick. They shoved him in the shower, dragged him down to the gig and pushed him on stage, just in time for him to do a perfect sax solo.

Anyway, as Bobby sauntered into our living room that night he looked as excited as a kid on Christmas morning. 'Guys, you are not going to believe this.' He grinned. 'I just found the most fantastic new way to do coke without fucking up your nose. Man, you are gonna *love* it!'

Bobby's new discovery was called freebase. He led us into the bathroom and showed us how to prepare it by mixing the coke with baking soda and heating it in water until it solidified into little rocks. You then flaked a bit off, put it in a water pipe and inhaled the fumes. I watched as Bobby and Ronnie had a go, and then it was my turn. Always up for trying something new, I sucked on the pipe and – *whoooooosh*! The feeling was an incredible rush: an insane, intense euphoria. *Wow*. But in moments it had gone. Immediately, I wanted to do it again – and again and again. It wasn't a physical craving, like heroin, but the hit was so short and so extreme that I was desperate to recapture that initial high.

For the rest of that night, under Bobby's expert tuition, we learnt how to prepare it ourselves – and it turned out that I wasn't just good at roast lamb, I was good at cooking freebase, too!

So began the transformation of our Mandeville Canyon home into Freebase Central for much of celebrity LA. At first it seemed like a dream of a drug. There were no physical side effects (apart from a total loss of appetite, but I wasn't really eating anyway), and sex on freebase was mind-blowing. We set up our own little home lab, complete with Pyrex flasks, test tubes, spatulas, glass plates and rubber tubing. Ronnie had never studied chemistry at school, so he used to joke that this was his way of catching up on his education, while I gave our freebasing sessions a typically fun Jo touch by putting food colouring and the little plastic people you get in Christmas crackers into the water pipe, so when you took a hit from the pipe they'd be bobbing about. It all seemed fun and fabulous, but when you realize that freebasing was an early form of crack you'll appreciate exactly what we were getting ourselves into. Nowadays, crack couldn't have a worse image, but back then no one had even heard of it and, initially at least, free-basing didn't seem any riskier or more harmful than our usual way of doing coke.

As the months went on, our freebasing expanded to include our neighbours: Sly Stone from next door, David Crosby of Crosby, Stills and Nash, John Belushi – in fact the whole of LA's A-list seemed to be doing it. Even Tony Curtis came round. I was very excited to meet him because he'd had sex with Marilyn Monroe – and now he was in our bathroom!

When we weren't freebasing at home, we found ourselves at the house of Alan Pariser, the bushy-bearded music producer who had been behind groundbreaking shows like the Monterey Pop Festival in the late 1960s, and who had taken Bobby's enthu-siasm for 'new' coke to a whole new level. He had put together a bespoke electric burner from an assortment of 1940s vintage parts and used ether rather than baking soda, which gave the freebase a distinctive flaky quality – the connoisseurs' freebase, if you will. I persuaded Alan to give me some of his vintage elements and, to Ronnie's delight, made a Pariser burner of our own, adding some improvements, including a dimmer switch so you could control the heat – those hours watching my dad make things as a child really paid off! As our freebase circle expanded, my little burner became famous and people would say to Ronnie, 'I'll give you an eighth [that's about three and a half grams] if Jo will make me one of her burners,' and soon I had a nice little business going on the side – although I had to beg Alan for more of the elements, and he was *really* stingy with them.

On one of our rare trips out of LA during this time – the kids safe at home with the blessed Jaye – Ronnie and I had a break in Miami, although it was a bit of a busman's holiday as we went to stay with a drug dealer. Rob, his name was – nice guy. This was before smoking was banned on planes, but I can only imagine what other passengers, not to mention the aviation authorities, would have done had they known that during this flight Ronnie darted into the toilet with a full-sized butane burner and cooked up freebase. After he'd been in there for what seemed like hours, he came back to the seat and whispered, 'Your hit's ready, Jo. I've hidden the pipe and burner under the sink.' So off I went for my share.

When we arrived in Miami I was so out of it that I forgot to pick up my suitcase from the luggage carousel, and when I finally remembered, I couldn't be bothered to go back and get it. I don't have many regrets in life, but that suitcase is one of them. I had some really great clothes in it!

We hadn't been at Rob's for long and were busy cooking when a black stretch limo pulled up, and out stepped a gang of heavy-looking older dudes in shades and suits. They couldn't have looked more like Mafia bosses if they'd been carrying violin cases.

The most senior of the bunch nodded at Ronnie. 'So what's da most you've freebased in a day?'

'I dunno,' said Ronnie. 'Maybe an eighth?'

'What were you doin'?' the guy scoffed. 'Sleepin' all day?'

And with that he got out a huge Pyrex flask, poured a whole bag of coke into it and started cooking up mountains of the stuff. When it was ready he put a bit into a pipe and beckoned to me. 'Hey, you, come here.'

I tottered over to where this guy was standing. I was drunk, high and had been up for days, so was in an ultra-silly mood. '*Hiiii*,' I trilled. 'I'm *Joooo*!'

He took a hit of his pipe, made me open my mouth, then took a straw and blew a mouthful of the fumes straight down my throat.

'Oh, my God!' I screeched. 'What did you have for breakfast?'

The whole room went quiet. With hindsight, telling a Mafioso that his breath stank *was* a stupid thing to do. But slowly the big dude started to smile. 'I like this girl,' he said to Ronnie. And that, thankfully, was that.

We were moments from the beach, but didn't leave Rob's house the whole time we were there. Then, after a week or so, our new buddies asked Ronnie to get hold of the Stones master tapes from the Paris studio so they could bootleg them, which was when we decided we'd better make a swift exit back to LA.

So, it was all crazy and fun and rock 'n' roll at first – but it doesn't take long for freebase to turn you into a loony. It's a very antisocial drug. While you're doing it you don't want to face the world, just the other people locked in the bathroom with you passing round the pipe. During one session I cut my finger quite badly on the glass tubing and blood was gushing everywhere, but instead of going to hospital, like a normal, sane person, I just bandaged the cut with gaffer tape and carried on.

And then there was the paranoia. You can't look at anyone when you're doing it as you're always keeping an eye out in case you've dropped a tiny precious crumb of the stuff on the floor. Ronnie banned meringues from the house after he'd tried to freebase sugar for the umpteenth time. The singer-songwriter, Bobby Womack, was a regular guest to the Wood bathroom and on one visit I realized he had disappeared. I found him in our hall cupboard, crouched cowering in the dark among all the coats.

'Bobby, what are you doing?'

'There's somebody outside,' he muttered.

'There isn't,' I said. 'It's all fine, just come out.'

'Yes, there is,' said Bobby, his eyes wild. 'I can't see them, but I know they're coming ...'

The drug started to affect my relationship with Ronnie, too. 'Ronnie not in best of moods. Seems really low,' I wrote in my diary, near the end of 1980. 'Something is bothering him, but don't know what. Wish he'd only let me know. Maybe it's me, or someone else. Just let me know so I can do something. Whatever way.' I made a little checklist of possible ways to help him out of it, and how pointless each of them seemed: 'Sex – not too keen. Affection – not wanted. Encouragement – no thanks.'

Ronnie was even more into the drug than I was – his freebasing period went on for four years – and he would stay locked in the bathroom for days at a time. I'd pass milkshakes through the window to him just so he'd put something in his stomach. One day I saw him and Bobby Keys out in the garden, crawling through the bushes, and when I asked what they were doing Ronnie furiously accused me of hiding a stash in the flowerbed.

There's an entry in my diary on 30 August that I obviously wrote in a rage – the pen pressed so hard against the paper that the indentation of the words is obvious well into September. 'I know that I'm not crazy but it still goes on,' I wrote. 'What must I say, what must I do for his trust! I AM NOT A LIAR OR THIEF!'

It was obvious our new hobby wasn't the wonder drug we had first thought. Even Keith, who must have sampled more narcotics than most, wouldn't touch the stuff. He said it was a revolting habit and that we were mad to do it. He was right, of course, but it's difficult to get much perspective on a situation when you're so heavily involved in it. Gradually, however, my world narrowed until its sole focus was freebasing. My diary for 1980 (my freebase year) is almost completely empty. There are just a handful of entries, including this scrawled under 11 June: 'Woke up this morning, I think.'

As you can imagine, all that cocaine didn't come cheap. We might as well have been burning our savings in that pipe. And Ronnie had never been good with money. When we first moved to LA he never opened any of his mail, just tossed it into a box. It was only when the pile of unopened letters started to spill over the floor that I asked Ronnie about it – shouldn't I at least check if there were any bills? He airily assured me that if anything important came up his lawyers would be sure to let him know. From then on I took care of the post.

At this time, Ronnie's *laissez-faire* attitude to our finances landed us in serious trouble. We had met an English guy living near us in LA called Seth Bigland, who described himself a 'businessman', although we didn't find out exactly what business he was in until it was too late. Seth seemed to be a huge fan of Ronnie and was always inviting us over to his house where he'd give us huge amounts of coke to freebase.

It was great at first – never look a gift horse in the mouth and all that – but after a while I started to get suspicious. 'He's giving us all this coke, but he's never asked for any money,' I said to Ronnie, one night. 'It's weird. He must want something in return.'

But Ronnie insisted it was just because he was a fan, so I shut up about it.

Soon we were going to Seth's house virtually every other day. Apart from all the free drugs, I never felt very comfortable there.

His wife was a curvy blonde called Trixie, who was obsessed with sex. Bizarrely, all the tins of food in her kitchen had been relabelled with weird sexual names, such as Canned Balls and Clit Chowder. On one of our first visits, Trixie had a friend visiting who sashayed downstairs soon after we arrived wearing nothing but stockings and suspenders. She was a chunky girl, as well.

'Hello there!' I said. 'I wish I'd known, I wouldn't have worn so many clothes!'

On Seth's birthday, Trixie sneaked me off to the kitchen to show me the ice-cream cake she'd had made for him. She fetched this huge box out of the freezer, opened the lid and there was this massive pink creation in the unmistakable shape of an open pussy. 'I had it modelled on me,' she said proudly. 'Vanilla and strawberry.'

'Oh, isn't that nice!' I said. 'I must get one done for Ronnie's next birthday.'

So the months passed, and Seth kept on inviting us round and then one day, as he was doling out the coke with this large silver shovel that he always used, he turned to Ronnie and said, 'I want to be your manager.'

And Ronnie went, 'All right, then.'

Just like that, he put his entire career into the hands of a man who turned out to be even dodgier than I could have imagined in my worst nightmares.

* * *

For a remarkably long time, I continued to be a fully functioning mother alongside the freebasing. It was a crazy time, but I know I was always a good mum. We never did drugs in front of the kids, but sometimes we'd still be high when they woke up, and I would try to sneak off to bed so they didn't see me. God forbid that they should see their mother like that. I was just so grateful that we had Jaye. I didn't see much of my family back in the UK during this time, but I know how worried my parents were. You just had to look at me to know I was in trouble. Mum never asked if I took drugs, but she's said to me since that she was convinced I was going to die.

The beginning of the end came with another knock at the door in early 1981. This time it was my friend Wendy Worth, who had come to find me after I'd cancelled our last few get-togethers. A few weeks earlier I'd had a seizure while freebasing, which had left me weak and frightened. So when I opened the door and Wendy laid eyes on me for the first time in ages, she looked shocked. The seizure, combined with the expression on Wendy's face, was the wake-up call I finally needed.

'Jo, look at you! You're so thin!' she gasped. 'When was the last time you went out shopping for some new clothes, or got your hair cut?'

I tried to laugh off Wendy's concerns, but inside I thought, *Oh, God, she's right. I haven't been shopping in over a year.* To my horror, I realized I hadn't done *anything* apart from that stupid fucking drug. So I stopped. To mark a new beginning, I went to the hairdresser and said, 'Cut it all off.' Gradually, I rediscovered life outside the bathroom.

I don't regret doing freebase. It was part of rock 'n' roll at that time, and my motto in life has always been, 'Bring it on!' But I certainly do regret wasting 18 months in the bathroom when I should have been spending more time with my kids. I'm just so glad that I managed to quit when I did.

Hey Jo

A few months after I gave up, I was in New York with Ronnie, and Bobby came over to freebase with him. They'd been at it for hours and were badgering me to join them: 'Come on, Jo, you've been so good. Just have one little hit, you deserve it.'

In the end I gave in. 'Okay, just one little hit …'

Some 12 hours later we'd run out of coke and I was scrabbling around the floor for stray crumbs. That was what the drug did to you – there was no way you could ever do *just one little hit*. It got hold of you and you wanted more and more and more. And at that moment I decided: 'I will never, ever do freebase again.' And I never did.

15

We were in desperate need of a family holiday. Just us, the kids, and *definitely* no drugs. Ronnie, Jamie, Leah and I boarded a plane with Jaye to St Maarten, a little jewel of a Caribbean island divided into French and Dutch territories that I felt sure would be far enough from the madness of LA to guarantee that the only powder we got near during our stay would be the white-sand beaches.

For the first few days we enjoyed some wonderful family time, playing with the kids in the warm water and building sandcastles, and when the sun went down the strongest thing Ronnie and I touched was the local rum cocktail. Then one evening he suggested a stroll down to the casino after dinner. We hadn't been there long when these two 20-something guys came over, clearly thrilled to spot Ronnie. 'Hey, Rolling Stone!' they cried, greeting us like old friends.

It's rare that Ronnie goes out without people coming up to him – one of the consequences of being in the world's biggest rock 'n' roll band. But while Keith hates being recognized – on tour the only time he would venture outside the hotel was at 5 a.m. when the streets were deserted – Ronnie quite likes it. He claims not to, but I know he enjoys the attention. When we were driving in the car he'd often open the window at traffic-lights so people could see him. A few years ago, we went to Ilha Bela, a tiny little island off the coast of Brazil, where not one soul cast an eye over him and he really missed the attention. I caught him staring at people in the street, trying to get them to look at him. Fame is a weird thing.

Anyway, that night in the casino Ronnie was his usual charming self and we got chatting to these two fans – Franco and Mustafa, they were called – who offered to get us some grass. We had a smoke with them (I didn't really count puff as a drug) and I assumed that would be the last we saw of them. But a few days later we were settling in for a quiet evening when they turned up on our doorstep with a couple of giggling girls. 'Hi, guys,' they said. 'We've come to party!'

My heart sank. I really didn't want a houseful of people – this was exactly what we'd come on holiday to escape from. And Franco and Mustafa were clearly dodgy. We've got some Polaroids from that night and underneath Mustafa's photo Ronnie has scrawled, 'Would you buy a used car from this man?'

But then Franco reached into his pocket and drew out a golf-ball-sized lump of cocaine. 'This is for you, Jo.' He smiled. 'A gift.'

I wanted to be good, I really did. But at that moment, in the face of 12 grams of coke, all my intentions about staying away from drugs just vanished.

'Well, what are you standing there for? Come in!' Ronnie said. I slipped the rock safely into my skirt pocket.

We partied all night, smoking joints, doing lines and getting through bottles of rum, while Ronnie played the guitar. In the early hours Franco and Mustafa asked if they could borrow our rental car to drive the girls home and we happily handed over the keys. They reappeared a little while later, we partied for a couple more hours, and then they left. Ronnie and I were still up when Jaye and the kids woke. Jaye was such a cool New Jersey chick, as tough as anything, that nothing ever shocked her. Honest to God, I owe her so much for everything she did for us.

It must have been late morning and I was sorting out our wardrobe, trying to get myself straight, when I heard a banging at the door and glanced out of the window to see the place was crawling with men. *What the hell?* Having had no sleep – and still being drunk and high – it took me a few moments to realize that it was the police.

I heard Ronnie downstairs talking to them. 'Hey, man, is this about the music? Sorry, we'll keep the noise down.'

'We have a warrant to search the premises,' came a voice. 'You have to come with us to the police station.'

As they started to turn the house upside-down I remembered with horror that Mustafa's rock was still in my skirt pocket in the wardrobe. I didn't know what the police had on us, but if they found 12 grams of cocaine in our possession they would throw away the key.

'I can't go to the police station like this,' I said, gesturing to my skimpy playsuit as one of the officers tried to lead me out of the door. 'I need to get changed.'

'Okay, but be quick about it,' he said – and followed me into the dressing room.

'You can't expect me to get undressed in front of you!'

He stared at me suspiciously. 'Okay, you've got one minute.' And, to my relief, he left me alone.

I changed into the incriminating skirt and followed the policeman downstairs, desperately trying to think of a way to dispose of the rock. My chance came when we were in the living room. I sat on the floor to put my sandals on and slipped the rock into one of Jamie's water-wings. It was a pretty smooth move, if I do say so myself.

As we were escorted out of the door, I shouted to Jaye: 'You've got to get rid of those water-wings, Jaye. There's a hole in one and I don't want Jamie wearing them.'

I could tell from her face that she knew what I meant and yet again muttered a silent prayer of thanks that we had her to help us.

When we got to the police station, they bundled Ronnie into one room and me into another. I felt surprisingly calm: now that the rock had been disposed of I couldn't imagine we'd be in *that* much trouble because, apart from perhaps a few traces of coke on the tables, they wouldn't have found any other drugs in the house. The hours ticked past and still nobody came to talk to me. At one point I heard Leah crying and realized that Jaye must have come to find out what was going on. The sound of my baby's cries tore me up, as you can imagine. Leah was just two. But I kept telling myself, *It's okay. This is a simple mix-up. Any minute now they'll let us go.*

The sun was beginning to set when, to my relief, a policeman finally came to get me, but instead of setting me free or taking me to see a lawyer, he escorted me across a dingy courtyard and into a tiny square stonewalled cell. It was empty but for a bucket and a raised concrete bench. The walls were covered with stains and the stench of sewage was overwhelming. By now, the drugs and booze had worn off and I was seriously worried. Nobody would tell me why we were being held and I had no idea what had happened to Ronnie. I just sat there thinking about him and my babies, and wondering how poor Jaye was coping with this whole terrible mess.

Thankfully, as I'd been up partying the whole of the previous night, I eventually managed to fall asleep on the bare concrete bench and woke early the next morning when a guard stuck a salami roll through the bars, with an official-looking document. It was mostly written in Dutch so I couldn't understand much of it, but the few words I could left me numb with terror: 'Trafficking in opium'.

They thought we were drug traffickers. I was going to be in jail for the rest of my life! And then another, even more horrific, thought hit me: did they have the death penalty in St Maarten? I flew to the bars and started yelling at the top of my voice.

'I want to see the boss! I want to see the boss!'

'You – shut up,' snapped the guard.

'I want to see the boss! I want to see the boss! I want to see the boss!'

It took a while, but I stuck with it and was eventually taken to see the police chief.

'I'll tell you everything I know,' I said, as soon as I sat down. 'But will you please give me another cell because that bed last night was really hard?'

'Fine,' said the chief. 'Now talk.'

I explained how we'd met Franco and Mustafa in the casino and that they'd turned up at our house uninvited and brought all this cocaine with them.

'I can assure you we don't usually do drugs, sir,' I added, meekly.

From the chief's questioning, it was clear that they weren't just holding us because they'd found a bit of coke residue in the house, but by the end of our meeting I was still none the wiser about why they thought Ronnie and I were drug traffickers – and they were showing no sign of letting us go any time soon.

At least I got my wish for different lodgings. When the guard returned he took me to a different part of the prison. To my horror, he led me to an open yard the size of a basketball court that was crammed with men. It was like something out of a prison movie: dozens of guys exercising, sitting at tables playing cards, just hanging out. When the heavy gate clanged shut behind me, every pair of eyes flicked in my direction. I was the only female in there.

I turned to the guard, horrified. 'You can't leave me in here!'

'You'll be locked up the whole time,' he said.

But I felt far from reassured as he led me through the crowds to a little open-barred cell in the corner of the yard, containing a canvas bed and a toilet. As he slid the heavy lock across and padlocked it in place, I sat down on the bed and tried very hard not to cry.

It didn't take long for my first visitor to arrive. A huge guy sauntered over to my little cell, followed by another, then a few more, until I could barely see out of the bars for the throng of bodies pressed in front of them.

'Hey – lady.' The ringleader knocked *tap-tap-tap* on the bars. 'Hey, you hear me?'

I nodded mutely, terrified at what was coming next.

'You know Keith Richards, lady?'

Well, *that* I hadn't expected. 'Yes, I know Keith,' I said, cautiously.

The guy broke into a huge smile. 'I was with Keith on the Stones' 'seventy-five tour!' He offered his hand through the bars for me to shake. 'The name's Malcolm, great to meet you.'

Malcolm and I became instant friends. He had ended up in prison for credit-card fraud, but was now clearly running the joint as, later that day, he managed to bring me a book, a loo roll and a bar of soap. On his next visit it was cheese, biscuits and a bar of chocolate, which I was hugely grateful for as the food was hardly gourmet. 'Lunch was a pile of rice mixed with chips and what looked like meat lying on top of it,' I wrote in the diary I kept during my time in prison. Just before bedtime Malcolm came back again, this time with a pillow and a towel. I slept far easier that night – and not just because I actually had a bed.

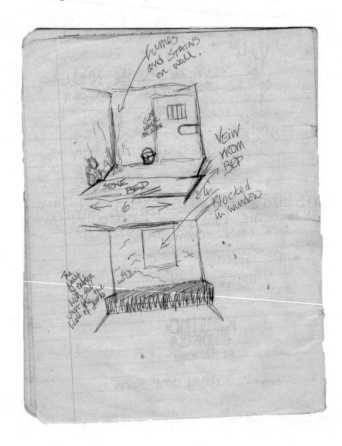

The next morning Malcolm slipped me a pen and scrap of paper. 'I'll get a note to Ronnie,' he promised. I wrote down what I'd told the police about Franco and Mustafa, so we could get our stories straight, told him how much I loved him and finished up with: 'Destroy this after reading.' I had clearly been watching too many thrillers.

Malcolm got the note to Ronnie by tying it to the end of a broomstick then standing on a dustbin to poke it through his cell window. A little while later, I was thrilled to get a reply. He signed off with: 'I love you Jo x ps. don't eat the meat.'

Malcolm became our go-between and sole source of information about what was going on with our case. He told me that because we were on the Dutch side of the island, we were considered guilty until proven innocent and had no option for bail. He explained that we would have to wait until we had a Dutch attorney before the legal process could start – and it sounded as if it might be a long wait. My fears worsened as I talked to the other guys. One of them had been imprisoned for eight months for having two joints on him; another had been there for almost a year after he was arrested with just half an ounce of grass. And Malcolm had been inside for two years and *still* hadn't gone to court.

'Jo, there's only one way you're going to get out of here,' Malcolm said to me, one day.

'How's that, Malcolm?' I asked.

'You're going to have to escape – and I've got a plan.'

'You're nuts – they've got guns! Someone will come and get us soon, I know they will.'

But lying in my little bed at night, listening to the heartrending sobs of grown men in the neighbouring cells, I began to think that perhaps we were stuck there for the long haul.

Little did I know that while we were languishing in what I christened the St Maarten's holiday camp, everyone in the outside world was going mad trying to get us out. Jaye had got hold of Ronnie's manager and lawyer in America, but then the police had cut off the phones in the house. As this was in the days before mobiles, it caused yet more delays as they tried to find alternative means of communication. When my family heard we were being held in jail my brother Paul was frantic with worry and rang Keith for reassurance. 'You can't do anything about it, Paul,' he said, calmly. 'She's most probably been gang-raped by now.' Cheers for that, Keith!

But, of course, I knew nothing of this. Sitting in my little cell, the hours dragged past like days. Thank God for Malcolm and the other guys, who used to gather round the bars every afternoon and ask me to tell them tales about my life. 'What's it like when you go on tour?' 'What does your house look like?' In return, they'd bring me cigarettes, snacks and magazines; I remember flicking through an issue of *People* and it was full of pictures of my friends. A bloke called Doris, who was as feminine as his name suggests, lent me shampoo and conditioner. Even the guards were quite sweet, bringing me clean clothes and an apple each day. Occasionally I'd catch a brief glimpse of Ronnie being marched past to the showers and he'd blow me kisses and mouth, 'Are you all right?' I missed him and the kids horribly. 'I just keep imagining what it's going to be like on the day we get out,' I wrote in my diary. 'I'm gonna run up to Ronnie and hold him SO close.'

Finally, on day four – progress. The lawyers arrived and I found out, at last, why we were being held. What had happened was this: when Franco and Mustafa had borrowed our car, they had stopped at a tree near our house and stashed a huge 22-kilo bag of coke in the branches for safekeeping. A security guard reported them to the police, who came and discovered the drugs. As Ronnie's signature was on the car-rental document, he was held responsible for crimes committed in the vehicle.

The following day the chief called me back to his office and I walked in to find none other than Franco and Mustafa standing there. They had apparently fled to a neighbouring island when they'd heard of our arrest, which was where the police had finally caught up with them.

'Do you know these men?' the chief asked me.

'Yes, sir.'

'Are they the men who supplied you with the cocaine?'

'Yes, sir.'

'And this was the first occasion you have done cocaine?'

'Yes, sir.'

Franco erupted in wild fury: 'You lie! You lie!'

'I am not lying,' I said indignantly, then turned back to the chief. 'Of course he's going to say that, sir, because he doesn't want to have to take all the blame.' (Okay, so I do feel a bit guilty about that, but the guys were professional smugglers – and they *had* landed us in jail.)

On the morning of day six I was ushered into a courtroom in front of a judge. He read out a long statement and told me that I was very irresponsible because I had a young family and should know better. 'May this experience be a lesson to you not to get involved with drugs in the future,' he said, gravely. 'I am not going to charge you, but you must leave this country immediately.'

And that was it. *I was a free woman!*

Without a chance to thank my new friends, I was immediately escorted outside where, to my utter joy, Ronnie was already waiting. We got into a car and went straight to the airport for an ecstatic reunion with the kids and Jaye. At the terminal I caught a glimpse of myself in the mirror for the first time in six days, and was shocked to see that I was covered with dozens of bites, but I didn't care. *I was free!*

We got a little charter to Miami and, as the plane took off, I vowed to myself that I was going to turn over a new leaf and quit the drugs – or, at least, seriously cut down. I'd encourage Ronnie to clean up his act, too. As the judge had said, the whole experience in St Maarten had been a wake-up call for me. But as we climbed into the clouds I heard Ronnie turn to one of the lawyers and say, 'Give us a drink and a line,' and I knew, of course, that it wasn't going to be quite so easy.

16

'Jo, get up! Get the fuck out of bed – NOW!'

My eyes flickered open, flinching at the light, and I struggled to sit up. *Oh, Christ, my head* … A couple of the Stones' security team were standing in the hotel room – they must have let themselves in. It wasn't until I managed to focus on the state of the room that I saw why they were looking so appalled. The place was absolute carnage, with empty bottles and glasses, clothes and shoes everywhere. The room was trashed. Ronnie was lying next to me fully clothed, still clutching a bottle of Jack Daniel's. It must have been a hell of a party.

'You're meant to be at the gig NOW!' said one of the guys. 'You've got twenty minutes!'

Oh, Christ … I jumped straight out of bed, threw on the nearest clothes, then phoned Housekeeping to bring up some black plastic bags, which they did straight away. 'Ronnie, get up, we've got to go!' I shouted, desperately trying to rouse him.

As I fished our possessions out of the chaos and started chucking them into the bin bags, I tried to piece together what the hell had happened. We were in Manchester – or was it Ireland? – and had been up for two, perhaps even three days since the Stones' last gig. Drinking, doing drugs, drinking, listening to music, smoking joints, laughing, being stupid, drinking. The last thing I remember was standing in our hotel room in the grey, early morning light, surveying the chaos and thinking, *I'll just have a little lie-down for an hour and then I'll get started on the packing …* That had been more than six hours ago. From that day onwards, no matter how tired I was, I always made sure I did the packing *before* we went to bed.

* * *

In September 1981, the Stones hit the road again in America for their Tattoo You tour, followed in the spring of the next year by the European leg. Compared to later tours they were quite short, just two or three months apiece, so I didn't have to spend much time away from the kids, but what they lacked in length they made up for in sheer craziness and debauchery. I remember coming home from that tour being so absolutely physically and mentally exhausted I spent a week in bed.

With the kids safely in LA with Jaye, Ronnie and I went on the road and off the rails. Mick and Keith had banned Ronnie from freebasing on tour, but one day in San Francisco he went missing and Keith was convinced he'd sneaked away to cook up some freebase. He was livid. I have this memory of Keith marching through the lobby of this huge hotel, turning the place over to find Ronnie. When he eventually appeared later – denying he'd been freebasing – the pair of them had a screaming row that ended in a proper punch-up. When Keith gets mad, he gets *really* mad.

I wish I could remember everything that went on during that tour, but I do know there was a hell of a lot of laughter. It was after the anarchy of Tattoo You that Mick laid down the law and decided that Stones tours needed to become far more professional and better organized, and by the time we hit the road again (not until 1989, thanks to Mick and Keith's feud over Mick's solo career), things were very different. For now, though, it really was sex and drugs and rock 'n' roll all the way. And the craziness seemed to infect everyone involved on that tour – roadies, security, drivers, the lot.

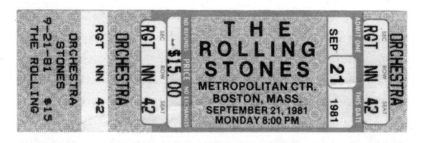

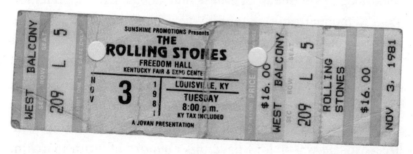

Much of what went on is not for the faint-hearted: those with a squeamish disposition should probably look away while I recount this particular episode. I was in our hotel in San Francisco after one of the gigs, walking down the corridor, and I heard laughter coming from Freddie Sessler's room. The door was open so I stuck my head in. There was a naked chick standing in the middle of the room, surrounded by roadies, while

Freddie waved a bag of coke in front of her. 'Come on, baby,' he was saying. 'If you want this, you gotta pull the string.' And I realized what he was trying to make her do – in front of all those blokes: take her Tampax out. I turned round and walked straight out again.

I had a new partner in crime for Tattoo You: Patti Hansen, Keith's soul-mate and soon-to-be wife. They had met a couple of years ago, after Keith took a shine to her when he spotted her picture in *Vogue*, and hooked up in the legendary Manhattan nightclub Studio 54 after meeting through mutual friends. I had never met Patti, but I knew her face from magazines and I loved her attitude. I remember reading an article in which top models had been asked their beauty secrets, and among the usual holier-than-thou responses – 'I drink 10 glasses of water a day' and 'I religiously cleanse, tone and moisturize' – one of the girls had said, 'I don't bother taking off my makeup before bed as I'm usually out partying all night.' *Now that's my kind of chick*, I thought – and the chick in question was Patti.

Keith took us to meet her when we were in New York and I remember her flying out of the door of their apartment, wearing nothing but a pair of men's pyjama bottoms, and jumping straight into Keith's arms. I thought she was fabulous, and adore her to this day.

Keith was crazy about Patti and one night on tour he dedicated a song to her. Apparently he said some really lovely, heartfelt things, but I wouldn't know because at the time Patti and I were backstage getting pissed in a Jacuzzi – Keith was understandably annoyed. The pair of us got up to all sorts of mischief together. It was great having another girl to play with, especially one who was just as up for it as I was. One night, after a particularly intense few days of partying, Charlie fell fast asleep on the couch in his hotel room, so the pair of us decided it would be funny to redecorate the room around him. Trying to stifle our giggles, we swapped all the furniture round and changed the pictures, the plan being that when he woke up he wouldn't know where the hell he was. Amazingly, Charlie slept through the whole thing. Perhaps all his drumming had made him deaf.

Of course, there were the usual groupies on tour, but by now I had perfected Jo's patented Anti-Groupie Technique™ (i.e. kill them with kindness) and, most of the time, everyone was too high and drunk to take much notice of any hangers-on anyway. Besides, Ronnie and I were always at our best when we were partying hard together, and because of that closeness, we had a great bond.

*　*　*

It was 15 March 1982, my 27th birthday, and Ronnie and I were in New York on a few months' break between the American and European legs of the tour. I didn't really feel in the party mood, though, as just a week earlier we had got the devastating news that my dear friend John Belushi had died. Ronnie and I had been driving from JFK airport into Manhattan when it came on the radio that he had been found dead in his room at the Chateau Marmont. A drugs overdose, the announcer had said. I was heartbroken, and what made it even harder to bear was that I felt a sense of personal guilt over his death. It turned out that the dealer who had injected him with the fatal shot of speedball – a mix of heroin and coke – was Cathy Smith, the crazy woman who used to hang around our house (the one Keith had threatened with a gun) and whom *we* had introduced to John. I kept torturing myself with the fact that if we'd been in LA John would have been hanging out with us, rather than with that awful woman. He was such a lovely man and very much missed.

So, my birthday was pretty subdued, as you can imagine – and that evening things got even worse. We had gone to a club with a group of friends and one of the guys brought along the model Kelly LeBrock. She was yet to find fame as a movie star in *The Woman in Red* and *Weird Science*, but her face was familiar to me from countless covers of *Vogue* and *Cosmopolitan*. Kelly seemed terribly sweet – Ronnie clearly thought so anyway, as he was all over her that night. We shared a limo ride home, and as I sat there, watching my boyfriend outrageously flirting with Kelly, I felt desperately insecure. I could cope with groupies, no problem, but this was a fucking supermodel. *Happy bloody birthday, Jo …*

Over the next few weeks Ronnie started to disappear for days at a time with no explanation. I assumed it was down to drugs as he was still doing freebase, but when I tried to talk to him one evening it turned into a horrible argument that ended with him storming off. Apart from a brief phone call to tell me he was okay, that was all I heard from him for more than a week. I had no idea where he was, although I had my suspicions, and was beginning to get seriously worried. In the end, I tracked down a studio where I knew he was due to be working on some material with Jimmy Cliff, and phoned them up.

'Oh, hi, this is Ronnie Wood's secretary. Could I please speak to him?'

'He's in the studio,' said the receptionist. *Well, at least I now knew where he was.*

'Is there any way you can interrupt him? I have an urgent message from London.'

'I'm afraid not,' said the woman. 'But his girlfriend is here with him – would you like to give the message to her?'

His girlfriend? I was so shocked it took me a few moments to find the breath to speak.

'Yes, that will be fine,' I said, quietly.

She put me on hold, and as I waited, I began to think that perhaps the receptionist had made a mistake, that everything was okay and Ronnie still loved me as much as ever, but then a woman's voice came on the line and in that moment my worst fears were realized.

'Hello?'

I slammed the phone down. I'd recognized the voice instantly; deep down I suppose I knew who it was going to be before she had even spoken. It was Kelly LeBrock.

I fled to Keith and Patti's apartment and holed up there. I was so devastated they kindly let me paint a huge mural on one of their walls, of people, flowers and kids. After a few days I felt ready to go back to our apartment, but I asked the model Janice Dickinson – who had become a good friend since she'd had a wild affair with Mick on the last tour – to come over for moral support. The two of us were sitting there, trying to make sense of what had happened, when the phone rang. To my surprise, it was Ronnie.

'Hey, Jo,' he said. 'What are you up to?'

I couldn't believe it. The guy was acting like everything was fine, like he hadn't just gone AWOL for 10 days with a supermodel!

Well, two can play at that game …

'Oh, you know, just hanging out. Janice is here.'

We chatted a while and then he said, 'I think we'll come over in a bit, okay?'

'Yeah, fine. See you then. 'Bye.'

I put the phone down and just stared at it in disbelief. Then I turned to Janice, who was clearly desperate to know what had been said.

'Ronnie's coming over,' I told her. 'And I think he's bringing Kelly.'

Sure enough, a few hours later, the pair of them turned up together. It was the most surreal moment, welcoming my boyfriend and his mistress into my house. Little did I know it, but the same thing would happen again almost 25 years later, but this time it would be an 18-year-old Ukrainian called Katia that Ronnie brought to meet me, rather than an American super-model. That night the four of us got drunk and high together and nobody mentioned how fucking weird it was, but I was struggling to hold back the tears. Every now and then when Janice could see I was about to lose it, she would take me into the bedroom, touch up my eye makeup, re-do my hair – at this time it was all short and spiky, like one of Duran Duran – and do her cheerleader bit.

'Come on, babe, you get back out there,' she said. 'You can do this!'

Janice was amazing that night and is still a friend to this day. She's really great. Insane, but great.

By 6 a.m., though, I'd had enough. I felt utterly broken and defeated. 'I'm going to bed,' I said to Ronnie. 'I'll see you later.'

Kelly stood up, too. 'Take me home, Ronnie,' she said. 'Let's get a cab.'

But Ronnie didn't move.

'No, you go on,' he said to her. 'I'm going to stay here with Jo.'

And that was it. He came up to our room and got into bed like nothing had happened, and that was the last we saw of Kelly. Ronnie later swore blind that he'd never touched her. I desperately wanted to believe him as I couldn't bear the thought of the alternative, so I didn't mention it again and our relationship was soon back on track. But although I didn't give Ronnie a hard time, I vowed to myself that I wouldn't tell him I loved him until he told me first. I think because he didn't grow up in an affectionate family, he had never been one for grand declarations of love. If I asked him if he loved me he'd say, 'Yeah, you know I do,' but it's not the same thing, really, is it? So it was important for me to hear those words from him, to know he truly loved me …

I waited for a whole year before I broke that vow. I stopped myself saying it so many times, but in the end I couldn't hold out any longer. Well, what can I say? I was crazy about the guy.

17

Just before Christmas in 1982 Ronnie and I had a few weeks in Barbados. It was a holiday of two halves – the first part was about family, then Jaye took the kids home, and Ronnie and I had a bit of a wild one – thankfully, we managed to avoid prison this time. We befriended a vacationing gang of English firemen and together we hung out and partied together, fuelled by rum and coke (the drug, not the beverage, obviously). It wasn't long after we got home that I started to feel suspiciously queasy.

I can't possibly be pregnant, I thought. *Not after all that partying …*

Then one chilly January morning I winced as the cold sent pain shooting through my nipples. A visit to the doctor confirmed it: I *was* pregnant!

I went to find Ronnie to tell him the wonderful news: not difficult to do at this time as he was so deep into freebase that I always knew exactly where he would be. I trotted down the corridor and stuck my head around the bathroom door.

'Honey, I'm pregnant!'

'Fantastic!' He beamed. Then went back to sucking the pipe.

By this time we had moved our family to New York. We had been spending more and more time in the city because Keith and Patti were now living there, plus Ronnie had managed to disentangle himself from Seth Bigland's clutches and had a new manager, an English solicitor called Nick Cowan, who was based in Manhattan. We found a fab brownstone on West 78th Street with plenty of room for the kids and Jaye: as she was originally from New Jersey, she was happy to head east with us. I loved being in walking distance of the Anglo-American school where we enrolled the kids – and, of course, the shops. After those months of freebasing, it had been a relief to leave behind the madness of LA for the relative calm of NYC.

Although the pace was a little less crazy, we still had a houseful on most nights. I might find myself cooking shepherd's pie for Bob Dylan (a sweet guy, but very quiet) or whipping up spag bol for David Bowie. Other visitors to the Wood residence at that time included Robin Williams, Andy Warhol (who hardly said a word all night, just went round taking photos) and Michael J. Fox. Our old freebasing buddy from LA, Sly Stone, stopped by whenever he was in town or out of jail, and on one occasion turned up wearing red leather trousers and a leather jacket with padded shoulders. 'Oh, my God, Sly,' I howled, on seeing the shiny monstrosity. 'What the hell is THAT?'

* * *

Physically, it was a really easy pregnancy: I didn't get any morning sickness and – as I'd been through it twice before – I knew exactly what to expect. But in many ways it was the hardest of the three. Ronnie was almost totally absent for those nine months, which was ironic as he was always at home. He had little interest in anything besides freebasing – and the more he withdrew from me, the needier I became. Chuck my raging hormones into the mix and you can imagine that my emotions were all over the place.

In the early stages of the pregnancy we went with Nick Cowan and his girlfriend (later wife) Julie to see John McEnroe play tennis at Madison Square Gardens. I remember saying, as we sat down, 'I'm in a foul mood so nobody talk to me.' The three of them chatted away for the entire match and – as commanded – didn't say a single word to me. My grouchiness lessened, but then I felt totally ignored and unloved. In the end I said, in a small voice, 'Can somebody please talk to me now?'

While I was pregnant, my daily routine almost looked like that of a normal mum. It was quite a novelty to be going to bed at night and waking up in the morning. Ronnie would still be awake, of course, having been in the bathroom freebasing all night. When he went to bed, I'd give the kids their breakfast and Jaye would take them to school while I got on with the household chores. At some point, usually just as the kids were getting home, Ronnie would emerge and I'd cook him breakfast. He'd often spend time drawing with the kids, which they loved, but I never felt able to leave Ronnie alone with them. If I needed to get some groceries I'd take them with me to the store rather than getting him to babysit. The problem was he had a very short fuse, especially when he'd been drinking, and would go ballistic about the most utterly trivial things, like if one of the kids touched his cassettes; but when it came to the important stuff, like manners and discipline – things you'd want a father to be strict about – he would totally ignore it. It was important to me that the kids loved their dad and didn't see a bad side to him, and it was easier to manage if I was around.

I tried to tell Ronnie that he should slow down with the free-base, but it was like talking to the wall. On one occasion he was having a meeting with record-company executives in our living room and kept popping out for another hit, leaving me to cover for him. 'I'm so sorry,' I'd say. 'Ronnie's got a really upset tummy. My poor Ronnie's been up all night!' But then he would come back downstairs and I'd take one look at him, his face like a crazy man's, and think, *They must know what's going on.*

It wasn't just the drugs: Ronnie was drinking so much, too. Probably no more than before I was pregnant, but now that I wasn't getting wasted with him I noticed it much more. He could be very moody when he was drunk – and for his part, he hated that I wasn't out there rocking with him. Ronnie had fallen for wild, crazy, dancing-on-tables Jo, not sober, sensible, having-a-nap Jo. In the later stages of my pregnancy we had tickets to a Tina Turner gig, but I was struck down with a really nasty bout of food poisoning. I remember dragging myself out of bed to get ready and being violently ill in the shower. It was so bad that I started to worry about the baby. Just before it was time to leave, Ronnie came into the bedroom to find me in a pale, shaky heap on the bed.

'Come on, Jo, we've got to go!' he said. 'Get up, get yourself ready.'

'I'm really sorry but I can't come. I feel terrible.'

'Well, I'm going on my own, then. See you later.' And he turned away.

I couldn't believe it. 'Ronnie, I'm really ill,' I said. 'I think I might need to go to hospital. Are you just going to leave me here on my own? I'm eight months pregnant!'

In the end he stayed, albeit grudgingly.

Throughout all this, though, I adored my man as much as ever – and I was positive he loved me, too. I really couldn't see much bad in him: the drugs and booze were to blame for the worst of his behaviour. It certainly never once crossed my mind that we should split up – Christ, no! I remember lying in bed one night, stroking my bump, and thinking, *If Ronnie dies before I do, then what on earth will I do? How could I exist without him?* And we were still having so much fun. We'd gone on holiday to Nassau when I was about five months pregnant and there's a photo of me lying on my front on the sand looking totally normal – I had dug a hole in the sand for my bump and lowered myself onto it. There were a lot of laughs, and life was generally pretty good.

* * *

As my due date approached I had a couple of false alarms, but when eventually I went into labour, on 21 August 1983, it happened *fast*.

'You're only three centimetres dilated so you've got a few hours to go yet, dear,' a nurse told me, when we arrived at the hospital. 'You just lie there and I'll see you later.'

As soon as she left I turned to Ronnie, who was getting busy with his sketchbook, and said, 'I'm having this baby right now, I just know it!'

'Sssh, keep still, I'm drawing you …'

Moments later, I felt the familiar pressure down below and hollered for the nurse. She checked me once again – and her shocked expression said it all. 'We need to get you to the delivery room,' she said. 'Now!'

So they ran me down there and in three quick pushes the baby was out. My darling Tyrone: a calm, peaceful baby who would grow into a wonderfully sweet-natured little boy. Ronnie had suggested the name – one of our friends, a keyboard player, was called Tyrone Davis – and I had instantly loved it, although it got a mixed reception from some of our mates.

'You can't call that kid Tyrone!' said one. 'Tyrone is that big black dude who lives on the corner of the block and when there's any trouble people say, "Quick! Get Tyrone!"'

I laughed. 'Well, he's just going to have to be the big white dude instead.'

* * *

It was my second day in hospital after Ty's birth and I was sitting up in bed feeding my little boy, feeling totally in love and at peace, when Ronnie rocked up.

'Hey, baby,' he said, dropping a kiss on my and his son's head. 'I've bought you something.'

Oh, my honey, I thought happily. *Could it be flowers? Jewellery, perhaps?*

Instead Ronnie handed me a packet of white powder. 'A little something to help you get back on track.' It was cocaine.

'Are you out of your mind, Ronnie? I don't want that! And you can't leave it here,' I added, as he went to squirrel it away in the cabinet. 'This is a *hospital*, for fuck's sake!'

The truth was that I was in no hurry at all to – as Ronnie put it – 'get back on track'. When I'd had Leah I couldn't wait to return to partying with the boys, but this time Ronnie had been doing so much freebase it had really put me off. I still wanted to have fun, to have a laugh and a line, but I was beginning to feel I wanted more in my life than just getting out of my skull every night. It was plainly obvious, however, that Ronnie didn't feel the same – and Ty's birth did nothing to change that.

Later that summer, we rented a house by the beach in the Hamptons. Friends dipped in and out, including singer, Billy Idol, and his girlfriend, Perri Lister – we'd been hanging out with them a lot in New York. During our stay a magazine commissioned the photographer, Ken Regan, to take some family photos of us for an 'at home' spread. On the day of the shoot I was running around, trying to get Leah and Jamie dressed, Ty snuggled up on my shoulder, when I realized that Ronnie had vanished. He still hadn't reappeared by late morning when Ken had already set up for the first shot.

I eventually found him sitting down by the water's edge knocking back tequila slammers on his own. I was so upset: we were lucky enough to be getting some really special photos with our new son and here he was, blind drunk, his hair sticking in sweaty clumps to his forehead. I'll say one thing for Ronnie, though: he can certainly pull himself together when he needs to. He looks absolutely fine in the photos. But I was furious.

* * *

'I can't live with Ronnie any more,' I sobbed to my friend, Lorraine. 'He's just gone completely insane. He spent the whole of my pregnancy in the bathroom.'

It was six weeks after Ty's birth and we had come to England to introduce the new arrival to our friends and family. We were staying with Lorraine, now married to the rock drummer, Simon Kirke, and I was pouring my heart out to her. I was no angel, true, but Ronnie's freebasing had got totally out of hand.

'You know what you should do, Jo?' she said. 'You should put Ronnie into rehab.'

'Rehab? What's that?' I had never even heard of it. This was the early eighties, remember, before a stint in rehab replaced the spa as the stressed-out celebrity's bolthole of choice.

'Don't worry, we'll find a suitable clinic and then you need to sit Ronnie down and confront him about the freebasing,' said Lorraine. 'I'm sure he'll understand.'

But Ronnie didn't understand. He went completely bananas.

'Are you fucking crazy?' he said. 'I'm not going to be locked away in some nuthouse! No way.'

Ronnie ranted and raved but in the end, miraculously, he agreed to give it a go for the sake of the family. A few days later, Simon and I drove him to the clinic in Devon that Lorraine had recommended. I must say, even at the most serious times Ronnie could be very entertaining. On the drive down he insisted we stop off at a few pubs and he was decidedly the worse for wear when we arrived. On check-in the receptionist asked for payment of £30,000. Ronnie turned round and said, 'Bloody hell, I didn't know I was that ill.' He had his blood tested, and the nurse asked what his sleeping pattern was. He said: 'Knit one, purl one ...' Simon and I just stood there, trying not to snigger.

He stayed for two weeks and when I drove down to collect him I was so proud that he had stuck with it. He made me stop at the first pub we passed so he could have a pint of Guinness, but he never touched freebase again.

Now, however, we had to deal with the fall-out from the Bathroom Years. The cost of all those drugs – not to mention Seth's highly questionable management technique – had left us completely skint. Ronnie's career and financial affairs were now in the hands of Nick Cowan, who would go on to manage him for the next 20 years. I liked and trusted Nick and enjoyed hanging out with him and Julie, but as a manager he would turn out to be another mistake. I would often catch him staring into space and assume he was deep in thought, dreaming up ingenious ways to make us money, but with hindsight I think his mind was just wandering.

We had been introduced to Nick in LA by a shady businessman, let's call him Harry, and somehow he, too, had become tangled up in running our affairs. I'm not sure what his official role was, but it was Harry who put us on a tight budget, giving me just $200 a week to run the household and feed the family. I was instantly suspicious of him, especially because the money he gave me always smelt of mildew. Once on tour he tried to talk his way into Keith's hotel room, but Keith couldn't stand him and said he would only let him in if he paid him 50 thousand in cash. A short while later Mr Mildew reappeared with a suitcase stuffed full of dollars. We were scrimping at the time, so this made me furious. I grew to distrust Harry big-time, but I was too young and too naïve to know how to deal with it. It was a struggle to keep to our tight budget, and it was new to us, but I was finally learning to live within our means – although occasionally I'd spot a fab pair of shoes and have to splurge. Ronnie found it much harder: he had no concept of money. Bill Wyman recently told me about the time Ronnie went to the guys in the band to ask for a loan, as we couldn't pay the kids' school fees.

After pocketing the cash he went straight out and bought himself a Rolex.

Then one day a debt collector turned up on our doorstep in New York and our problems suddenly got much worse.

'You owe Seth Bigland a hundred and fifty grand for cocaine,' grunted this heavy, who was almost as wide as he was tall. 'And I'm here to see that he gets it.'

It turned out that Ronnie's ex-manager had ended up in jail after police had raided his home and found a huge vault containing a coke lab and dozens of guns and bombs. I was just surprised that sex-mad Trixie, his wife, had let the officers get out fully dressed.

My first instinct was to go straight to the police and tell them this bloke was trying to extort money from us. After all, we had done nothing wrong; we didn't have anything to hide. But Nick Cowan was adamant we should get out of the country while he and Harry cleared up the mess, so we packed up the family and got on a flight to Mexico.

I can think of worse places to be a fugitive than an ex-president's house on a beach in Cancún. Ty was six months old and we spent our days playing with the kids in the surf and hired a jeep to explore the area, which was then largely an undeveloped expanse of palm-fringed white sand. It was our second visit to Mexico that year, as a few months earlier the Stones had gone there to film a video for their new single. Over the years I had nagged and nagged Mick to let me appear in one of the videos and, to my amazed delight, this time he finally gave in. The song was 'She's So Hot' – although in the video I look far from that. I was to play a little old lady in a grey wig, shawl and long floral dress alongside Bill Wyman as my equally doddery husband. *Gee, thanks, Mick ...*

On the day of the shoot I was shown to the set, where Bill and I were going to be sitting in front of a large window in our rocking chairs. I couldn't understand why the scenery was surrounded with all this plastic sheeting until the director yelled, 'Action!' I heard a loud rumbling, then thousands of gallons of water broke through the window with such force that I was pushed off my chair. I was drenched, and the shock you can see on my face in that video is entirely genuine.

We were in hiding in Cancún for six weeks, and when we got back to New York the Seth problem had disappeared – but our financial situation was worse than ever. We were trying to sell our house in LA and, thanks to Mick and Keith's spectacular fall-out over Mick's solo ambitions, it looked highly unlikely there would be another Stones tour for the foreseeable future, which meant Ronnie's main source of income had dried up.

We needed to make some money – fast. Ronnie was an undeniably talented artist and had always enjoyed drawing and painting as a hobby, and now seemed like the ideal time to see if he could make it work as a day job. He borrowed an art studio in San Francisco and for two weeks he shut himself away and threw himself into his work. That first creative frenzy produced some great woodcuts of Chuck Berry and John Lennon that Nick Cowan had no trouble selling, and pretty soon the money started to dribble in.

*　*　*

By Tyrone's first birthday it really felt like Ronnie and I were back on track. After Ty's birth he had given me a beautiful ring set with five diamonds: 'One for each of us.' Sure, we'd had a few bumps along the road, but I knew our love was still rock-solid. Things were good – no, they were great. As our seven-year anniversary approached in September 1984, we went to Jamaica to stay with Keith and Patti to celebrate. And it was here that my life would take another totally unexpected turn.

18

'Ronnie, what the hell is wrong with you?'

We'd been at Keith and Patti's house in Ochos Rios in Jamaica for three blissful weeks, but in the run-up to our anniversary Ronnie had been acting really weird. Sort of shifty and twitchy, as if he was up to something he didn't want me to know about. I'd tried to ignore it and dearly hoped that whatever it was would just blow over, but if anything he was getting worse – and now that the two of us had some rare time alone together, I was determined to find out what was up.

We were having an anniversary dinner at a restaurant Keith had described as the most romantic on the island. Our candlelit table was right next to a waterfall and surrounded by lush greenery twinkling with fairy lights: all pretty idyllic, except that Ronnie had barely spoken to me since we'd sat down and was now staring at the menu as if it was written in Chinese.

'Ronnie?' I tried again, raising my voice over the rush of water. 'Please, just tell me – what's the matter?'

'Nothing, nothing,' he muttered, still avoiding eye contact.

The waiter came over, pen hovering expectantly over his pad, but Ronnie irritably waved him away and went back to the menu.

And then, just as I was giving up any hope of a romantic evening, he suddenly blurted out: 'Jo, will you marry me?'

Well, I certainly hadn't been expecting *that*.

It wasn't the first time Ronnie had proposed – during the early years of our relationship he had frequently popped the question, but I had always turned him down. Not because I didn't love him enough – the man was my whole world and I adored him – but he had never asked in a way that was romantic or even sincere: usually just a drunken 'Come on, Jo, marry me.' More to the point, I was perfectly happy being his girlfriend; after all, marriage hadn't exactly worked out well for either of us the first time round. So, because I'd turned him down so many times, I'd assumed Ronnie had given up asking, but now, as I looked at his gorgeous little face peeking over the top of the menu, all hopeful and worried, I just thought, *Well, why the hell not?*

'Oh, all right, then,' I finally said. 'Now, are you going to have the fish or the chicken?'

*　*　*

Keith always claims full responsibility for our wedding. Flush with happiness after his own marriage to Patti, he had apparently been nagging Ronnie about proposing to me the whole time we'd been in Jamaica. He virtually jumped on us as soon as we walked in the door after dinner. 'So come on, come on, did you do it, then?' I don't really know who was happier that night: the future Mr and Mrs Ronnie Wood or Cupid Keith.

I arranged the whole wedding from scratch in three weeks. We returned to England in December for Christmas and, with Lorraine's help, threw everything together in time for the big day, which was to be 2 January 1985. I designed my white lace and satin dress and had it run up for just £300. I carried a bunch of red roses: the scarlet woman getting married. Leah and Domino, Lorraine's daughter, were bridesmaids, wearing little lace dresses, my sister Lize was chief bridesmaid in a vintage lace dress, and Jamie and Jesse were our pages. I put them – and Ronnie – in tuxedos and red bow ties, and found a vintage knitted outfit with a red woollen cap for Ty. I really enjoyed getting the whole thing together.

I had wanted to be married in church, but being a Catholic/Jewish-ish divorcee made this out of the question, so we decided to get the official bit done in a register office, then go for a blessing in a C of E church. We picked one in Denham, Buckinghamshire, not far from where Ronnie's parents lived so we could use their address. In the run-up to the wedding Ronnie and I had to meet the vicar every week so he could talk to us about the sanctity of marriage and the importance of regularly attending church, *blah blah blah* ... Pretty much wasted on a couple who'd been living in sin for seven years and had already clocked up four kids between them.

On the night before the wedding I went to the theatre and dinner with the girls, then stayed at Lorraine's house, sharing a bed with Lize. Meanwhile Ronnie took his mates, including the comedian, Peter Cook, and my brother Paul, out for his stag. The group roamed around various seedy joints in Soho, but because it was New Year's Day nothing much was open and after they'd been thrown out of a strip joint for rowdy behaviour, they ended up drinking champagne in the lobby of the Ritz. They stayed there, boozing and banging away on the grand piano, until the hotel's genteel clientele started wandering down for breakfast.

Paul was so epically hung-over that day that he barely remembers surviving the wedding.

Like most brides, my memories of my wedding day are just brief snapshots rather than a detailed video. (We had an actual video, but a few weeks later Ronnie helpfully recorded the snooker over much of it.) I remember kneeling with my new husband at the altar, swapping delighted grins and stifling giggles, as the vicar droned on and on. 'There are many stars in the sky,' he was intoning gravely, 'but some give off little light. Just as there are many stars here in the congregation today' – he gestured to the famous faces lining the pews – 'but always remember that stars can dwindle and die ...' It was a car-crash of a sermon; I think there might have been actual heckling from the direction of Peter Cook and Rod Stewart.

When it was over, the two of us bounded out of the church, high on love and adrenalin, and into the white Bentley waiting to whisk us to the reception at a nearby pub, the Bull. But before we could head off, Keith jumped in too and, instead of the usual bottle of champagne to toast the wedding, whipped out a little packet of coke. Someone in the car behind us later told me they had watched as our three heads dipped in unison for a celebratory line. I was actually furious with myself for doing it, as I knew it would kill my appetite at the reception. Sure enough, I couldn't eat a thing at dinner. Dad was sitting next to me and kept asking why I wasn't eating and I had to come up with some lame excuse about being too excited. I can't even remember what we had. Something to do with melon? God knows ...

It was a perfect day. Peter Cook made a very funny speech, and when the Dirty Strangers took the stage after dinner, Ronnie and Keith got up and played and then I stormed up there too, and sang 'And Then He Kissed Me'. As well as our families, friends had flown in from all over the world, including the boys from the band (although Jerry had just given birth to Lizzie and Patti was about to have Theodora, so they couldn't come), Rod Stewart and Kelly Emberg, Ringo Starr and his wife Barbara, Peter Frampton and Jeff Beck. For this special day, I only wanted the people I loved most in the world around me. (Our old friend Harry, Mr Mildew, had tried to bribe me with $10,000 for a wedding invitation, but I'd turned him down flat.)

The celebrations went on until 6 a.m. and then Ronnie and I fell into bed at the Bull, still with enough energy to consummate our marriage. Lying cuddled up together, watching the sun rise, I was surprised by how different I felt now that I was Mrs Ronnie Wood. We had been together so long and been through so much that I assumed being married wouldn't change a thing. But with hindsight I realized I'd never truly felt totally secure in the relationship until now. Our wedding rings had made it official: he was my man.

For our honeymoon we went to the island of Bora Bora in the South Pacific. It was somewhere I'd always wanted to go, my imagination fuelled by images of vivid turquoise water, coconut palms and locals diving for black pearls – and the reality didn't disappoint. The place ticked every desert-island fantasy. We stayed in a little hut built over the sea on stilts, beneath which you could see huge, colourful fish swimming around the coral reef. Ronnie's not a great swimmer – he can get quite panicky in the water – so we didn't do any diving or snorkelling, but we did go out on a boat for a day's fishing with a handsome young local we'd met on the beach. He was very attractive, all bulging muscles and long blond curls, and so flirty and charming with me that I think Ronnie got a twinge of jealousy. We were out on the boat for hours, and eventually I announced that I was 'dying to spend a penny'.

Tarzan just cupped his hands and said, 'Spend it in here, Jo.'

I squealed with appalled laughter. 'What? No way!' Ronnie looked as if he was about to explode. I don't think we saw our friend again after that day.

It was a fabulous holiday. One day I persuaded Ronnie to join me in a fishing tournament, even though it started at 5 a.m. As we headed out to the deep waters of the Pacific the captain of the boat said, 'Jo, you need to bring us good luck. As the only female here, you need to sit on the lures.' So I happily sat on all of them. It obviously worked, as we landed a heap of fish that morning, including some tuna.

By midday I noticed that Ronnie was a little peaky. 'I've had enough,' he groaned. 'I wanna go back.' For the rest of the holiday we kept our sea-legs on land.

One day we hired bikes and set out to explore the island (or, rather, the island's bars). Ronnie bought me a beautiful black pearl. But really it was all about the drinking. Southern Comfort and lemonade and Cuba Libres were our holiday tipple. Nowadays I wouldn't touch either as I find them revoltingly sweet, but back then those were our drinks of choice. On our first day Ronnie got so drunk he had the most violent attack of hiccups. After trying every remedy we could think of to get rid of them, he came up with a fantastic idea. 'I'll stand on my head,' he declared. And with that his legs flew up into the air as he wildly tried to get his balance. Unsurprisingly, he ended up in a heap on the floor. Our honeymoon might have been low on textbook honeymoon romance, but it was definitely high on fun.

19

Although the restaurant scene in New York was booming in the eighties, one of the few dishes you couldn't get was a decent curry. So when a new Indian restaurant called Nirvana opened in midtown Manhattan soon after we got back from our honeymoon, we immediately booked a table for a Jalfrezi fix. The kids came too, with a friend of mine called Melissa.

The evening started really well. The restaurant was situated a few floors up so you got into an elevator off the bustling Manhattan sidewalk and, moments later, emerged into a spice-scented oasis, as if you'd just been magically transported to India. The kids had got stuck into the poppadums and we were looking at the menus when Melissa excused herself to go to the loo, which was on the floor below. A waiter came to take our order, then our drinks arrived, but Melissa hadn't reappeared. 'What the hell is she doing?' I whispered to Ronnie. Then, as I was starting to worry, the elevator doors slid open and Melissa flew into the room, covered with so much blood that her white blouse had turned red.

Once we had calmed her down, she explained what had happened. When she'd walked into the Ladies she'd come face to face with a guy holding a big chunk of wood. He'd demanded all her money and she'd given him the $20 she had in her pocket, but as she'd turned to go he had whacked her on the back of her head before running off. For me, though, the most disturbing part of the story was that when she'd got back into the elevator, looking like something out of *Nightmare on Elm Street*, none of the other occupants had blinked an eyelid. I guess this kind of thing wasn't that uncommon in New York in the days before Mayor Rudi Giuliani cleaned up the streets.

Later that night, after I had taken poor Melissa to hospital to get her head stitched up, I was lying in bed, thinking, *I really don't want my kids to grow up here*, when I heard a loud crash outside. Ronnie had gone to the studio, so I stuck my head out of the window and saw a gang of kids smashing the hell out of an expensive car. I shouted, hoping to scare them away, but instead they just waved their knives at me – and that was when I decided the Wood family had to get the fuck out of the Big Apple.

I'd actually been feeling homesick since arriving back in New York. I loved our place on West 78th Street and had just finished putting in a fab new kitchen, but I'd spent so much time with our families at Christmas and the wedding that I realized now just how much I'd been missing them. Ronnie could work on his art and music anywhere; it felt like the only thing keeping us in New York was that Keith and Patti were nearby. The following morning I said to Ronnie, 'We've got nobody here. All our family is in England. Can we please go home?'

And he just went, 'Okay, let's go.'

We didn't even bother waiting until we'd put up our house for sale, just packed all our worldly goods and flew back to England to stay with Lorraine and Simon until we found a place of our own. Keith was not happy that we were leaving Manhattan – in fact, he was furious – but the time was right for us to go home.

By the end of 1986 we'd found a lovely house in Wimbledon. It wasn't at all grand, but it was cosy and homely with a studio/den in the garden for Ronnie. All our possessions had been in storage and when the boxes arrived at the new house they were accompanied by a couple of Customs officers; I guess the fact that Ronnie was a Rolling Stone was enough to make them suspicious. As the removal men brought in the crates, they would pick a box at random and go through it with forensic diligence. This would have been nothing more than a minor inconvenience but for the fact that while I was packing up the house in New York I had found a huge lump of hash, about the size of a CD case but an inch thick, and stashed it inside a cushion. I knew we would be in serious trouble if they found it – not exactly the start to our new life in England that I had hoped for. In an attempt at organization I had labelled each box with a letter, so when the Customs officer turned his gaze on Box H ('H' for hashish, obviously) my heart was thumping so loudly I was sure he must be able to hear it, but then – *thank God* – he waved the crate past. 'Just bring that box upstairs,' I said, as casually as possible to the removal man, then hid it out of sight until our visitors finally left, thankfully none the wiser about the cannabis cushion.

Jaye didn't come to England with us: she stayed in the States and went to work for Mick and Jerry. I missed her hugely, of course: she had been an absolute life-saver over the years. I hired a very sweet girl called Myfanwy to be a part-time nanny, but she left after six months and the agency sent an Australian girl in her place. Well, that was a disaster. On her day off I had expected this girl would want to get out and see London, but instead she'd spend the day sitting on the couch watching TV. 'Don't mind me, Jo. I'll just have these tinnies,' she'd say, cracking open a beer. One day I came downstairs at breakfast time to be met by the most rancid stink – and there was the nanny, just about to give Tyrone a mouthful of scrambled eggs. 'Those eggs must be off!' I screeched, grabbing the spoon. 'Can't you smell them?'

She stared at me blankly. 'Nah, I don't eat eggs,' she said. 'I thought maybe they were meant to smell like that.' She was gone the next day.

That was when I turned to my sister Lize, then in her early twenties, and asked if she'd like to move in with us to help look after the kids. The arrangement worked brilliantly for everyone: Lize got a pad in London (the cottage at the bottom of our garden) and a job, while I had someone I trusted completely to help babysit the children and look after them when we had to take brief trips abroad for Ronnie's fledgling art career. She lived with us for several years.

While Wimbledon might have been a big change in terms of location, it was business as usual as far as our lifestyle went. We always had a houseful, with people coming and going: Terence Trent D'Arby was a regular guest, Keith crashed with us for a bit and Bobby Womack came to stay, too. But our most frequent visitor – who would become a regular fixture in our lives – was the snooker player, Jimmy White.

The kids had all settled into their new schools and had easily adjusted to life in Britain. I'd been waiting to collect Leah from school on an afternoon a few days before Christmas when I noticed a man standing nearby whom I recognized instantly. It was Jimmy, whose match Ronnie had recorded over most of our wedding video.

'My husband is a big fan of yours,' I said to him. He seemed lovely and I couldn't wait to get home to tell Ronnie I'd met him.

I found him in his studio. 'Ronnie, guess who I met today at the school and who'll be at the nativity play tomorrow?'

Needless to say Ronnie was in the audience the following day – and not just to see Leah playing Mary.

Ronnie and Jimmy instantly hit it off and arranged to go out drinking together the following day. Ronnie didn't reappear for another 24 hours, by which time it was late on Christmas Eve. God knows what the pair of them got up to, but it can't have been very much because they were so monumentally legless when they eventually staggered home.

Jimmy started hanging out so much at our house that he might as well have moved in. Now, I love Jimmy, but he and Ronnie just spent their time getting blind drunk. Ronnie, too, had settled back into British life, and knew every pub in our area. It was through Jimmy that Ronnie met another snooker legend, Alex 'Hurricane' Higgins, who was even more of a nutter. On one occasion his chauffeur sat outside our house for a whole day, waiting to take Alex to see his two young kids, while he boozed and went down the betting shop with Ronnie. In the end I had to go behind his chair and tip him onto the floor to get him to leave.

I'd try to stay up with Ronnie for his all-night sessions with Jimmy and the boys, but I just couldn't do it any more – and, in all honesty, I didn't really want to. I wanted a normal life in which my husband didn't come to bed at five o' clock every single morning. So many times I'd be lying in bed in the early hours thinking, *Is Ronnie ever going to come up to bed?*

One morning I came downstairs to the kitchen and spent a good few minutes trying to work out where an awful smell was coming from. I went and found the boys, who were still up from the night before. 'Ronnie, I think there's a problem with the drains,' I said. 'There's the most terrible smell in the kitchen.'

'Oops, sorry, love, that might have been me,' said Jimmy, from where he was slumped in an armchair. 'I threw up in your dustbin.'

Another morning I had just opened my eyes when I heard a loud banging at the front door. Jamie answered it and I heard a woman's voice saying angrily, 'Where is he?' It was Maureen, Jimmy's long-suffering wife and mother to his five kids. I jumped out of bed and went to the bedroom window in time to see Jamie leading her to Ronnie's studio, where the boys had spent the night drinking and playing music. When Maureen finally managed to wake him up, Jimmy smiled up at her and said, 'Morning, love! Cup of tea would be nice.' He was so drunk he thought he was at home in bed. As you might imagine, he didn't get that cup of tea.

Although we were now based in London, we still spent a lot of time travelling back and forth to the States. In January 1989 Ronnie was invited to play at the inauguration ball of President George Bush Sr because one of his key political advisers, Lee Attwater, was a fan. After the ball we headed off to a Washington blues club with a little group, including the square-jawed secret-service guys who had been assigned to us for our stay. After a really long night, we got back to our hotel at 5 a.m. The place was deserted except for a guy who was polishing the floor. I was desperate to get to my bed, and reached the elevator first as the others dawdled along behind me. I spotted something on the floor and bent down to pick it up. It was an envelope that was covered with columns of pencilled numbers – and when I peeked inside I saw that it was full of cash. *A lot* of cash.

I tucked it into my bag, and when we got back to our room I went straight to the bathroom to count it. One thousand, two thousand … seven thousand … eleven thousand – $12,000. I couldn't believe it. A thousand dollars for every year I'd been with Ronnie. It was a sign – it must have been meant for me all along!

I went back into the room. 'Guys, you'll never believe this,' I said. 'I've just found an envelope with three thousand dollars in it!' (Well, come on – if I'd told them how much was *really* in it they would have expected me to share it!)

The secret-service guys – Brad and Chip, or whatever their names were – went straight down to Reception to ask if anyone had reported losing any money, but nobody had.

'If I was you, Jo,' Brad told me, when they got back, 'I'd hold on to it. From the look of that envelope, it's either drug or gambling money. Either way, I doubt anyone will be coming to ask for it back.'

And despite us leaving our contact details with the hotel, they never did. So I put that money into my Halifax account – and it's still sitting there to this day.

20

We'd been in Wimbledon a couple of years when Nick Cowan, Ronnie's manager, approached him to front a new live music club in Miami. I was instantly suspicious: we weren't asked to invest any money and I knew that Harry was involved so it was bound to be a bit shady, but Ronnie loved the idea. The club was in the up-and-coming South Beach area – well, up-and-coming might have been pushing it. It had once been a beautiful art-deco neighbourhood, but the buildings – like the area's aged residents – were now elegantly crumbling away. But the potential was definitely there, and when we saw the derelict hotel that was proposed as the site for the club, we agreed to take on the project. Woody's On the Beach was born.

I suggested Biba's Barbara Hulanicki, whom I had idolized since I was a teenager, to design the interiors. (Barbara moved to Miami to work on the project and still lives there, so at least someone got something positive out of it!) She created a very cool deco-themed hangout with an impressive bar, a VIP room and a huge stage. The waitresses wore sexy little bra tops and skirts with the Woody's logo. Bobby Keys was appointed the club's musical director. Then we started rocking.

We had the maddest times at Woody's. It was all about the music and the good times. We were flown back and forth from London to Miami at great expense, but at no cost to us. Ronnie and I would pop over to Woody's, get the craziness out of our systems, then be much better behaved when we got back to London – well, I would, at least!

After one of those mad trips we were staggering through Customs at Heathrow, totally exhausted, when a voice barked, 'Hey, you two, over here.'

The Customs guy took an instant dislike to Ronnie. 'I'm going to find out what you've had for breakfast,' he said menacingly.

The fact that Ronnie sniggered didn't really help. As the man started rooting through our bags, I turned to Ronnie. 'Have you got anything on you?' I whispered.

'Yep.'

'How much?'

'Three and a half grams.'

Fuck …

By this time the Customs man had finished checking my suitcase, leaving the contents heaped in a huge pile on the table, and had started on Ronnie's.

'Where is it?' I muttered to him.

'In my pocket.'

'Okay, try and get it into my bag,' I said.

I turned to the Customs officer, all sweet and innocent. 'Excuse me, sir, have you finished with this suitcase?'

He grunted that he had, so Ronnie flicked his little package right into the top of the suitcase and I quickly zipped it up. They then took us off and strip-searched us but, of course, found nothing. Yet again, we'd had a lucky escape.

After two years of rocking, the fire department closed down Woody's On the Beach – for noise pollution, unsurprisingly. But it was great fun while it lasted. All Ronnie's mates appeared on that stage – Ray Charles, Fats Domino, Jerry Lee Lewis – a succession of music legends. At the time Jerry Lee was hooked on some downer and refused to go on stage until we got him his weird drug. Cue frantic calls round all the dodgy doctors and pharmacists we knew. We eventually got it and he went on stage and just smashed it. It was a fantastic night.

I'd met Jerry Lee a few years previously and we'd really hit it off, though Jerry was an undeniably dark character. One day he took us to see his apartment in his Cadillac, with a number plate that read 'NO WIFE', and he was showing us around when I noticed a huge hole in the wall by the stairs.

'Hey, Jerry Lee, what happened here?' I asked.

'That's where I missed her.' He smirked.

Another time we were hanging out in Jerry's Winnebago when, to Jerry's obvious delight, three very young and pretty fans came in.

'Hey, Jerry,' one said, in a sweet Southern drawl. 'You smell *niiiice*. What's that you got on?'

To which Jerry replied, 'I got a hard-on, but I didn't know you could smell it.'

*   *   *

I loved watching Barbara Hulanicki designing and bringing together Woody's and it stirred something in me. In a way, I suppose I was a little bit jealous that it wasn't me who had the chance to work on it, even though I knew I wasn't qualified. I've always had a love of design and architecture from those early years watching my father in his studio, and I started to think how fabulous it must be to be able to do that for a living. But I had three kids to look after – I was a mum. Nevertheless, I was now in my early thirties and wanted to do something for myself again – not that I knew what that *something* was going to be. Besides, Ronnie would never have been keen on me going out to work. When we got together, *he* became my job. Ronnie was a demanding guy and useless at looking after himself and, as I've always been quite a motherly person, I happily took on that role and made him the centre of my world, putting my own career and interests aside. At the time it suited me just fine, but looking back I wish I hadn't let myself get so consumed by him and had focused more on my own ambitions.

On our first New Year's Eve back in England, we threw a big party and invited everyone we knew. Among the guests was the *Monty Python* star, Graham Chapman, whom we had first met in LA many years before. Back then he had invited us to his home to see the first edit of *The Life of Brian* and Lil Wenglas Green – who was with Keith at the time – laughed so hysterically throughout that in the end Graham had to ask us to leave as we were disturbing his mother, who was trying to get to sleep upstairs. Graham was producing a lot of films at the time and while we were chatting at our party I seized the opportunity and asked if I could have a role in one of them. It started as a bit of a laugh: 'Come on, Graham,' I begged. 'Put me in the movies, make me a star!'

I didn't think he'd take me seriously, but at the end of the night he came over and handed me a piece of paper. 'These are the details of an audition on Monday,' he said. 'I'll call the casting director and tell him you'll be coming to do a reading. Okay?'

When I bounded into the film company's Soho production offices a few days later, I was sure the most I'd get out of the audition would be a funny story to tell Ronnie and the kids. On discovering I was up for the role of a drug addict my confidence picked up a bit – after all, I'd been around enough junkies in my life to play one convincingly. Still, I couldn't have been more stunned when the director turned to me at the end of the audition and asked if I would be free for filming in Devon later that year.

'You won't let us down, Jo?' he said. 'You can really do these dates?'

I nodded enthusiastically.

'Okay,' he said. 'We'll be in touch tomorrow with more details.'

I wandered back to my car on autopilot, trying to take in what had just happened. It looked very much like I had just landed a role in a movie.

The film was *Love Potion*, a low-budget horror flick about a heroin-addicted girl, whose parents send her to a rehab clinic for treatment where, as the poster put it, 'the mystery cure is more dangerous than the addiction'. My character, Lottie, was one of the other patients at the clinic. As the movie unfolds all these terrible things start to happen, like a guy sneezes during a meeting and blood starts gushing out of his face. In another scene one of the patients dies horribly during a party. There was plenty of sex and gore – your classic B-movie material – but with a twist. The girl is so shocked by the horrors at the clinic that she gets better. Then, at the very end, you see all the other patients sitting behind the scenes, putting on their makeup, and you realize they were actors employed to help the girl clean up.

We were on location in Devon for five weeks, all the cast and crew staying together in a big house. I missed Ronnie and the kids, but it was a brilliant experience. I didn't have that many lines because my character was so out of it the whole time, but at the end the director told me he wished they'd given me a bigger part because I was so good, which gave my confidence a real boost.

It was after we'd filmed a graveyard scene in which we buried one of the clinic's patients that I got back to the house to a phone call from Ronnie telling me his dad, Archie, had died. Ronnie didn't cry – neither did he shed a tear when his mum and brothers passed away (in fact, the only time I've ever seen Ronnie cry out of grief was when our Great Dane's puppy died) – but I knew the two of them had been close. For my part, I'd always got on fine with Archie. He was quite a character. The first time we'd met I'd leant over to give him a beer and with a grin he'd pinched my bottom. 'I could give you three yet, girl.'

'Archie!' I giggled. 'You're a very naughty boy.'

When I first met the Wood family, I found it fascinating to be around them. A quiet night in at the Wood house was like a rowdy night down the pub. They would always be drinking, singing and entertaining – a really boozy bunch. My dad would have one or two drinks at Christmas, maybe a nice cider when it was hot in the summer; but Ronnie's family cracked open the Guinness in the morning and the booze would flow until early evening when they would move on to vodka, brandy, whisky or whatever else they had in their little bar. As I said, I was fascinated at first; but later, when I saw how badly Archie treated his wife, Mercy, when he was drunk, it started to worry me. He had been so horrible to her over the years that she refused to go to his funeral.

I was beginning to worry Ronnie might be going the same way as his dad; his drinking was getting out of control. We had gone on a really wonderful holiday with Keith and his family, sailing around the Caribbean on a huge motor yacht. On one of our first days we pulled into a harbour and Ronnie came back to the boat carrying a bottle of local Pusser's rum that was nearly 100 proof. In other words, about the strongest alcoholic drink you can buy. Settling himself on deck, he downed glass after glass after glass, like he was on some sort of mission. I tried to get him to slow down – even Keith told him he was nuts – but that afternoon he polished off the whole bottle. Ronnie gave himself such severe alcohol poisoning that for the next few weeks if he had even a sip of booze he was violently sick.

I tried to sit down with Ronnie and explain to him how worried I was about his drinking, but he's a hard man to talk to. If he didn't want to face something, he'd somehow twist the conversation until we ended up talking about what *he* wanted to talk about. Either that or he would go off and have a drink – and if I kept trying to force the issue he'd get angry, and suddenly I was the bad guy. Instead I'd pour out my emotions in my diary in the form of poems.

> *I found him in bed with a bottle*
> *Gently licking the rim*
> *I found him in bed with a bottle*
> *Whispering, 'Oh such a sweet, sweet thing.*
> *I love you, I want you, I need you*
> *With me every day.*
> *I'm gonna keep you near me,*
> *Come whatever may.'*

He held the bottle close
With tears in his eyes
I found this quite romantic
To my complete surprise.
Then he drank the liquid with lust and put the
     bottle to his heart
 It was then I lost my trust
And decided to depart.

His drinking was getting so bad I was worried for our relation-ship, but most of all I was worried for Ronnie's health. As it turns out, it should have been *my* health that I was more concerned about.

* * *

By 1989, Mick and Keith had called a truce and another Stones tour was on the cards. With a long-overdue payday approaching for Ronnie, Nick Cowan suggested we rent a place in Ireland for a year to lessen the tax hit. We ended up in County Kildare, look-ing around a beautiful old house called Sandymount. As we explored the outhouses, stables and acres of lush grounds, I turned to Ronnie and said, 'Forget about renting it. We should buy it!' So we did.

We did a lot of work to that house. Ronnie turned the stable into a pub and the cowshed into recording and art studios. I designed and supervised the building of a swimming-pool, with a steam room, sauna and Jacuzzi. I used to love swim-ming laps or having a steam and sauna while listening to music.

There were some mad parties too, of course; it wouldn't have been a true Wood residence without them! To celebrate the opening of the pool we got in an Irish fiddle band and laid on serious amounts of food and drink for the guests, who came from far and near to see us. The actor, John Hurt, stripped off to christen the pool with a skinny dip, swimming lengths sedately on his back.

It was great to have Sandymount as our refuge in the country and a place we could share with friends. The sleepy pubs of County Kildare had never seen anything like it. The Stones recorded there a few times, U2 dropped by and we had Guns N' Roses guitarist Slash to stay with his first wife, Renee; they became great friends after the band supported the Stones on tour. During one of our visits to their home in LA there was an earthquake and as the four of us cowered under a doorframe (apparently one of the safest places to be in a quake) my main concern was that Slash's extensive collection of giant snakes might escape out of their tanks. I'm still very close to Slash and his second wife Perla, who conceived their son at our house and named him London accordingly.

*   *   *

Back in 1989, there weren't many great restaurants in Ireland, but one night we found a fabulous little Lebanese place and went there for dinner with the horsy crowd. Our main courses had arrived and the wine was flowing freely when I was suddenly struck by an intense wave of nausea. I had a sip of water and tried to carry on chatting, but within moments I was feeling even worse. Excusing myself from the table I went outside to get some fresh air. An agonizing pain shot through my stomach, leaving me bent double and dry-heaving in the street.

It had come on so violently that my first thought was food poisoning, but as the pain grew unbearably intense I began to worry that it was something serious.

That night Ronnie took me to hospital, where the doctors started muttering about appendicitis. The thought of surgery made my heart sink. Not because I was nervous but because I was due to fly to Morocco with the Stones in two days' time: the boys were going to perform with the Jajouka band, a team of traditional Moroccan musicians, that they had last played with in the sixties. I had been looking forward to it and there was no way I was going to miss it because my appendix was playing up.

'No, it's okay. I'm sure I'm fine, really,' I said to the doctors. 'In fact, I think I'm beginning to feel a bit better!'

The next morning they discharged me with some tablets for the pain and strict instructions to return *immediately* if it got any worse. Off we went to Morocco. I felt okay on the trip – not totally back to normal, although there was no way I was going to admit that in case Ronnie sent me home – but when we got back to Ireland I had another attack. I went back to the hospital where I was eventually diagnosed with Crohn's disease, an inflammation of the intestine. It was incurable, the doctors told me. I was put on a cocktail of steroids and anti-inflammatories to keep it under control. It was two years before they found out what was *really* wrong with me.

21

S itting at my dressing-table, I stared miserably at my reflection. Who was this woman in the mirror? I didn't recognize her any more. The high doses of steroids might have been keeping the Crohn's under control, but they had wreaked havoc on my appearance. My face was red and bloated and my skin felt weirdly bumpy. I had tried hard to put some life into my hair, but it was hanging dull and lifeless around my fat little face. I tried out a smile, but it didn't reach my eyes. I was 35 but looked at least ten years older. Worse than the physical changes, though, was that the steroids had destroyed my spark. Little by little they had eaten away at the life in me until I was just a cardboard cut-out of a woman. I didn't want to laugh or be silly, but I wasn't feeling depressed either. I wasn't feeling anything. The steroids had taken my soul.

It was a miserable time, but my kids helped me through. I would never have dreamt of complaining to them, but Leah and Ty could tell when I was unhappy and would kiss and cuddle me and tell me how much they loved me. Ronnie felt sorry for me, I could tell, but there was no way he wanted to be stuck at home with the boring, bloated housewife I'd become, so he'd head off clubbing in Dublin most nights. He never told me I looked ugly – although he didn't reassure me I looked okay either – but my confidence had taken a beating. In later years I asked him if there was ever a point he'd thought of leaving me, and he said immediately, 'Yes, when you were ill.' Gosh, that would have been awful. Thank God he didn't go through with it then, as I really don't know how I'd have coped.

We'd had the house in Ireland for nearly a year when my dad came to stay while Mum flew to South Africa to see her relatives, the first time in many years. As I drove her to the airport, I had a really weird feeling that her plane was going to crash, and that I'd never see her again. That week in Ireland with Dad in November 1990 was one of the few high points during what was a pretty awful year. I remember it especially fondly because he was unusually affectionate. We were sitting by the fire one evening and I'd brought him a cup of tea, when he said, 'Thank you, Josephine. I love you.' I was stunned. I knew he loved me, of course, but he'd never been one for actually *saying* it! At the end of his visit we all flew back to London together, to stay at our Wimbledon house for a few days, and during the flight he was proudly boasting to the air stewardess about Ty and Leah. It was unlike him to be so emotional.

The night we got home Jimmy White and a bunch of Ronnie's mates came over to the house, and when I got up the following morning to take the kids to school they were still boozing. Dad had woken early and was now in the living room, sharing some joke with the boys – although he was on nothing stronger than tea. After the school run I went back to bed and was just dropping off when one of Ronnie's friends, Brian, burst into my bedroom.

'Get downstairs, Jo, quick! It's your dad.'

I raced down to the living room to find Dad lying on the floor, with Ronnie and Jimmy trying to resuscitate him. The boys later told me that Dad had been sitting there with them, laughing and joking, when suddenly he just choked and fell to the floor – and that was it. Talk about sobering them all up … Within minutes the paramedics arrived, tried to get his heart going with a defibrillator, then rushed him off to hospital.

We knew that Dad suffered from an enlarged heart because of all the chemical fumes he had breathed in during his years of model-making. The doctors had told him he could have an operation to help the condition, but he had refused.

I was sitting in a hospital waiting room with my brother Vinnie, struggling to take in what was happening, when the doctor came in. 'Where's our father?' I said, jumping up.

'I'm afraid he's passed away,' said the doctor.

'Well, just give him a new heart!' It had all happened so shockingly suddenly I wasn't thinking straight.

'I'm sorry,' said the doctor, kindly. 'There's nothing more we can do for him.'

* * *

It's the weirdest feeling when someone dies, like a sort of vacuum. The crushing grief would come soon enough – I would cry for days – but right then I just needed air. I pushed past the doctor and went out into the hospital grounds. It was cold, but the sky was bright blue and cloudless. Whenever we get weather like that now, it always reminds me of that day.

The phone call my brothers, sister and I had to make to Mum in South Africa to tell her Dad had died was the hardest we ever had to make. I was so distraught I couldn't speak.

The funeral took place in Devon, near my parents' home. It was a wonderful affair: a beautiful horse drew a carriage with the coffin to the sound of a jazz band. If a funeral can be nice, this was as nice as it was going to get. We drove down there on the day and had intended to stay the night but Ronnie wanted to get back to London and, stupidly, I agreed. As he had been drinking, I had to drive, with Leah and Ty in the back. It was dark and I was totally drained and emotional from the funeral, so it's little surprise that as we sped down the motorway in the pouring rain I swerved to miss a traffic cone and lost control of the car.

Ronnie had taken the insane decision to stand in the road and wave his arms to warn oncoming traffic when another vehicle collided with ours and clipped his ankles, resulting in a fractured fibia. I had been trying to get the kids out when it crashed, but thankfully they escaped with a few minor cuts.

That night I remember lying in hospital, staring at the ceiling. *My dad's just died. I've got Crohn's disease. And now we've had this terrible accident. Things can't get any worse …*

We eventually got home from hospital to find our bedroom ceiling had fallen down. Someone up there clearly had a very black sense of humour.

*   *   *

It was about a year after my diagnosis with Crohn's that the press found out about my illness: 'Stone's Wife In Incurable Disease Shocker,' ran the cheery headline in the *Daily Express*. But the response to the article was overwhelming. Hundreds of readers sent me letters, sharing their own experiences of Crohn's and offering advice. One in particular caught my attention – and it wasn't just because of the erratic handwriting. The correspondent was a herbalist called Gerald Green, who said he was quite sure he would be able to put my disease into remission for life. Days later, bubbling with an optimism I hadn't felt for months, I drove to his home in Hastings.

Gerald's house was called Shangri-La, although I was unsure whether the place would really prove to be an earthly paradise. I had seen various specialists, but all of them had said the same thing: it was Crohn's and there was nothing they could do, except keep the symptoms at bay with steroids. Perhaps this would turn out to be another false dawn.

Once we were sitting down in his cosy living room, Gerald's opening question surprised me: 'Tell me, Jo, what do you eat?'

'Oh, pretty much anything,' I said. 'Ordinary stuff like chops and roast dinners, whatever I get at the supermarket. I sometimes have those slimming ready-meals. I mix up packet stuff. If I can't be bothered to cook I like Kentucky Fried Chicken and McDonald's.'

Gerald was nodding wisely while I spoke, then sat back in his chair and smiled at me. 'I'm afraid, my dear, if you want to get better you'll have to stop eating all of those foods.'

I nearly got up and left right then, but Gerald started telling me about how the synthetic chemicals in food can cause the body's immune system to break down and start attacking the body itself. He explained that I would have to change my diet radically – no wheat, dairy, processed food, sugar or red meat – and eat only organic produce.

'And, er, is alcohol allowed?' I asked, nervously.

'Better if you don't, but if you must then stick to organic vodka, which is the cleanest alcoholic drink.'

To my utter relief, Gerald also told me I must stop taking the steroids. 'Those pills will kill you before your disease will,' he said.

In the three hours I sat talking to him in Shangri-La, Gerald changed my life for ever. With his help, I weaned myself off the steroids, cleared my kitchen cupboards of all processed food and started obsessively to hunt down organic food – not easy, in those days. Holland & Barrett stocked organic dried goods and I met a girl who knew somebody who worked on an organic farm and she'd bring me weekly boxes of produce. It was a start. I planted my own vegetable patch in Ireland, too. Then I heard that if you make a request to supermarkets for a certain product they have to listen, so I went on a one-woman mission to get organic food on the shelves of my local Tesco. At one stage I was seeing the manager nearly every week. 'You've got organic goat's cheese,' I'd nag, 'so surely you can get organic butter and milk as well.' I eventually wore him down and the number of organic products on the shelves slowly increased.

I became obsessed – I am to this day. When I went out to a restaurant I wouldn't necessarily go for what I fancied but instead order whatever sounded purest and least processed, which was usually fish. I tried to make every meal that came out of my kitchen organic. 'This spaghetti Bolognese is totally organic,' I'd say, proudly presenting it at the table. Ronnie and the kids got heartily sick of my preaching, although I noticed they didn't have any complaints when it came to eating the food.

As my system got rid of all the toxins my skin cleared up, I lost the extra weight, my eyes sparkled and my hair shone. Best of all, I felt like Jo again. In two months, the change in me was nothing short of miraculous.

But then: disaster. I was at Lorraine's house when suddenly I doubled over in pain. It was back, that same gut-wrenching agony.

'I can't believe it, not again!' I whimpered. 'What's happening to me?'

Lorraine made me an appointment with a doctor friend of her father's, an intestinal specialist called Professor Farthing, and with a heavy heart I went to see him, fearing he'd put me back on the dreaded steroids. But after a load of tests, he came back with a surprising conclusion.

'I don't think you've got Crohn's disease.'

'*What?*' I couldn't believe it. 'But all those doctors, the specialists, they said …' I trailed off as something else occurred to me. If it wasn't Crohn's, why had I been feeling so terrible? *Oh, God, not cancer …*

'The only way we're going to find out what's wrong is by having a look inside you,' said the professor, as if reading my mind. 'I'd like to book you in for exploratory surgery next week. Hopefully we'll then have an answer.'

And the answer was a perforated appendix. They whipped it out while I was in surgery, along with parts of my small and large bowel. The doctors said that all the steroids had prevented it bursting, but if I'd kept taking them they would have continued to mask the symptoms until it did burst – and that was often fatal. So Gerald's advice to clean out my system and quit the steroids had effectively saved my life.

'So I'm going to be better?' I asked the professor.

'Yes, you'll be fine. We're going to keep you in for two weeks, but after that you'll be able to live a normal life.'

I know that doctors would deny a link, but I truly believe that I'd brought my appendix problems on – in part at least – by all the poison I'd put into my system over the years: all the drugs and booze. I had treated my body terribly for the best part of 20 years, so it was no wonder my poor battered appendix had decided enough was enough. Lying in hospital after the operation, I made a vow to myself: from then on I would live a wholly organic life.

The knowledge that you've cheated death changes your outlook. I wanted to be healthy and have a better quality of life. I still wanted to enjoy a drink or two, but the most important thing for me now was that Ronnie and I lived long and happy lives and enjoyed everything we had worked so hard for. The problem was, I was far from convinced that Ronnie would see things the same way, and whenever he came to see me in hospital, smelling of booze from having stopped off at a pub on the way, it never seemed the right time to talk about it. And while I recognized that the operation had been a turning point in my life, it wasn't until years later that I saw it had been a turning point in my relationship with Ronnie as well.

Ronnie didn't prove to be much of a carer. I thought back to those weeks after our car accident, when he had lain in bed with his legs in plaster for days just doing coke and shouting orders at me: 'Bring me a cup of tea! I need a drink! Get me that book!' I had waited on him hand and foot. I tried not to feel resentful: after all, I was his wife, it was my job to look after him. And, despite the ups and downs, I was going to stick by him.

As I was lying there after my operation, a pretty blonde Australian nurse came in, took a look at my chart and told me I needed more painkillers. As they worked through my system over the next few moments the strangest thing started to happen. I was fully conscious, but I couldn't move my body. Even opening my eyes was a huge effort. I began to panic. This definitely wasn't right. As the sensation intensified, I started to freak out. Eventually another nurse came into the room and it took all my rapidly dwindling strength to croak, 'Help!'

When the nurse grasped what was happening, she ran out of the room to fetch help, and within moments I could hear a doctor in the room. He injected me with something else. It was the weirdest sensation, like freezing cold water shooting through my veins, and in a minute or two I was totally back to normal. I later discovered that the nurse had miscalculated the amount of drug she was administering and had given me too much. I never saw her again.

It wasn't until later that my sister Lize admitted to me that while I was laid up in hospital, Ronnie would invite the pretty young nurses who had been helping to care for me – including the blonde Australian – back to our house for parties. To this day I wonder if that nurse messed up the dose because she was so hung-over from partying with my husband. Who knows?

22

Imagine stepping out onto a stage in front of a crowd of 100 thousand fans all screaming their appreciation at you – and this is before you've even started doing anything. If it happened to you night after night, year after year, you'd start to think you were pretty fucking special. Now, of those 100 thousand fans, let's assume half are women. At a conservative estimate (and rock stars aren't a very conservative breed), a third of those women are going to want to sleep with you. So that's tens of thousands of girls, many of them young and beautiful, ready to jump into your bed at a nod. That's a pretty potent gift to know you have in your possession. It's no wonder that sex and rock 'n' roll go together like Jack Daniel's and coke.

On the road with the Stones there were always girls willing to do anything for Ronnie – and he never got bored of the attention. In the early days of mobiles, soon after Ronnie got his first phone and when texts were still a novelty, I sent him a message as a bit of a joke: 'Hi, Ronnie, this is Mandy. I got your number from a friend. I'm such a huge fan, it would mean the world to me if you'd text me back!!!'

I assumed Ronnie would immediately know that I'd sent it; after all, I was the only person who had his mobile number at that point. But moments later 'Mandy' got a long, saucy text in reply and I realized he hadn't a clue who it was. I wrote back an even flirtier message and almost instantly he responded again, this time suggesting we meet up. I sent him a final one-line response: 'It's your wife, you fucking idiot.'

By the early nineties we had moved out of our Wimbledon home – the place was scarred for me with the memory of Dad passing away in the living room – and moved to a beautiful townhouse a few miles away in Richmond. I loved it, but I have good and bad memories of living there. I had come to terms years ago with the fact that groupies were a fact of life on tour, but it was around this time that Ronnie's infatuation with young girls had started to creep into our everyday lives. Whether we went out or had people to the house – which was virtually every night – Ronnie would flirt continuously and blatantly with whichever female was around, be that a waitress, another party guest or just a random girl in a bar. She didn't even have to be that attractive.

Ronnie started to complain that he felt trapped in the Richmond house as there wasn't enough space and used this as an excuse to disappear to Ireland for weeks at a time while I stayed in London with the kids. Sandymount became his escape from family and responsibilities. He was so much freer than I was – like most mums, if I wanted a big night out I'd have to plan it well in advance and book a babysitter. I remember lying in bed on so many nights wondering where my husband was and why the hell he wasn't answering his phone. When I finally got hold of him he'd usually tell me he'd been out clubbing. *Why on earth would a married man in his fifties want to hang out in night-clubs?* I asked myself, over and over again – and I'd always reach the same disturbing conclusion: *The only reason he'd go clubbing is to fuel his ego ... or look for a shag.* But Ronnie had an answer and excuse for everything – and I always wanted to believe what he said, as I couldn't bear the thought of the alternative. One time I went up to join him at Sandymount after one of his extended disappearances and found a drawing he'd done of our bed in Ireland with three girls asleep in it.

'Ronnie,' I said, as calmly as I could in the circumstances. 'That's our bed.'

He shrugged. 'Well, I'm allowed to draw from my imagination, aren't I?'

The flirtations sometimes became infatuations. I could always tell when Ronnie became obsessed with a girl because he immediately turned against me. Well, of course he did – I was in the way! First there was a PR girl called Katrina. Then, a few years later, he got a crush on Lee, a girl he'd met in a nightclub. I think she was about twenty. He dropped her name into conversation the whole time, talking about how much they enjoyed hanging out together. I'd overhear him on the phone: 'Can't wait to see you, babe ...' He was never that clever about hiding it.

Ronnie met Lee in Ireland while he was working on one of his solo albums and I could never listen to it: I wasn't sure whether a couple of songs on it were written for me or her. Their 'friendship' had been dragging on for months by the time I finally got hold of Lee's number and sent her a text, telling her she was coming between my husband and me. She wrote back: 'I'm sorry, I won't have anything more to do with him.'

That wasn't the end of Lee, though. While we were on tour in Europe, Ronnie disappeared for a night in Spain and when he finally reappeared he said to me, 'Guess who I bumped into in a club? My mate Lee!' *Here we go again ...*

I'd blame the booze for the worst of Ronnie's behaviour. There was a time when he went off to Los Angeles to do some recording with the Stones and after two weeks – during which I'd heard worryingly little from him – Keith rang me up.

'Jo, get your fucking arse over here now,' he said.

'Why? What's happened?'

'Your husband is out of control,' said Keith. 'You need to get out here and sort him out.'

It turned out Ronnie hadn't been going to the studio to do his overdubs and had even checked out of the hotel where the rest of the boys were staying. My brother Vinnie, who had gone out there to look after him, was beside himself because he hadn't a clue where he was.

I flew to LA the next day and when I finally found Ronnie, he was in a terrible state. He had spent the past week downing bottles of whisky and hanging out with a hooker. 'She's just my mate,' he said defensively, when I caught up with them in their hotel room. 'We've been drinking together and went to this crazy party up in the Hills ...'

I managed to get Ronnie back on track by making sure he ate and slept and took his vitamins, but he wanted the hooker – his 'drinking buddy' – to stick around. I had to be nice as pie to that weird bird, all the while hoping and praying she hadn't been shagging my husband. She most probably had. But I never knew anything for sure and Ronnie always trotted out the same line: *We're just drinking buddies.*

But while I put on a brave face and turned a blind eye to whatever was going on, it made me increasingly unhappy. I loved

Ronnie so much that I always wanted to believe what he said, so I forgave him. But with each of these passing flings, or infatuations or whatever they were, the more insecure I felt about myself. I began to feel ugly. It chipped away at my self-confidence. If I'd known then what I do now I'd have made sure I was more independent in our marriage and kept more of a sense of my own identity, but I was so caught up with looking after Ronnie and raising our kids – the people that gave my life meaning – that I didn't focus on myself at all.

I often think that if it hadn't been for my kids I'd have ended up a total mess. Jamie, Ty and Leah, not forgetting Jesse, were, and remain, the most important things in the world to me. They helped keep me sane through the insanity of my life with Ronnie. He got so much public adoration that I think he struggled with one-to-one relationships. He was in his own world, at the centre of his universe, and the rest of us were in his orbit. It is very hard to get love from a performer who is adored on such an enormous scale. So it was the kids who were my great love, my stabilizer and my reason to keep plugging on through the tough times. When I was having a bad day I would gather them up in a huge cuddle, shower them with kisses and think, *If it wasn't for you, my babies, I'd probably have lost the plot a long time ago …*

My three children were growing up into such different characters. There was Jamie, Mr Extrovert, whose naughty streak would get him into trouble in a few years' time. From a young age he had boundless confidence. I remember once there was a problem with the tube on his journey home from school, so he knocked on the door of the first house he came across and asked if he could use their phone to call me. He's never had any fear. Jamie was the strongest academically of the kids, so it was unfortunate he got expelled from school for smoking pot. He took the blame for some other lads, though, which is typically loyal of him.

Leah could make anyone laugh. She had loads and loads of friends at school – and still does today. Everybody loved Leah. She was queen bee. When we were in New York, her teacher called me one day and told me Leah would only play with the girls whose dresses she liked. It was a relief when we came back to London where they had school uniforms! I was really proud that she stayed on at school to do her A levels.

And then Ty, my cute little honey. From a young age he was incredibly self-sufficient. I would put his cereal and milk on a tray in the bedroom and in the morning he'd get out of his little bed, come into our room and make his cereal, then turn on our TV and watch cartoons while we had a bit more sleep. Like me, he hated school. The first day I left him at the nursery near our home in Wimbledon he cried and cried, and it just broke my heart. From then on, I would let him bunk off school at the feeblest of excuses.

'Mum, I'm not feeling too well today,' he would say.

'That's okay, darling. You stay at home.' Just like my mum had done with me.

Being a mum is my proudest achievement and I would happily have had more kids, but I never got pregnant again. I was quite surprised, really, as I'd had the others so easily.

* * *

I hadn't been on tour for the best part of a decade so it was a very different Jo who got back on the road with the Stones in the early

1990s. Not only had my illness made me reassess what was important in my life, I'd spent nearly 10 years at home with my kids – and the thought of leaving them for months at a time nearly killed me. There was a moment on Steel Wheels in 1989, our first tour for many years, when the kids came for a brief visit. When it was over we all went to the airport together, where they were to board a plane to London and Ronnie and I were to fly to New York. We said tearful goodbyes, and as I watched their three little heads disappearing into the crowd, accompanied by an air stewardess, I made a decision. *From now on, whenever we go on tour, the kids come too.* And when I started bringing our kids along, Patti brought her girls, Theodora and Alexandra, and Jerry brought James, Lizzie, then later Georgia and Gabriel. Charlie's daughter, Seraphina, came too. There would still be groupies and Freddie Sessler, but now there were nannies and tutors as well. From now on, Rolling Stones tours would become a family affair.

23

Back in the old days I had to worry about just one thing when the Stones were on tour: having fun. And I was really good at it. Sure, I helped out with Ronnie's stage outfits and ran errands for Chuch, but only in a pretty haphazard way between all the partying.

Nowadays, however, I had four roles to perform on tour: Jo the mum, Jo the wife, Jo the PA and, last but by no means least, Jo the rock chick. While the fun might have had to take a back seat every now and then, we still had a laugh and partied hard, even if I was on organic wine rather than Southern Comfort and lines of coke. After all, what could be more of a blast than travelling around the world on a magnificent magical adventure with all the people you love best in the world? There were a few far-flung places to which the whole of the Stones establishment – the band, the crew, the staff and the extended entourage – would fly together and we'd all get on this specially chartered jumbo jet on which I would know every single passenger. That's something like 350 friends. As you can imagine, trips to the bathroom took some time: 'Hey, Jo, stop and have a chat!' 'Jo, how are you?' 'Do you want a drink?' And so on …

It was on one of those long-haul flights that Keith suddenly declared he loved the word 'labia' so much that it should be the name of a country. By the time we had landed he had come up with a national anthem – 'Labia, oh, Labia, the place I long to be!' – and formed a government. Ronnie was going to be Minister for Internal Affairs, Keith was going to be Minister for Foreign Affairs and I was the female Cunt-stable. I'm not sure if Keith ever got round to designing the flag.

So, my overriding memory of being on the road with the Stones is laughter. As I wrote in my diary during the Voodoo Lounge tour, 'The best thing about my life is I have a good laugh nearly every day – and that is great.'

Nevertheless, from the band's first 'professional' tour – Steel Wheels, in 1989 – until A Bigger Bang nearly 20 years later, I took my responsibilities as Ronnie's PA very seriously, and not just in terms of organizing his wardrobe and schedule. On later tours I had the far more challenging task of trying to keep him sober. And when there were tough times, usually thanks to big nights and bigger egos, I'd try to remain my sunny, silly self; one of the riggers, Kenny, used to say I made his day because I was always smiling. He let me try out his harness once and I remember swinging from the scaffolding, several storeys high above the stage, while Ronnie and Mick played far beneath me. *Wheeee!* I'd always try to inject a bit of fun into the day's jobs, such as leaving funny little notes for Spin, the guy who was in charge of the band's luggage, to let him know how many bags we had that day:

Hey Jo

What's this box, Jo?
It's okay Spin, it will go.
I tried to pack in cases, you know,
But the case just said NO.
So in a box to Hamburg it must go.
Don't worry, next week to London this box will
  blow!
With a total of 17 in all, packed and ready from
  me, Jo x

We spent much of the nineties on the road and my diaries give a good idea of what life was like as I tried (usually pretty successfully) to juggle my various responsibilities. Here's an extract from 1995, during the Stones' Voodoo Lounge tour:

10 July – LONDON
Phone woke me about 2.00 p.m. and didn't
stop. Sorted tickets, tour bus, etc. Went to
Waitrose with Leah and saw Georgia May
[Jagger] with nanny and cook. Made dinner
and phoned to arrange tickets for Ronnie's
cousin. Ronnie drove me mad with wanting to
talk to Keith. Watched Jack Dee – v funny.

21 July – SPAIN
Left Richmond around 3.15 for Gatwick. Leah,
Ty, Ronnie and me arrived second after Charlie
and Shirley and then we were off to Gijón. Not
a good hotel as Keith LET IT BE KNOWN HIS

ROOM WAS TOO SMALL. Went to dinner and had paella – very good. Ronnie finally got out of Keith's room around 3 a.m. and into my arms. ☺

25 July - LISBON
Up with a cough most of last night. So today I felt rough. Did a lot of sleeping. Ronnie went off to record with the guys. In the evening I packed up everything while Leah and Ty went with Richard the tutor to see an old refugee camp.

26 July - FRANCE
On the way to the hotel after the flight our driver hit the crash barrier. Really scary! We are staying at the most beautiful hotel in a medieval village. Had birthday dinner for Mick. Keith pulled a moody at 3 in the morning. Ronnie and me saw a star move 45° (i.e. 10 o' clock to 1 o'clock) then dull and disappear. I wonder if anybody will believe us? I waved.

28 July - SWITZERLAND
Left at 4.30 today for Swiss-land. Good hotel. Alexandra's birthday – 9 years old! Bought her and Theo a fab doll each. When we arrived I took the girls (Theo, Alex, Leah, myself and one male, Ty) to dinner on river, then joined by Patti, next Keith, then Ronnie. Afterwards

entertained the Black Crowes – Johnny (bass),
Mark (guitar), Chris (LV) [lead vocals]. Keith
left about 4.30 a.m. to be attacked by his loo
seat in the dark!

29 July
SHOW DAY in Basel. V. hot. Kids to show. Gave
Jamie his new kick-ass T-shirt at gig. He loved
it. Tomorrow kids leave at 9 a.m. for the Sound
of Music tour – it will be a good break for them.
Party night number two with Black Crowes.
GREAT NIGHT. ☺

30 August – NETHERLANDS
LAST SHOW. Party in our room in Amstel
Hotel in Rotterdam. I dressed up to shock!
Finished work now and I am his wife again.
Just having fun doing it! ☺

31 August
Party still going on, so I had to stay up cos
I had to pack …

It might sound like a recipe for grey hair and high blood
pressure, but I can honestly say that being a parent on tour was
wonderful. The first that we went on as a family was the
international leg of Steel Wheels in 1990, when Leah was 10 and
Tyrone just 6 (although Jamie, then 16, had to stay at school in
England). It was surprisingly easy to manage two young children
on the road. They would usually stay awake for the show – if Ty

grew sleepy we'd just make him a little nest on some chairs backstage – and then I'd take them straight back to the hotel and put them to bed. Any attempt at a strict routine would have been pointless, as we were living in hotels and jumping on flights every few days, but there were loads of fascinating distractions and a whole bunch of fun grown-up friends to keep the kids entertained. Leah, in particular, adored the whole experience: helping me with the packing, going into Wardrobe to prepare the costumes, watching the riggers set up the stage, seeing the sights of whatever city we ended up in that week and hanging out with her unofficial big sister, Lisa Fischer, and, of course, big brother Bernard Fowler, the band's backing vocalists. On later tours the kids would have a tutor with them to keep up with their schooling, but life on the road really did provide its own education.

As the kids got older they would have their own hotel rooms (although I always made sure they were next to ours and that I had a key) and they would hang out with their friends, watching movies. On one occasion Ronnie and I were going out to dinner, so I told Leah and Ty to get whatever they wanted from room service. It wasn't until I saw the bill that I discovered that, instead of burgers or club sandwiches, they had ordered several hundred dollars' worth of caviar – with French fries and ketchup, naturally. Clearly, our kids had rock 'n' roll in their blood. I suppose I should have been grateful they hadn't chucked the TV out of the window!

Of course, it wasn't all fun and games on tour. I never let my children run wild; in fact, I was quite strict. They always said it was the glint in my eye when I was angry that made them behave, but occasionally I needed more than that to keep them in order

– especially as they hit the teenage years. During the Voodoo Lounge tour we were in Boston and, having finished my jobs backstage, I decided to go and watch the show from the mixing desk, which is situated in the middle of the stadium and is where security always put any VIP guests. I made my way there through the crowd to see who was around and found Lenny Kravitz, who had opened for the boys that night, sitting with his arm around my teenage daughter.

'Um, hi, Leah,' I said, warily.

'Hi, Mum!' Leah beamed up at me.

It wasn't like they were snogging, but I was a little concerned; while Lenny was in his thirties, Leah had just turned 15 and was very innocent for her age. The following day the phone rang in my room.

'Hello?' I said.

'Hey, Leah, I'm waiting for you downstairs on the bike.' It was a man's voice – and I recognized it at once.

'This is Leah's mother, Lenny,' I said, sternly. 'I'm afraid she won't be coming downstairs.'

'Oh, hey, Jo, sorry, I thought this was Leah's room.' He quickly put the phone down.

Well, I went straight round to see Leah. 'What do you think you're doing?' I asked. 'You can't go out on a motorbike with a grown man!' She was upset with me, but I didn't care. No way was my young daughter getting mixed up with a rock star – especially not one who was 20 years older than she was. I knew exactly what those boys were like ...

It was sometimes hard to enforce strict rules on our kids when they knew what their parents had got up to over the years. Things calmed down dramatically on the later tours, but this was the Rolling Stones: it was hardly going to be early nights with a mug of cocoa. And we were working so hard that at the end of the day we just wanted to let our hair down with a drink or two. One night in Florida we were having a late-night party in our hotel room when Spin stumbled through the window.

'Spin!' I shrieked. 'How the hell did you get here?'

'I took the outside path,' he said, nodding to the window.

'But we're on the third floor!'

It turned out there was a ledge running around the outside of the hotel and Spin had been so drunk he'd simply climbed out of his window and strolled all the way round to ours.

Another particularly memorable incident happened while we were in Memphis. In our room Ronnie and Keith were playing together while I fussed around, lighting candles and being barmaid. After a while, Keith noticed the guitar that Ronnie was playing.

'Where did you get that from?' he asked.

'It's one I borrowed from Mick,' said Ronnie.

Without a word, Keith got up, fetched two pillows from our bedroom, put one against the wall, laid the guitar against it, put the other pillow over the top, then opened his doctor's bag and took out his gun.

'Keith,' I shrieked, 'what are you doing?'

'I'm going to shoot that fucking guitar.'

'You can't do that in our room!'

'Why not?'

'Why not? Well …' Really, there was no point in trying to argue with Keith. 'Oh, all right, then,' I said, 'go on.'

So he did. He shot a bullet straight through the guitar, leaving a perfect hole with pillow fluff sticking out of it. The gunshot was so loud I still can't believe that nobody came up to find out what was going on.

The next day at the gig I went to find Pierre, Keith's roadie.

'You won't believe what Keith did to Mick's guitar last night!' I said, and told him about Keith using our room as a shooting range.

'Which guitar was it?' asked Pierre. 'The acoustic? Dark brown?'

'That's right.'

'That wasn't actually Mick's guitar,' he said.

'It wasn't?'

'No,' grinned Pierre. 'Mick borrowed it from Keith.'

*   *   *

As Leah spent many years watching her dad get up on stage, night after night, it's no surprise that she caught the performing bug. She was developing a really nice little voice and in 1998, on the Bridges to Babylon tour, would sing backing vocals with Lisa Fischer during rehearsals. She was good enough to impress Keith, who one day said to her, 'Come on, Princess, I want you up on stage to sing with me on my song.'

I don't know who was more thrilled – Leah or her very proud mummy. I wrote in my diary:

*I saw Lisa holding Leah and taking her on
stage for Keith's first song, 'Thief in the Night'.
At first I was worried, but then oh so happy.
My girl was singing and looking SOOO good
up there. It was wonderful. It just went too fast.*

I wanna see it all again … I could not control
my smile. Oh! Oh! Oh! I loved, felt, smiled,
smiled, chuckled, watched, knew, SO chuffed
or whatever the words, I need better ones …

Of course, it wasn't just the music on tour that influenced the kids. Although I always kept them away from the worst of it, they had obviously been exposed to far more rock 'n' roll behaviour than the average kids. When we lived in New York, Jamie tiptoed downstairs one morning to get a bowl of cereal and found Christopher Reeve, the *Superman* star, passed out on our sofa, clutching a bottle of booze. My poor child marched straight up to our bedroom in floods of tears. 'Mum,' he howled, 'you killed Superman!' He didn't forgive me for days.

When they reached an age at which they might experiment with drugs I took the decision that it was better in the first instance if they got them from me. I know that many people might be shocked to hear that, but it made sense to me that I should educate my kids about drugs rather than just say, 'Drugs are bad, don't do them,' because I knew damn well that they would. Besides, it would have been hugely hypocritical if I'd lectured them about the evils of drugs when they knew full well that their parents (and all their parents' friends) had been doing them for years.

My plan met with varying degrees of success. When Leah was 15 I offered her a puff of a joint, but she was horrified and stormed out of the room: 'I can't believe my own mother is offering me drugs!' So that totally backfired. A few years later, when Ty was 16, I found a little packet in his room of what looked like grass but was actually dried herbs, so I made sure he tried the real stuff in order that he would know what he was buying next time. I also gave him a small packet of coke to try one evening. Irresponsible? Perhaps. But I would much rather he learnt about these things under my roof, where I could keep an eye on him, rather than in some dodgy club taking God knows what.

Jamie went through a really terrible period in his late teens. After getting expelled from school, he fell in with the wrong crowd and started getting into trouble; nothing serious at first, but then he discovered heroin. His addiction got so bad that I was sure he would either overdose or end up in prison. And despite my years of experience, when my son started shooting up I just didn't know how to handle it.

'Put him on a boat and send him to sea,' said Keith. 'That'll straighten him out.' While hardly a practical suggestion in this day and age, it got me thinking. Keith was right: we needed to get Jamie away from his 'friends' and keep him distracted with some physical work. In the absence of a merchant navy vessel with an opening for a ship's mate, we found the modern equivalent: working backstage on a Stones tour.

So, in August 1994 Jamie joined the crew of the good ship Voodoo Lounge as it set sail in the States. He was given all the dirty, tedious jobs that no one else wanted to do: shifting furniture, laying carpets, setting up dressing rooms, cleaning. He didn't get special treatment because Ronnie was his stepdad – quite the opposite. One day I come down to the gig to find my baby totally filthy and stinking like a sewer. 'I've just unblocked a toilet,' he told me, miserably.

After a couple of months, Jamie begged me to let him go home.

'You've got no idea how the other guys treat me,' he said. 'They tease me the whole time. They're really awful to me. Please, I can't do it any more, Mum.'

But there was no way I was going to let him give up. 'Jamie, you cannot let me down. You can't just walk away. You owe it to me and to yourself to prove to everyone that you can do this.'

So he stuck with it – and a few months later it was as if something just clicked into place. Suddenly he wanted to earn everyone's respect by working hard and doing a really great job. From then on he went from strength to strength, and at the end of the tour he came to Ronnie and me with a business proposal. The guy who supplied the backstage furniture for all the tours had approached Jamie to ask him if Ronnie would be interested in investing in his business. But Jamie had realized that, rather than asking us for money on someone else's behalf, he should set up his own business.

With Ronnie's help, Jamie set up Inner Sanctum, a furniture-hire business for concerts, and within a few years he had not only taken the Stones business from the other guy (well, obviously), but had started doing Madonna, U2 – all the big tours. He made a huge success of it.

It was a very different Jamie who came to see me on the verge of tears one day. 'How can you ever forgive me for all the bad things I've done to you?' he asked. 'I've stolen money out of your purse, I sold stuff of Dad's. How can you have me as your son?'

I hugged him. 'Because I love you and I knew that you'd be all right in the end.'

I hadn't really known that, but I'd dearly hoped so – and Jamie, to his immense credit, came through.

24

The Fiji Four

The Fiji Four arrived tired and weary,
With aching bones and eyes all bleary,
They looked at the sky full of rain
And thought the weather might be a pain.
The following day the skies were blue
And they settled in to a holiday anew …

An island cove they did discover
Occupied by them and no other,
With music, booze and loads of food,
They quickly got that island mood.
They drank and laughed, they swam, they ate,
All their needs on the island were met …

Until just one of the Fiji Four
Decided that he wanted more,
To climb a tree and swing from a branch,
He thought he might have a chance
To be as young as he could be
So he swung right out of that old tree …

Oh boy he came a cropper
And whacked his head, good and proper,
So for a couple of hot days
He hid his pain in so many ways,
But, alas, he was flown afar
Where he turned the hospital into a bar.
So the Fiji Four then became just two,
With two on Fiji, the other two flew …

But the memories that they had
Were really good and not all bad,
And when Fiji one is better and well
They'll sit together and will tell
Of the island cove they did discover
And the love they had for each other,
Cos the Fiji Four will rise together
And will be four in hot weather,
As where there's sun and sea and sand
The Fiji Four will find that land …

*　　*　　*

From 1989 to 2006 the Rolling Stones spent years on the road and travelled the globe many times over. It was a real privilege to be part of such an incredible experience. As you can imagine, all the different tours merge into one in my mind. I have so many memories, so many tales – so many blanks! We'd usually spend a few days in each place, then move on to the next, so life was a disorienting blur of flights, dressing rooms and hotel foyers. I would wake up in the middle of the night in another hotel room and not have a clue which country I was in.

One night in Rome, Spin got up needing to pee, opened a door that he thought was the bathroom and found himself out in the corridor. Before he realized his mistake the door had closed behind him, leaving him stuck outside, stark naked. He eventually managed to find a service closet and had to go downstairs to get a spare key wearing nothing but a chambermaid's apron. I hate to think what the view was like from behind …

I'd always tried to make our hotel rooms feel like home, but now we were spending so much of our lives on the road I travelled with a little two-ring electric stove, a frying-pan and a saucepan so I could prepare home-cooked meals. I had really gone off room-service food, and not just because I was getting more health conscious: the boys were often smuggled out of hotels through the kitchen to avoid the crowds and some were so disgusting, you really wouldn't have wanted to eat anything that was produced in them.

I transported my stove wrapped in a towel, but one day I opened it to find a burn on the towel and realized I should come up with a safer alternative. I worked with a designer to create a fabulous custom-made portable stove: dual-voltage with drawers for a kettle, toaster and pans, plus storage space for organic dried goods, like pasta and beans. When we arrived at a hotel I'd nip out to the nearest organic store to stock up on ingredients while waiting for the luggage, and then I was ready to knock up anything from mincemeat stew to fish with rice. If Ronnie suddenly declared he was starving at 1 a.m. in the Ritz-Carlton I'd just whip up bacon and eggs. I had a bit of trouble with fire alarms at the beginning, so I'd put a shower cap over the sensor before I started cooking. We rarely used room service on tour again.

*   *   *

The best ever Stones gig, in my mind, was Buenos Aires. The band played there on several occasions, but the first and most memorable time was in February 1995. The Stones were the first major international group to perform live in Argentina and the fans were hysterical before we'd even touched down. In scenes reminiscent of Beatlemania, thousands of people were waiting behind barriers to see the boys at the airport, and as we drove out of the airport's gates to Buenos Aires, our convoy was surrounded by vehicles. Ronnie and I were travelling with Charlie and Shirley, and we all stared open-mouthed as cars swerved as close as they could so their passengers could manoeuvre their whole bodies out of the window to try to touch our car as we sped down the motorway.

It was even crazier when we reached our hotel: thousands more fans were waiting outside. As our car inched through the crowd, they started banging on the doors and trying to climb on the roof. It was actually quite scary. Then, suddenly, one of the fans managed to slide down the window and grabbed hold of Charlie, who totally lost it. 'Fuck off!' he screeched. It's the only time I've ever seen Charlie Watts lose his cool.

I had never been to Argentina before and was stunned at the beauty of Buenos Aires; its Baroque buildings and tree-lined boulevards bringing to mind a South American version of Paris. I was lucky enough to be able to get out for a bit of sightseeing, but the fans were so crazy that the boys were confined to the

From a very young age I have always loved to cook. Even when we were living in the States – this was in New York – I liked to cook a proper Sunday roast with all the trimmings.

I love this picture of Ronnie with Jamie and Leah. It was taken while we were on holiday in Barbados – we had so many happy family holidays in the Caribbean.

Barbecuing in our back yard in New York in the mid eighties. When it came to cooking, I was always in charge! My brother Vinnie was living with us at the time.

The Blessed Sister Josephine on tour.

Below: At the end of every tour the band threw a party for the crew and spent the night waiting on them – which is why I'm dressed up like a waitress.

Ronnie serenading me in the early eighties. I'm wearing a chamois leather dress that I designed myself.

On holiday in St Maarten, shortly before our arrest, wearing the skirt in which I had hidden Franco and Mustafa's rock.

My lovely sister Lize.

My best friend Lorraine.

My 40th birthday party at the Hard Rock Café in Japan with some of the boys from the crew. We didn't get to bed until 10 o'clock the following morning.

Chuch Magee: my tour teacher, hero and dear friend.

Bad boys when they're awake, angels when they're asleep…

I love this picture of
Keith cracking up while
I played Tarzan in a tree
in Jamaica. We'd been
up all night and went to
a beach called Laughing
Waters near Keith's house
to continue the party.

Me and the girls:
the faaaabulous
Jerry Hall and my
wonderful friend
Patti Richards.

2 January 1985. Just married – with our darling Ty in his vintage knitted outfit. My dad and Jamie are in the background.

One of the very rare shots I have of us with all our children: Jamie, Leah, Ty (just a few months old here) and Jesse.

The King and Queen of Mandeville Canyon, Los Angeles.

At the Rio Carnival in my silly shiny tights about to do the samba (well, try to anyway).

Stopping for refreshments way out in the bush on safari with Jesse, Ty and Leah.
I fell in love with Kenya and have wonderful memories of this holiday.

Sundowners on the side of a mountain in Kenya in the early noughties.

My 50th birthday party. We had a marquee in the garden with dinner cooked by Jamie Oliver and entertainment courtesy of three male strippers (organised by my eldest). So embarrassing, but very funny!

Way up in the mountains of Tibet. I had to get a photo with this wonderful woman. The Tibetan way of life fascinated me.

Hanging out with the girls (and pretending to do a bit of sewing) at Swallows village in Bangladesh.

I had the most amazing time on *Strictly Come Dancing*. I was so proud that I lasted six weeks on the show, even though I can't dance!

My first publicity shots for Jo Wood Organics. I was so proud of my products and everything we achieved.

Here's me with my gang. *Top, left to right:* Charlie, my eldest grandson; my granddaughter Lola; Kitty, my niece; Arthur, my grandson; Elian, my nephew. *Bottom, left to right:* my nephew, Teddy; Kobi, my grandson; me; Maggie, my granddaughter; my grandson, Leo. Missing in this line-up are Bill and Ben, my brother Vinnie's sons.

hotel for two weeks. It was like the time we were in Singapore during the SARS outbreak: total lockdown. Mick, Ronnie and Charlie had terrible cabin fever, but it suited Keith perfectly as he never liked leaving his hotel room anyway: if you asked if he wanted to come out to a restaurant he'd say, 'Why do you need to go out for dinner when you've got perfectly good room service?'

The band played eight gigs in Argentina in 10 days. On show day the doors of the venue would open at 11 a.m. and all the fans ran in, positioned themselves right next to the stage and stayed there, peeing and crapping into plastic bags, then tossing them on to the floor, until the Stones went on at 11 p.m. And when the show eventually started – well, I've never seen an audience reaction like it. I spent most of those shows watching the crowd rather than what was happening on stage. This huge mass of people would jump in time to the music, all moving and swaying as one; at one point, they unfurled an enormous Argentinian flag with the Stones tongue logo in the middle and stretched it right across the stadium over everyone's heads. Security had to wear plastic raincoats because the fans showed their appreciation by spitting and the guys at the front ended up drenched. It was mind-blowing.

Just like in Argentina, the Stones were the first major Western music act to play in China – although here the audience's reaction was rather more muted. The Chinese authorities blacklisted a number of Stones songs with sexually suggestive lyrics, but otherwise they treated the band as honoured guests.

Shanghai reminded me of Gotham City, all smog and skyscrapers. On our last night we had a roomful of people all desperately trying to get rid of their stash of weed before we flew out to Australia the following day. I hadn't touched the stuff for ages, but had one little puff, then promptly turned green and had a panic attack. I had wanted to hang out with my family that evening, as the kids were all going home the next day, but I had to go straight to bed. That was one of the last times I smoked a joint.

*   *   *

When we were on tour we all used to rate the shows as to which had been the best. If Buenos Aires had exceeded expectations, the one in Johannesburg definitely failed to live up to them. We had all been excited about going to South Africa, most of all me because of my family's link with the country, but in the event the audience was subdued. While we had expected to see lots of black African faces, the crowd was predominantly white. I had invited 25 of my cousins to the gig, none of whom I'd met before, but in the event they ignored me and spent the whole time talking to Ronnie – I was a bit miffed about that, too!

You could generally predict how audiences would react, depending on where you were. America was always reliably fantastic: that whole *yeah, man, rock 'n' roll!* attitude. Germany was another place where you knew the fans were going to be brilliant: they would always be totally transfixed by Mick, their faces intently following him around the stage. But for me the most fascinating people were the Japanese, especially the first time we went there in 1989 before the country became more Westernized. Rather than needing lots of security at the front of the stage, Jim 'JC' Callaghan, the Stones' head of security, would just point to a line on the floor and tell the fans not to cross it – and they never would. During the show the audience would applaud after each song, then fall silent as they waited politely for the next one to start, and at the end people would file out row by row without being instructed to do so.

What they might have lacked in bad-ass attitude, however, they more than made up for in other ways. The Japanese fans worshipped the boys, showering them with presents: one little girl made these incredibly detailed Jo and Ronnie dolls. And they were always so sweet and gentle and welcoming to us. I had my fortieth birthday in Tokyo and, despite my horror at reaching this grand old age (I wrote in my diary, 'seems like a joke – I'm 26 or no age'), I had a wonderful party at the Hard Rock that continued in our hotel room well into the next day. The Japanese promoter had jackets made for Ronnie and me with 'Party Central' on the pocket, as our room was always packed with people.

Our visits to Tokyo started my love affair with Japanese cuisine. I've never been squeamish about food, so I happily tried whatever was offered to us – even the more exotic dishes. During one of the many incredible sushi banquets, I was presented with a little green morsel presented on a shell. 'Lobster brain,' smiled our host. It tasted surprisingly sweet. Another delicacy we tried was *fugu*, the famously poisonous blowfish that kills if it's not meticulously prepared. It was nice: very mild and fishy. Nowadays, whenever I go out for sushi I'll always skip the salmon and tuna and go for the more interesting options.

I'd always be up for trying the regional delicacies wherever we were, such as croc burgers in Australia (which tasted like fishy chicken) and fried crickets in Mexico (exactly like peanuts). Sticking to the local cuisine was a strategy that paid off. In India the band's accountant, Coach, got terrible food poisoning from a cheese sandwich, but I had vegetable curry and rice and was absolutely fine. I loved India, but we had a sticky moment when we were travelling between Mumbai and Bangalore. Our plane was sitting on the runway waiting to take off when I looked out of the window and saw a chunk of metal hanging off the wing. Some men were clustered around it, looking like they were trying to fix it back on, but that did little to reassure me. A ripple of unrest passed through the plane as more and more people noticed what was going on. I pointed this out to Keith, who watched the men hammering away for a few moments. Now, Keith is not prone to panic – quite the opposite. We once flew through a cyclone en route from Australia to New Zealand and, as we rattled around the plane like beans in a can, I totally lost it.

'I hate this!' I wailed. 'We're all going to *diiiiiie!*'

Keith turned round to me, cool as anything, and said, 'If you don't like it, darling, you shouldn't come on tour.'

This time, though, Keith slowly picked up his bags and stood up. 'I'm going to get off this plane,' he announced to the other passengers. 'Everyone who wants to come with me, we're leaving now.'

Every single person followed him.

Over the years I had grown to hate flying: you go on enough flights and you're bound to have a few hairy moments – and those were enough to put me off planes for life. Once we were island-hopping in the Caribbean in a small plane and had to circle during a storm while waiting for permission to land. As we ricocheted around the clouds and I readied myself for the crash that I was convinced was about to happen, I looked at the kids, trying desperately to summon some motherly words of reassurance: Leah was fast asleep and Ty was busy with his computer game. My little boy glanced up and gave me a big grin. The pilot later told me it had been the worst conditions he'd ever flown through, but I don't think Ty had even noticed.

It's difficult to pick a favourite out of all the countries we travelled to over the years, but I fell deeply in love with Brazil. On one of our visits we met an artist who offered to lend us his house in Recife, the country's most northerly town, so off we went, Ronnie and I, with the kids, and Leah's friend, Becca, who luckily spoke Portuguese. We had been driving for ages and it was late at night when we turned onto a little dirt track that plunged into the jungle. As the road got bumpier and the vegetation got thicker, Ronnie was freaking out. 'Where are you taking me? You don't know anything about this place!' I tried to reassure him, but then we passed a couple leaning up against a tree having sex and I began to wonder if I'd made a huge mistake.

What am I doing dragging my little Rolling Stone out into the wilderness?

Just as I was thinking of turning back, we rounded a final corner and the track opened out onto a stunning starlit beach, at the end of which sat the most beautiful little house. It was a magical place. Ronnie still wasn't happy, though. He loves being around people, and here we were, so far from civilization that the few people we did meet had no idea who he was. Then one afternoon, after we'd been in Recife for a few days, he came back from a wander along the beach with a huge grin on his face.

'You won't believe what's happened to me,' he said, excitedly. 'I was walking down the beach and I bumped into this guy who said, "Your album is the only one I've brought on holiday"!' They'd had a long chat – and now he knew there was a fan in the vicinity Ronnie's mood perked up no end.

On our last night I was packing the bags and tidying up when I heard Ronnie calling from outside. It was about 3 a.m.

'Jo! JO! Come here now!'

I rushed outside to find him staring up at the sky.

'Look at that star,' he said, pointing. I was stunned to see what looked like a cluster of lights hovering low over the sea, the beams reflected on the waves, gently pulsing.

'Ronnie, I don't think that's a star, I think it's a UFO. Quick, go and get your glasses.'

But as Ronnie ran inside, the star – or whatever it was – suddenly shot across the horizon at a 45-degree angle, stopped dead, then zoomed off into space. From the unearthly way it moved and the speed it went, I knew it could be nothing other than some kind of spacecraft. The next day the headlines in all the papers read: 'UFO invades Brasilia'. Clearly hundreds of other people had come to the same conclusion.

On another trip to Brazil, Ronnie and I were lucky enough to watch the Rio carnival as guests of Brahma beer. On our first day there we were chatting with the head honcho of Brahma and I made some throwaway remark about how I'd love to be in the carnival.

'You want to be in carnival, Jo?' he said. 'Okay, I'll send you the outfit tomorrow.'

Yeah, right, I thought. *Like that's going to happen.* People prepare for months – sometimes years – to be on the carnival floats. They were hardly going to let some 40-something English chick wobble along with them.

But the next day I was in my hotel room when I got a call from Bobby Keys, who was on the trip with us. 'Hey, Jo,' he said. 'Your carnival outfit is in my room.'

I couldn't believe it. It was actually happening! 'What's it like, Bobby?' I was *so* excited.

'Well, lemme put it this way,' he said, in his Texan drawl. 'It's two dots and a dash.'

He wasn't exaggerating. The 'costume' consisted of a white G-string and two very small shells, plus an enormous white and silver headdress covered with shells, glitter and feathers. Beautiful, but worryingly brief.

'I can't wear this,' I told the Brahma guy, when he called later. 'I'm a mother!'

'You English girls.' He chuckled. 'I knew you wouldn't go through with it …'

I paused. It seemed I had no choice. 'Well, I'd better try it on, then,' I said finally.

I was to appear on the Mangueira float, from the world-famous Brazilian samba school, but it didn't leave until 7 a.m. so at midnight I went with Ronnie, Bobby Keys, Nick Cowan and his wife Julie to watch the rest of the parade, carrying my little outfit with me in a bag. I watched the floats going by thinking, *That's going to be me up there soon!* I was so excited I didn't even have a drink. At 5 a.m. I was taken away to get changed, Julie with me for moral support, but when I opened the door of the dressing room to find 12 gorgeous girls shimmying into the same outfit as me, I got a serious case of stage fright.

'Julie, I can't do it,' I muttered, staring in horror at my fellow hot-bodied dancers. 'Look at them! They're eighteen years old – I'm in my forties! This is nuts.'

'Jo, you can't walk out now,' said Julie, although I could tell from her appalled expression that she was thinking exactly the same thing. 'Come on, you can do this.'

An hour later I found myself walking along the street towards the Mangueira float in my two dots and a dash. I'd decided to wear shiny tights, but had forgotten that my tummy would be on show so had ended up with shiny legs and a bright white midriff. *Never mind*, I thought. *I'll probably be hidden away at the back.* But when I reached the float one of the girls pointed to a little platform in the shape of a large shell about 15 feet off the ground and told me, 'You're going up there.'

As I started to climb the ladder, I suddenly realized I hadn't a clue what I was supposed to be doing when I got up there. 'I don't know how to samba!' I shouted to the girl on the ground. 'What shall I do?'

'Don't worry, Jo,' she yelled back. 'You just gotta move!'

So, as the music started and the float started to make its way along the parade, I did as I was told. And as the sun started to come up and the crowd cheered wildly I just danced my little white dash off. It took about an hour for the float to make its way along the carnival route and I was literally buzzing when I got off. Everyone else was knackered, and Ronnie was moaning, but I was on this incredible adrenalin high. When we got back to the hotel I rang my mum, Lize and anyone else I could think of to tell them *I'd just been in the Rio carnival!* I felt very lucky to have had this amazing experience.

Despite my Rio groundwork, years later, when I was on the BBC's *Strictly Come Dancing* it was during the week of my samba that I crashed out of the competition with the lowest score ever. 'A complete dance disaster,' was the verdict of the judges. So, clearly, there was more to it than 'You just gotta move'!

25

'This house is too small,' moaned Ronnie. 'I feel claustro-phobic and I've got no room to hang my paintings. Jo, we're running out of space.'

I loved our place in Richmond, but I could understand what he was saying: we had definitely outgrown our house. The kids were bigger and we had accumulated loads of stuff over the years – there was barely room to move in Ronnie's office. After spend-ing most of the nineties on the road we had a happy bank manager, so although I didn't really want to move, when my brother Paul pointed out that perhaps we should get a bigger place I could see the sense in his suggestion. In 1998, halfway through the Bridges to Babylon tour, we bought Holmwood in Kingston, a magnificent 20-room hunting lodge in three acres of tree-filled grounds that had been given to Queen Victoria and Prince Albert as a wedding present in 1840.

To be honest, when we first saw the house it didn't look like much had been done to it since then. It was in serious need of some TLC, but that just made it all the more appealing: it was a totally blank canvas for us to create our perfect home. There was plenty of room to create a music and art studio for Ronnie, plus space for a huge organic vegetable patch. The possibility of a whole new life opened up before me. I had visions of getting all our family together for Sunday lunch around a huge table, of our kids (and grandkids) filling the numerous bedrooms, of Ronnie and me snuggling up in front of a blazing log fire. I wouldn't have admitted it to anyone, but I had high hopes that moving to Holmwood would not only solve our problems with space, it would fix the problems with Ronnie's drinking as well.

Soon after we moved, Ronnie's manager, Nick Cowan, came round for the evening. After dinner, Nick raised a toast to our new house and our future. Thanks to the Stones tours, Nick informed us, we were in the incredibly fortunate position of never having to worry about money again. 'You've got enough to last you for the rest of your lives, unless, of course, you go out buying yachts!'

We laughed along with him: it was such an amazing feeling to be debt-free and financially secure.

'It might be worth thinking about investing some of your money,' Nick went on. 'Put it to work, so it's not just sitting in the bank.'

And he just so happened to have what he believed was the perfect investment opportunity. Nick had met a guy called Andrew Edwards, who owned a fabulous building in South Kensington – the former Pineapple dance studio – that they thought would make a perfect private members club. It was to be called the Harrington Club after the street it was situated on (although Ronnie wanted it to be called 'Somewhere', so people would jump in a cab and say 'take me to Somewhere'). Nick was looking for 10 investors for the project, but had come to us first. It looked like a terrific idea – and we totally trusted Nick's judgement – so we signed on the dotted line.

Three years later we had lost everything.

As I've mentioned before, business acumen had never been one of our strengths. In the eighties, just as Ronnie's art was starting to take off, he'd had a show at a gallery in Sweden and the organizers gave us the option of whether to take £25,000 or a brand new white Volvo as payment. We took the car. Eight months later I heard a helicopter hovering low above our house and the police turned up on our doorstep, sirens blazing. It turned out the Volvo had been a hire car that the gallery had 'forgotten' to return to the rental company. Gosh, when I think of all the times I'd driven around London in a stolen car! We really should have taken the money.

We originally put a million into the Harrington on the understanding that there would be other investors, but Nick was struggling to find anyone else – and by this time the building was being gutted. I suppose we should have backed out there and then, but I'm never happier than when I'm poking around a building site in a hard hat, so we put in another million and kept going. Besides, Nick, the business expert, didn't seem concerned: why should we be?

I had caught the interior-design bug in a big way after doing up our Mandeville Canyon home, so when they asked me to design the club's interiors I jumped at the chance. I was aiming for a homely, comfortable atmosphere with an eclectic mix of modern and vintage pieces; I've never been much into minimalism. The ground-floor bar had the feel of a traditional English club, with book-lined shelves and leather couches, but with feminine touches too, like lots of fresh flowers and pretty objects. Upstairs was the restaurant, quite a simple space but with quirks, like picture frames without pictures and Ronnie's painting,

Beggars Banquet, his portrait of the Stones, as the centrepiece. The menu, all organic, would change according to what was in season and would use produce from my vegetable garden. We hired a brilliant young chef called Arthur Potts Dawson, whose stepfather was Mick Jagger's brother, Chris, and gave him free rein. Next to the restaurant was a private dining room, a little jewel with the most beautiful chandeliers, and at the very top of the club was the library, where you could go in the morning to relax with coffee and the papers on comfy sofas.

My proudest achievement, however, was the basement spa. I interviewed and hired all the beauty therapists myself; I sourced organic beauty products from New York, and hunted down the best of everything, including organic cotton towels, beautiful massage beds for the four treatment rooms and massive Hawaiian crystals as the centrepiece for the steam room.

As the bills started piling up, we had to plough in yet more money. The Harrington had to look great: people would be paying a lot of money for membership so we couldn't do it on the cheap. Besides, Ronnie and I were paying for the furniture and decorations out of our pocket on the understanding that anything we bought for the club would belong to us. I even borrowed furniture from our home, including our living-room couch, to ensure the place lived up to my vision.

There was a real buzz about the Harrington Club when it opened in September 2000. I was so proud of what we had achieved: it had all come together beautifully. Ronnie and I made sure we were there every night and were often back in the morning for breakfast and a massage, too. We had some really great nights there. You might find Mick and Jerry dining in the restaurant, Tess Daly having a facial in the spa or Mick

Hucknall break-dancing in the bar (he was actually quite good). We started with 300 members and the number grew to include the likes of Eric Clapton, Frankie Dettori, Geri Halliwell and Kate Moss – the members and their guests were as eclectic as the vibe.

Kate had become a friend after I'd met her at a party at Noel Gallagher and Meg Mathews' house, Supernova Heights, for Noel's birthday. It was the mid-nineties and we'd settled so well back into London life. The Brit Pop scene was thriving, we were meeting new musicians and artists – it was a really fun time all round. We arrived and the house was rocking. Every room was jammed with interesting people. As I was getting a drink – passing a huge fish tank that ran all the way up the stairs – I bumped into Keith's son, Marlon. The little boy I used to look after in Paris and dress up as an alien had grown into a tall, handsome and brilliant man with the most beautiful wife, Lucie.

'Hello, darling,' I said, putting my arms around his neck and giving him a kiss on the cheek.

'I've got someone I want you to meet,' said Marlon. 'You're going to love her.' He led me into the other room and there was Kate Moss. We clicked immediately.

Over the next few years Kate became very much part of our lives. A few weeks after our first meeting, she brought her gorgeous boyfriend, Johnny Depp, over to our house. While Johnny and Ronnie played guitar in the living room, I took Kate upstairs to see my attic of clothes, and we bonded over a love of vintage fashion and a good party. I was really sad when Johnny and Kate split up, as they made such a wonderful couple. We remained friends with Johnny, though, and intro-

duced him to Keith, who famously inspired his movie character, Captain Jack Sparrow. One night in Paris we were all sitting
round drinking and I admired Johnny's grey check shirt. 'It's
yours, Jo,' he said – and immediately undressed to give it to
me.

I literally took the shirt off Johnny Depp's back.

*   *   *

The Harrington hadn't been open for many months when alarm
bells started to ring. Ronnie and I were footing the bill for everything – staff wages, overheads, food and booze – and not seeing
a penny in return. On top of that, we were paying Andrew
Edwards half a million a year in rent. Then Andrew said he
wanted to manage the place, so Nick drew up a contract and told
us we had to look at the bigger picture and invest more money.
I don't think Andrew had ever been a manager of a club before
and I began to worry about some of his decisions, like making
his wife the membership secretary.

When the Harrington had first opened we didn't have a late
licence so the drinking had to stop at 11 p.m. – far from ideal for
a club – but Andrew had assured us it was just a formality and
we would have it any day. A year later we *still* didn't have that
licence. I started complaining loudly and frequently to Nick
about Andrew's management and in time, incredibly, we were
banned from our own club.

Then one day, out of the blue, Andrew called to tell us we
needed to put in more money.

I was stunned. 'But we've already invested millions!'

'Well, you need to invest more or pull out,' he said.

It was then I realized that something was seriously wrong. How could we be expected to keep pumping in money without getting anything in return?

I phoned Jamie, who was proving to be a brilliant businessman.

'Honey, I need your help.'

'What for, Mum?'

'It's the Harrington. Andrew has just asked for more money, but I have no idea why.'

'Okay, let's get hold of the contract and run it by another solicitor, but don't tell Nick what we're doing.'

The solicitor told us that the contract was seriously flawed. It turned out we weren't ever going to make any money out of the club, and if we decided to walk away we would not only leave with nothing, we would actually have to *pay* several hundred thousand just to disentangle ourselves from the lease. To make matters even worse, according to the contract everything in the club belonged to Andrew Edwards, so we no longer owned any of the beautiful things we'd bought – not even the items I'd borrowed from our home, Holmwood.

In the end, the Harrington stayed open for two years at a personal cost to us of £10 million. It was a disaster. At least we knew that Nick had kept some of our money to one side. But when he came to see us during a trip to Ireland, where we had gone to get as far away as possible from the whole nightmare, he looked like a broken man.

'There's nothing left,' he said, quietly.

Ronnie and I exchanged worried looks.

'What do you mean?' asked Ronnie.

'Your money. It's all gone.'

So we had nothing. For the next week I had a headache down the side of my face from sheer stress. We had to remortgage Sandymount and Holmwood; if there hadn't been another tour coming up we'd probably have had to sell them. We fired Nick Cowan as Ronnie's manager and hired Jamie in his place.

My elder son had always been good with money. When we lived on a budget in New York I'd take Jamie to the supermarket with me; as I put the food in the trolley he'd be totting up the cost in his head. If I was over budget when we reached the checkout he'd make me put stuff back on the shelves. Now Jamie got us back on a budget and quickly made huge inroads into sorting the mess of our finances. Amazingly, thanks to my son's talents, we would pull through again, and a year later Jamie produced another miracle for us – my first grandchild, Charlie.

I have to admit, when I learnt that Jamie's girlfriend, Charlotte, was pregnant and that I was going to be a *granny* at the tender age of 44, I was horrified. I felt a bit uneasy right up until the day of the birth, which I was lucky enough to attend. Charlotte had just given birth to a perfect little boy when joy turned into terror as she started to haemorrhage. The doctors, who were clearly extremely concerned, handed me the baby and rushed Charlotte off to the operating theatre. As I looked down at him I felt such an overwhelming rush of love for this beautiful little boy that being a granny suddenly seemed like the best thing ever. Within a few hours Charlotte was fine – and I was still on my blissful grandmotherly high.

Charlie was the start of a whole new generation of children for our family. My brother Paul already had a son, Teddy, who was six, but now they came thick and fast. My sister Lize had a son, Elian, and a daughter, Kitty; my brother, Vinnie, had two sons, Bill and Ben; Leah and Jack now have Maggie; Jamie has Leo and Kobi with his wife, Jodie; and Jesse has Arthur and Lola – by the time this book comes out, he and his girlfriend, Fearne Cotton, should hopefully have made me a granny for the seventh time. While Jesse's then wife Tilly was pregnant with Lola in 2005, his mum (and Ronnie's ex-wife) Krissy died tragically from a drugs overdose. Krissy and I had become friends and I was devastated that she would never see her granddaughter, so I swore that I would be a granny in her place – which I'm honoured to say I have become. I adore each and every one of my grandchildren and now all I need is for Ty to complete the set – although he's currently insisting he's going to stay a bachelor for life!

26

It was well past midnight, but it was still so warm that I was perfectly comfortable sitting outside in just a summer dress. The buzz of cicadas and the scent of cinnamon and rose petals filled the air, and while our table was dotted with candles, the full moon would have provided more than enough light on its own.

It was 2003 and Ronnie and I were in Udaipur, our latest stop on a magical holiday around India with Keith, Patti and Jane Rose. We'd ridden elephants, shopped for saris and jewellery and stayed at the fabled Lake Palace Hotel – although a drought had dried the lake into a dustbowl when we arrived. Tonight we were at a restaurant having dinner with a large group of people, some of whom I knew well, such as our friend, Dilip, an Indian cricketer turned rock promoter, and others we had met that evening. The food was fabulous and the wine was flowing freely – a little too freely in the case of Ronnie, who had already started on the vodka. To my dismay, he was well on the way to getting wasted.

I could always tell when Ronnie was on one of his binges. He got this crazed look in his eyes, although he wasn't able to look at you directly, and all he wanted to do was drink and tell funny stories and entertain everyone. Ronnie is an extremely lovable guy and such a charmer – if he walked in the door now he'd charm the pants off you – and he was an extremely charming drunk, too. All his drinking buddies thought he was fantastic. They would never have believed he had a darker side: 'Ronnie ever get angry? *No way!*' But while he was Mr Charisma with everyone else, the booze could make him unbelievably nasty to me and to those closest to him.

When Ronnie signalled to the waiter for more vodka I decided to risk a quiet word. 'Ronnie,' I said, putting my hand on his arm. 'Don't you think you've maybe had enough to drink?'

As he turned to me I knew I should have stayed quiet.

'You fucking cunt,' he said, making no attempt to keep his voice down. 'Don't you fucking tell me what to do.'

I flushed with embarrassment, acutely aware of the glances from the other guests sitting nearby, but I just tried to laugh it off. 'Ronnie, I don't—'

'Didn't you fucking hear what I said? Shut the fuck up!'

By now I knew the whole table must have heard, although I was too ashamed to look up to check. I was mortified at being spoken to like that, especially in front of people we'd only just met; I would hate them to think of me as some sort of *victim*. But the last thing I wanted was to make any more of a scene so I shrugged and rolled my eyes and the moment blew over. Ronnie went back to his vodka and the woman sitting on the other side of him. But as I reached over to top up my water, I caught Jane Rose staring at me from across the table. The expression in her eyes made me want to cry. She looked concerned and sympathetic but, worse than that, she looked like she felt sorry for me.

* * *

Despite the hopes I'd had for Ronnie and me to share a healthier future, our lives had taken very different paths in the years since my illness. I wanted to live a normal life when we were at home, but for Ronnie it was still all about drink and drugs and rock 'n' roll – and the more he drank, the less I wanted to: I could cope with him better if I had a clear head. Getting pissed out of my brain didn't hold much allure for me any more: nowadays, I got far more excited about getting into the car and driving to a lovely hotel in the country for the weekend. I tried hosting dinner parties at Holmwood, but Ronnie would always want to stay up all night, so I'd get up in the morning to find all these blokes still snorting, drinking and smoking, and wonder, *What happened to my lovely sophisticated dinner party?*

The last years of our relationship were ruled by Ronnie's alcoholism. The following is taken from my diary in 2005, but it really could have been from any year during the last decade that we were together.

7 January
After six days of sticking to his New Year's Resolution and not drinking Ronnie slipped. What a shame, he was doing so good. Here we go again ...

17 January
Woke today at 8.30. The old man lay still sleeping and stinking of booze but he woke feeling positive and said he was gonna get back on track. Great, I thought ... But when we sat down to dinner R was well on his way and

*getting louder. I added water to his strong
drink and he went mad and left the table.*

12 February

*When we got home Ronnie was horribly drunk.
I had to undress him as he lay on the floor then
he threw up all over the bathroom floor, so at 3
in the morning I was mopping up sick. This is
fucked up. Or rather, he is VERY ILL.*

14 February

*Cooked Valentine's dinner mainly because can't
bear to go out with Ronnie cos he's drinking.
UGGH …*

2 March

*Went for dinner with Jimmy and pals at River
Café … Ronnie drunk before we even got there.*

6 March

*Ronnie drunk on sake. Very pissed. Another
awful night.*

8 March

*Got a migraine last night – must have been
when I saw how pissed old man was getting.
Cooked dinner for Lize and Leah, Ronnie, Ty
and all his pals. In the night Ronnie started to
choke and gurgle. I got him out of bed and into
the bathroom where he fell over like a toy*

soldier. Oh my, it was awful. But got him up,
made him sleep on his side, he knew nothing of
it!!!

For the whole time I'd known him, Ronnie had always drunk huge amounts, but when we'd got pissed together in the early days we'd had a real laugh. Now, more often than not, Ronnie's binges would end with him laying into me about something. Maybe his body couldn't tolerate the alcohol as well now that he was getting older – or perhaps it was just me that he couldn't tolerate.

I actually find it so sad to think about the bad times. One night I was asleep when Ronnie burst into our bedroom at Holmwood, drunk as a skunk, and turned on all the lights.

'There's no fucking vodka in the house!' he yelled. 'Where's the fucking vodka?'

'Ronnie, please,' I said, pulling the covers over my head. 'I'm asleep! Just leave me alone.'

On that occasion he *really* lost it. He came over to the bed and the poison just started pouring out of his mouth.

'I'll throw acid in your face ... You'd better watch out because I know people ...'

It was like he was possessed (which, in a way, he was).

After he went back downstairs I cried myself to sleep, feeling broken-hearted and totally helpless, and when he eventually woke up the next day I asked him if he remembered what had happened the night before.

'No,' he said, sleepily. 'Was it a good night? Coffee would be lovely, Jo ...'

When Ronnie was on a real roll he would go on drinking for days and days until he literally collapsed from exhaustion, but when he woke up it was like I had my old Ronnie back. For the next day or two he would be absolutely great and I'd begin to relax, but then the drinking would start again and he'd be such hard work that I couldn't imagine putting up with another day of it. But that's typical of living with an alcoholic.

My worst fears were coming true: the booze was making Ronnie treat me in the same way that his dad had treated his mum. And while I usually got the worst of it, he'd occasionally freak out with the kids, too. I had managed to protect them from it when they were growing up, but now they were older they were far more aware of what was going on. I remember a holiday in Barbados when Leah was upset because Ronnie refused to leave a bar. They ended up screaming at each other in the street and I had to break it up.

I had been sucked into Ronnie's alcoholism and had become his co-dependent: covering for him, caring for him and trying to keep our lives together while all the time I was being dragged down with him. My sister Lize would get so angry about the way he talked to me and kept asking why I put up with it, but I would just make excuses for him. 'Oh, he was drinking last night … He hasn't had much sleep … He's been working really hard …'

I became so caught up in Ronnie's illness that at times I felt like I was drowning in his alcoholism. It was a horrible, hopeless feeling. I lost all my confidence and became this meek, apologetic woman who would do anything just to keep the peace. On Lize's wedding day Ronnie decided he'd had enough at 10 p.m. and wanted to go home, but instead of staying on to enjoy myself alone I left without question. On my own sister's wedding day!

You might wonder why I stuck with Ronnie through all this, but when someone talks to you so badly it eats away at your self-esteem until you don't feel you're worthy of anyone else. While I knew I didn't deserve to be treated that way (and that it was making me deeply unhappy), it didn't cross my mind for a moment to leave Ronnie. In the early years we had done all these stupid things together – tangled with the Mafia, police, drugs, prison – yet I had always been totally unafraid. It was always 'Wooo, let's go!' But I wasn't fearless now: I was full of fear. Full of fear that I was going to be on my own, that I wouldn't be able to cope. Ronnie's alcoholism had crushed my spirit and reduced me to an insecure wreck. And when I look back at photos of the two of us from this time, my arms always wrapped tightly around Ronnie's neck, clinging on as if for dear life, I just think, *Oh, Jo, what the fuck were you doing?*

Throughout all this I hung on to my conviction that the booze was to blame for the worst of his behaviour; in my mind all I had to do was get him to quit and we'd be back on track. In 2000, Ronnie acknowledged he had a drinking problem and, to my immense relief, checked himself into the Priory for a week, but it wasn't long before he had slipped back into old habits. This began a pattern over the next few years of him going into rehab, staying sober for a few weeks and then relapsing. In 2002 he flew to Cottonwood, a famously tough clinic in Arizona, to prepare for the Stones' Forty Licks tour, but straight afterwards we went to a spa for a few days and he ordered a white wine spritzer. He thought he'd be able to control it, but from there it was just a short hop back to vodka.

Ronnie tried his best to stay clean for Forty Licks and A Bigger Bang and had counsellors and life coaches with him on the road to keep him on the straight and narrow, but he never managed it completely. During our marriage, I think the longest he ever stayed sober was about six weeks. I would see him on stage, know instantly that he'd had a drink, and my heart would sink. Mick had decreed that one of my responsibilities as Ronnie's PA was to keep him sober, but I'd had no training in how to achieve that so it was an absolute disaster, an additional pressure on our relationship that we really didn't need. Suddenly I was watching Ronnie at every moment of the day, petrified he was going to have a drink – and, of course, the more someone feels they can't have a drink, the more they want one. Then Mick would find out and all hell would break loose again.

'I'm so tired. I argued with Ronnie about his alcoholism till the early hours,' I wrote in my diary, while we were on tour in Denver. 'He's been taken over again. On the plane R had a couple of vodkas, by the time he got to the hotel he was gone … He hated the room (which was nice) and marched out. Here we go …'

Then I jotted down a poem:

I hate my husband's alcoholism, I really do.
I hate the way he talks to me, I really do.
I hate it when his illness takes over him, I really
   do.
I want Ronnie back, I really do.

I would work as hard as I could when we were on tour, but nothing was ever good enough for Ronnie when he was drunk. I remember many nights when we'd be in the car driving back to the hotel, with security sitting in the front pretending not to listen while Ronnie yelled at me about something or other.

But the instant he got up on stage all was forgiven. He was my guitar hero. Sometimes I'd stand in front of the stage, look up at him and think, *I'm married to a genius*. I was totally in awe of his talent. In those moments I was so proud to be his wife that it seemed worth putting up with a bit of crap. I hated the way the alcohol made Ronnie treat me when he was 'taken over', as I put it in my diary. And what kept me going through all the bad times was my rock-solid belief that one day I would help Ronnie stop drinking. When he was sober, our problems would be over and we would be happy together. After all, our lives over the years had been such a fabulous fairytale, surely we'd get the happily-ever-after, too.

27

Every time we passed through Los Angeles on tour I would always visit this fantastic organic supermarket called Mrs Gooch's, just off Rodeo Drive. I still remember the first time I walked through its doors: for an organic addict it was like entering Nirvana. Piles of organic vegetables still covered with soil! Freshly baked organic sourdough bread! Even the air in the shop smelt like it was doing me good. I hadn't been so infatuated with a shop since I'd walked into the Ragged Priest all those years ago – except this time I was lusting after organic carrots rather than velvet hot-pants. But the real revelation was Mrs Gooch's huge selection of organic beauty products. Nowadays you can buy organic shampoo in Asda, but back then such products were far from mainstream in the UK, so I would bulk-buy organic face cream, toothpaste, deodorant, bath salts and shower gel to take home.

It wasn't until my brother Vinnie gave me a book called *The Fragrant Pharmacy*, about the benefits and uses of essential oils, that I had the idea of making my own organic beauty products. In the book the author, Valerie Ann Worwood, explains how you can easily make your own moisturizer, face scrubs, bath oils, perfume, even tooth powder. It sounded fun, and far cheaper than shipping those boxes back from Mrs Gooch's. So, with the help of my new assistant, Emily, who had worked in Jamie's office for years and would soon become my invaluable right-hand woman, we ordered a load of essential oils, base oils, droppers and bottles and I stuck a piece of wood over the bath in one of our spare bathrooms and set up my own little lab. Once I got started, I couldn't believe how easy it was to create your own products. Take some hazelnut oil, add fifteen drops of rose and five each of camomile, lavender and lemon – *et voila!* I designed labels for my bottles of 'Jo's Oil', burning the edges for a vintage feel, and gave them to my girlfriends as presents. As I learnt more about the different oils, I began experimenting with recipes to get them just right. It was just like 20 years earlier when I had locked myself away in the bathroom for hours at a time to freebase, except 100 per cent organic and a hell of a lot less antisocial.

I'd had my home laboratory for a couple of years when Donna, who worked in our office, suggested that I think about producing the oils professionally. I laughed. *As if I have time to do that! Who's going to look after Ronnie and the kids?* But, though I didn't realize it at that moment, she had planted a seed.

A few weeks after this conversation with Donna I returned to Holmwood after a trip to the supermarket. The house was totally silent. Ronnie was in his studio working on a painting and having his obligatory pint; Leah was out with her friends; Ty had gone travelling; Jamie had left home ages ago and had his own family – just as the other kids would before long. And as I stood in the kitchen, unpacking the endless bags of shopping and planning dinner, I became aware of a little voice inside my head.

Is this it for you, Jo? Just shopping and cooking? Is this how you're going to spend the rest of your life?

And then, as if in reply, another voice piped up: *Perhaps you should try to make a go of those oils, after all …*

* * *

I rang up my friend, Josephine Fairley, who had been a beauty editor before she'd started the organic chocolatier Green & Black's, and she gave me the name of Dr Colette Haydon, a French cosmetologist. I took Colette two of the original oil blends that I had mixed in my bathroom lab, one fresh and citrussy, the other musky and woody, and we got to work. The next step was to set up a meeting with a PR company. At this point I didn't have anything to show them – not even any visuals – but I wanted to know if they thought my concept for a line of organic yet luxurious beauty products had potential. There was already a small selection of organic products on the market, but the packaging tended to be either rather stark and minimalist or hippie-ish and homespun. I wanted to create beautiful, high-end products that felt like a luxury purchase: in other words, organic products that didn't actually look organic.

The meeting was a disaster. I was hopelessly out of my depth. I had travelled the world and chatted to all sorts of people, but when it came to promoting my own venture my confidence deserted me. I don't think I said a word for the entire meeting apart from 'Hello'. I just sat there smiling inanely, silently furious with myself, while the girls from my office, Donna and Emily, did all the talking on my behalf.

Unsurprisingly, the PR girl was unimpressed. 'Oh, we have lots of things like this,' she said. 'Wives of rock stars coming in and wanting to set up their own business. It never works.'

Ronnie was equally dismissive. 'You'll never get that together,' he said. His lack of confidence in my idea didn't put me off, though – quite the opposite. The more people told me I couldn't do it and it wouldn't work, the more I wanted to prove them wrong. But although I had full confidence in my concept, we didn't exactly get off to a flying start. I didn't have any experience in setting up a business – or in the beauty industry – so it took Donna, Emily and me a while to find our feet. Put it this way: we kissed a lot of frogs before we found our princes.

In the early days a businessman – let's call him Len – came to meet us to discuss a potential licensing deal. We were sitting around the table, deep in conversation about royalties and projected demand, when without warning Len abruptly changed the subject.

'You know, I love nothing better than going down on a lady,' he said.

'I'm … Er – sorry?' I assumed that I'd misheard.

'I was just saying that I really enjoy giving head,' purred Len.

Donna, Emily and I looked at each other with wide eyes, clearly all thinking the same thing: *What the fuck?* There we were, hoping to get a licensing deal, and Len was talking oral sex. I have no idea why he brought it up; perhaps he thought us 'ladies' would be so impressed by his generosity as a lover that it would seal the deal. Somehow we managed to get through the rest of the meeting, but after he left we just cracked up. Needless to say we didn't go with Len – in either sense.

From the very beginning I was involved with every aspect of the process. I put together a business proposal and approached the bank for a loan, on which Ronnie acted as guarantor. I worked closely with Colette on the formulation of the products, using my two original oil blends as the basis. I had clear ideas about the look of the packaging too, which I wanted to have the vintage feel of the black and gold Biba logo, so I put together a mood board with sketches and cuttings for the designers.

Once we'd got some samples of the products and the packaging, it was time to tackle the big question: would anyone actually want to *buy* the stuff? Our first stop was a meeting with the buyer at the legendary London department store, Harvey Nichols. By this time I had grown in confidence, yet even so I felt utterly terrified as we sat in that meeting taking her through the samples. I had invested so much of myself in the project that I knew I'd take it personally if we got a negative response.

'So what do you think?' I asked nervously, once we'd finished our pitch.

'Well, I can see it's not quite ready yet,' said the buyer. 'But, yes, I think we'll take it.'

Oh. My. God. I was so shocked that I don't think I said anything for the rest of the meeting, just smiled and nodded; but once we got out into the street I just screamed my head off. It was such an incredible feeling. We'd done it!

* * *

2005 was a big year for me. Not only did I turn 50 but in October I gave birth to my fourth baby: Jo Wood Organics. The range consisted of soap, bath oil, body lotion, body spray and body oil in two fragrances, *Usiku* and *Amka*, which are Swahili words meaning 'night' and 'awake', a nod to Mum's African heritage. We had naïvely reckoned the process would take about six months from start to finish, but in the end it took nearly three years to get the products into the stores. What really held things up was my insistence that we had to get the products certified as organic and that all the packaging should be recyclable. There was no question that we would go any other way but it meant we had to endure a few delays.

In the run-up to the official launch I was promoting my products like crazy. At first I found the prospect of press interviews terrifying, but when I discovered how friendly and interested people were, I started to relax and enjoy myself. To my delight, my products popped up in *Vogue, Elle* – all the glossy mags. My friends really got behind the range, too: Jerry and Patti spread the word, and Kate still asks for one of my salt scrubs whenever I see her. I was getting such fantastic PR coverage it was worth millions in advertising.

In August we hit the road again for the American leg of A Bigger Bang and this time I wasn't only working as Ronnie's PA: I was busy promoting my products as well. At every major city we stopped in, I set up appointments with buyers at the big department stores and press interviews with all the beauty editors and local TV stations to spread the word about Jo Wood Organics. Of course, when it came to getting press coverage, it helped hugely that I was the wife of Rolling Stone Ronnie Wood. I knew I had a fantastic product, but he was my foot in the door. But while Ronnie might have seemed supportive to the outside world, I never got the impression that he was particularly keen on his wife's new venture. He liked me safely tucked away in the background, looking after him, not out there getting attention for my own achievements. Perhaps that was why he made little digs at me, telling me I was fat or that my hair looked like a dog's ears.

I had a really fabulous party at Holmwood for my fiftieth birthday in March, with a marquee in the garden, male strippers (a gift from my elder son) and Jamie Oliver himself doing the catering, but the following day Ronnie looked at me and said, 'I never thought I'd ever be married to a fifty-year-old.' It was the *way* he said it: not even with a smile and a chuckle, but a despondent shake of his head, as if I had somehow let him down by daring to get older. They were just throwaway comments, but they really hit home, making me feel increasingly insecure about the way I looked.

In Ronnie's eyes, I think there was room for just one star in the family – and that was Ronnie Wood. When we were in LA on tour, staying at the Four Seasons, I arranged a meeting with the buyers of Neiman Marcus to see if they'd be interested in stocking my products. We didn't really have parties in our hotel rooms that often any more, but the night before my meeting Ronnie invited literally everyone up to our room, knowing that I had to be up early the next morning. He partied tirelessly (and noisily) well into the early hours. I begged them to keep the noise down but I got hardly any sleep that night. Was it jealousy or just pettiness? I have no idea. But I'm sure Ronnie could sense that working on my business was helping me to regain my confidence and get my mojo back again. I was slowly emerging from his shadow and finding my feet as an independent woman. And, bearing in mind what would happen to me in the next few years, I'm so thankful I did.

*   *   *

The launch party for Jo Wood Organics was on 26 October 2005. The Stones were still on tour, so I had to leave Ronnie in North Carolina, from where they were heading up to Canada, and fly back to London by myself. Incredibly, it was the first time I'd flown anywhere on my own for 30 years.

The party was held in Harvey Nichols's Fifth Floor Bar, fuelled by crates of champagne and dozens of chocolate cupcakes decorated with the gold Jo Wood Organics logo. Loads of people came, not just friends, such as Cilla Black and the fashion designer, Betty Jackson, but all the magazine editors as well. It was a brilliant night, but at the end of the party, the culmination of years of hard work, I suddenly got so possessive over my products that I didn't want anyone to take the goodie bags!

Looking back I still feel immensely proud of what we achieved. Nowadays everything organic is in the mainstream – and I do feel a little bit responsible for that. When I go into the supermarket and see shelves and shelves of organic products I think that perhaps I helped to get them there. And having seen the incredible benefits an organic lifestyle has brought to my body and mind, I'm still as 'addicted' (thank you, Keith!) as ever.

*   *   *

The day after my party I flew to Canada on a high from the successful launch. I was excited to see Ronnie and tell him how well it had gone, so I dumped my bags at the hotel and went straight to the arena. When I finally found him he wasn't alone. He was all over a group of giggling young girls – and, judging by their body language, they obviously all knew each other pretty well. I kept my distance for a moment and heard them laughing about a party Ronnie had thrown the night before and what a wild time they'd had. I had so desperately hoped that I would come back to find that he had missed me and was thrilled to see me – but, no, here we were again. It was such a horrible feeling.

Come on, Jo, I thought wearily. *Put on a smile and get over there. Go and laugh and make friends with these girls who are young enough to be your daughters ...*

It was what I'd been doing for the last 30 years, but while Ronnie and I had got older, the girls had stayed the same age. Ronnie swore blind nothing had happened with them, of course, just as he always did. And yet again I chose to ignore my doubts and fears and to believe him. The alternative was just too painful to consider.

28

I n January 2008 we went on a family holiday to Kenya. I flew
out first with Leah and her fiancé, Jack, as Ronnie had to stay
in London for the launch of Martin Scorsese's Stones film,
Shine a Light. I was excited about returning to Kenya: we had first
visited after my dad had died, a wonderful holiday during which
Lize ran off with our safari guide and ended up living in Africa for
six months with a pet bush-baby. This holiday was going to be a
particularly special one, though, as it was the last I would be
taking with my daughter before she and Jack got married in June.

When I'd been there for a few days, I called Ronnie to see how
he was getting on. When he answered the phone I could hear
loud music and voices in the background. He explained he was
staying in a hotel in London.

'Why?' I asked. 'We only live in Kingston.'

'I'm with Jimmy White,' he said, dodging the question. 'Man,
we've been out drinking for days ...'

I felt a horrible, twitchy anxiety in the pit of my stomach.
What was he up to? But I knew from experience that there was
no point in giving him the third degree, so I just told him I was
looking forward to seeing him in a few days and left him to it –
whatever it was.

Ronnie flew to Kenya with Jamie, who was still working as his manager and had proved himself the best of the lot. His business instinct was always spot-on: in a few years he'd turned Ronnie into the biggest-selling print artist in the US. When the pair of them got off the speedboat at the resort, my first thought was that Ronnie looked awful. His skin had a grey tinge and he had an infection in one eye, which was swollen and weeping. I settled him into a hammock near our little hut on the beach where he promptly fell asleep, then went back and started his unpacking. Jamie appeared at the door.

'Mum,' he said, quietly. 'Do yourself a favour and break the Sim card in Dad's phone.'

'Why?'

'I can't tell you,' he said. 'But make sure you do it, or you're not going to enjoy your holiday.'

Jamie flatly refused to give me any other details but he clearly felt it was important, so I promised to do as I was told. Ronnie usually clung to his phone for dear life, but I noticed the charger was plugged into a socket in our room so I followed the lead to a pocket of one of his shirts that was hanging on the back of a chair with a pile of towels covering it. I retrieved the phone (I admit I thought about sneaking a look at his texts but was worried he'd wake up), took out the Sim card, gently snapped it, then quickly put everything back the way I'd found it.

Ronnie started to stir. 'Hi, honey!' I said. 'How are you doing? Good sleep?'

'Oh … yeah … hi …'

'I'm going up to the restaurant for lunch,' I said. 'Shall I see you there?'

Some 10 minutes later Ronnie appeared at the table, absolutely furious.

'What the *fuck* is wrong with this phone?' He held it out to me, his face like thunder.

'Ooh, goodness, don't ask me. I'm useless with things like that,' I said. 'You could always use my phone or the landline?'

He spent the rest of that afternoon trying to work out what was wrong with it, but I'd snapped the Sim in such a way that you couldn't tell it had been tampered with. His terrible mood lasted a few days, but eventually he calmed down and we had a lovely-ish holiday, but I couldn't get it out of my mind.

We had been back in London for a week when I was woken at 4 a.m. by the beep of Ronnie's phone, which was now working. He was snoring away, totally oblivious (and I was still curious about what Jamie had asked to do me in Kenya), so I reached over and looked at the screen. It was a text: 'Hi Ronnie. Not been working. Keeping myself to myself. Please send money. E.'

I stared at the message. *What the hell was that about? And who was 'E'?* I took down the number and then, in a panic at being discovered snooping, pressed delete.

When Ronnie woke the next morning I told him I'd picked up his phone in the night to stop it beeping and thought I might *possibly* have deleted a text by accident. He went absolutely mental – 'Don't you ever fucking touch my phone again!' – and stormed out, but later that day I overheard him asking our housekeeper, Jenny, to get him some cash. The twitchiness in my stomach got worse.

In the months before Leah's wedding, Ronnie's behaviour grew even shiftier than usual. He went to Ireland for a few days, then phoned to tell me he was back in London and had checked into a hotel – but when I got to the hotel he wasn't there. Then, suddenly, he acquired another phone, which he said had been given to him by Steve Bing, the producer of *Shine a Light* (and father of Liz Hurley's son). I didn't want to think about his reasons for needing two phones.

Leah had told Ronnie that she didn't want him walking her down the aisle if he'd been drinking, so to my relief he agreed to go back to the Priory in preparation for the wedding. As usual, I thought the booze had been to blame for his weirdness.

A few days into his stay, the Priory called the house to ask if Ronnie was there.

'Of course he's not,' I said. 'He's with you.'

'I'm afraid he's disappeared,' they said. 'We can't find him, so we assumed he must have gone home. We can't reach him on his phone. I'm sorry, Mrs Wood, but we don't know where he is.'

Frantic with worry, I kept trying his phone and eventually he answered.

'Ronnie, where the hell are you?'

'Oh, I couldn't take the Priory any more,' he said. I could tell he was drunk. 'I've checked into a hotel in Richmond.'

'But Richmond is five minutes away from here!' I said. 'Why didn't you just come home?'

'Look, I'm coming home now, all right?'

He appeared at the door with a weird mark on his cheek, clearly wrecked. I fixed him up, but soon after that he disappeared again – just walked out and didn't come home for days. It was such a stressful time. If I hadn't had the preparations for Leah's wedding to keep me busy I would have had so many sleepless nights.

I was at a promotional event in Fenwick's, the department store, for the launch of my new product range, Jo Wood Everyday, when my close friend, Fran Cutler, rang.

'Jo, can you talk? There's something I think you should know.'

I'd first met Fran back in the nineties at one of Mick and Jerry's parties and we'd instantly felt like we'd known each other for years. She's one of my best girlfriends and I trust her totally. Fran told me she had been at a gig in Hammersmith and had seen Ronnie there with another woman. My initial thought was that the girl would have been one of a group of his mates and I told Fran as much, but she was adamant there was more to it than that.

'I promise you, Jo, everyone in London knows what's going on,' she said. 'You're the only one who doesn't. I'm so sorry.'

'Come on, Fran, don't do this to me.'

I was standing in the middle of the beauty hall in Fenwick's, people hovering nearby, waiting to talk to me, and my friend was basically telling me – what? That my husband was having an affair? I'd learnt a long time ago not to listen to rumours, so I told her not to worry and that I'd call her later.

But when I got home to discover that Ronnie had disappeared again, I found it impossible to get what Fran had told me out of my mind, and when I noticed that Ronnie had left the Steve Bing mobile behind I had an idea. I dug out the number I'd copied down from the text message from 'E' and rang it from his phone.

'Hello?' A girl's voice, but in the background I heard a man say, 'Who's that, then? Another of your boyfriends?' It was Ronnie.

'Put him on the phone,' I said, as calmly as I could.

'What?'

'I know Ronnie's with you. Put him on the phone right now.'

She hung up, so I called Ronnie straight back on his mobile.

'What's going on, Ronnie?'

'Listen, she's just my drinking buddy,' he said. 'She's a really sweet girl – you'd like her.'

'Well, if she's a really sweet girl, why don't you bring her home? Let's all meet this new drinking buddy!'

And, an hour later, that was exactly what he did.

*   *   *

The pair of them fell out of the taxi onto our drive in a drunken heap. The girl – who couldn't have been more than 18 or 19 – seemed totally wrecked. As she picked herself up, I was staring at her, thinking, *Surely my husband's not sleeping with this ... child? Fran must have got the wrong end of the stick. They must be drinking buddies, like Ronnie said. They can't possibly be having sex ...*

I led them into the kitchen, where Ty, Leah and Jack, who had been at home and knew what was going on, were waiting around the table.

'This is Katia,' said Ronnie, beaming at us.

The girl slumped at the table and started fumbling with a packet of cigarettes.

'What are you doing hanging out with our dad?' said Ty. 'He's old enough to be your grandfather.'

'Age makes no difference to me,' she slurred, sticking a cigarette into her mouth, then going to the stove and lighting the hob.

Oh, go right ahead! I thought. *You've taken my husband – why not help yourself to my gas?*

She bent down to light her cigarette and – *whoosh!* The front of her hair went up in flames. Quickly (perhaps a little too quickly, with hindsight) I grabbed a dishcloth and damped it out. I'm not sure she'd noticed she'd caught fire.

'Hey, let's watch the Eurovision Song Contest!' she suddenly said.

This was turning into the most surreal encounter of my life.

As we walked to the living room she tripped and fell, then staggered to her feet and plonked herself on my couch.

'Ain't she funny, Jo?' Ronnie was looking at her fondly. 'She reminds me of you when you were young.'

'She does?' *Oh, God …*

And then she passed out, swiftly followed by Ronnie.

I went back to the kitchen. 'Jack, let's call a cab and get her out of here,' I said, wearily. I went up to bed, utterly exhausted.

The next day all my attempts to talk to Ronnie about the girl were met with the same response: drinking buddy, drinking buddy, drinking buddy.

A few weeks before the wedding, Ronnie and I went to the Myar clinic, a health farm in Austria, for a bit of R and R – and, considering I drank nothing but herbal tea and ate only dry bread and sheep's milk yogurt, I'm definitely not talking Rock 'n' Roll.

We arrived in our room and were unpacking when Ronnie pulled out a stuffed owl from his suitcase and laid it tenderly on our bed.

'Ronnie, what's that?'

'This? Just my little owl.'

'I can see that,' I said. 'But why on earth have you got it with you?'

It wasn't even a *nice* stuffed owl – it looked cheap and highly flammable.

'Oh, it's just from some fan.' He shrugged.

'Ronnie, you're nearly sixty-two. Why would you bring a stuffed toy on holiday? It's just weird.'

He eventually agreed to put it back in his suitcase, and we had a nice week together – until the last day. I strolled back to our room in a relaxed haze after a wonderful massage and walked in to find Ronnie sitting with our dinner and, to my astonishment, a large neat vodka.

'I just got this as a little treat for us!' he said.

Quite how he'd found vodka at a health farm I have no idea.

Sunday, 1 June, was Ronnie's 62nd birthday. The whole family was there: all the kids and their kids. In the morning, Ronnie and I dug up new potatoes and picked cabbage from the garden, then Jack and I cooked roast lamb and chicken. When we'd finished eating, the grandkids crowded around Ronnie at his end of the table and led the chorus of 'Happy Birthday'. All the next week, the two of us hung around Holmwood together. I was finishing decorating one of the rooms; Ronnie was watching TV, sketching, playing the guitar – with not a single sip of booze, a single line of cocaine. *Please*, I kept telling myself, *just keep it up* …

*   *   *

It was the night before Leah's wedding and the house was full. My siblings and their families were all staying; my best friend Lorraine had flown in from New York with her kids; there were people camped out in every room. The reception was going to be held in a huge bamboo marquee in our garden, where we would be hosting an organic dinner for 150 and an after-party for at least double that number. I was so excited about our daughter's wedding day, and preoccupied with everything I still had to organize, that I didn't really have time to worry about my strong suspicion that Ronnie was drinking again. At least he wasn't *visibly* drunk. That evening I cooked a huge dinner for everyone, then slept with Leah in her bed. It was lovely to be able to cuddle up with my daughter on her last night as a single woman.

I was up early the next morning to deal with the invasion of caterers, florists, makeup artists and hairdressers. There still seemed to be an awful lot to do and I was standing in the garden deciding exactly where a gorgeous display of lilac, white and orange flowers should go when Mum came bustling over.

'Josephine, I need to speak to you.'

'Not now, Mum, please.'

'It's important. It can't wait.'

I sighed. She wasn't going to give up. 'What's wrong?'

'Well, I came downstairs last night at about two to get a cup of tea, and as I walked past the breakfast room I could hear Ronnie on the phone.'

'Yes?'

'He was saying, "Don't worry, darling, just wait until the wedding's over. Then everything will be sorted and we can be together."'

My first thought was: Katia. Oh, God, I really didn't have time to deal with this now … Perhaps Mum had made a mistake. Besides, whatever *had* been going on with that girl,

I was pretty sure it hadn't been some big romance. The thought of a teenager going out with a man of Ronnie's age was too ridiculous.

'Mum, I'm sure you misheard. Don't worry.' And I left it at that.

* * *

It was a beautiful service at Southwark Cathedral and the reception was a huge success, but although I'd had a wonderful day, I felt weirdly unsettled. Maybe it was because of what Mum had said to me, or perhaps because I'd had to rush to get ready and didn't feel confident about how I looked in my orange vintage dress. But there was also a strange feeling in the air, a sense that something was ending. Jimmy White had come over to me at one point and put his arm round me. 'I just want you to know, Jo,' he said, 'that you are and always will be a really good friend of mine.' Later, when I'd asked Ty if he'd seen Ronnie (who had, unsurprisingly, disappeared), he had said, 'Mum, you know I'll stand by you whatever happens.' I was confused, tipsy and emotional, but it was Leah's day and there were hundreds of guests to entertain, so once again I put my fears to one side and partied until 6 a.m.

The following day we had a family lunch at the hotel where Leah and Jack had spent the night, then everyone came back to Holmwood for a swim. Ronnie was on great form, sitting in the Jacuzzi and entertaining everyone with funny stories. I struggled up to bed around 9 p.m. and was deeply asleep when Ronnie came in, gently prodded me awake and said, 'I'm going out. To see Damien Hirst.'

'But it's so late, Ronnie,' I said, looking at the clock. 'Damien doesn't even drink – why would a sober guy be going out at this time of night?'

'I'm going out,' he said again.

In that moment, all the stresses and fears and frustrations of the past few months combined into a fireball of fury and I just exploded. I screamed at him, told him all this craziness and lying had to end. Finally, Ronnie admitted he was going to see 'Kat'. He said he had to see her, to 'call it off with her', and tell her she couldn't 'nag' him into leaving me and our family. He showed me a text message from her, calling him a 'mad dog'. And he stayed.

*   *   *

The following afternoon Ronnie went to see a new counsellor – he'd seen dozens over the last few years to help with alcoholism – and sent me a text telling me he'd be home for dinner. By nine o' clock he hadn't turned up.

Here we go again ...

I kept calling his mobile until he finally picked up.

'Where are you?'

'Oh, hey, Jo, I'm at a Spanish bar in Beauchamp Place.'

'Fine. I'll come and have a drink with you.'

I jumped into my car and drove straight to Knightsbridge. My patience had finally run out. I wasn't prepared to put up with the lies and games for a moment longer. But when I got to Beauchamp Place – no Spanish bar!

I phoned him. No answer. I kept ringing and ringing until eventually he picked up.

'Ronnie, there is no Spanish bar in Beauchamp Place.'

'So I lied,' he said, his voice flat and emotionless. 'I'm in the Haymarket, at a bar, not sure which one.'

By this point I was in a desperate state. I *had* to know what was going on, even though I was sure I wouldn't like it. Ronnie was clearly just going to lie and lie, so I had to confront the situation head on: it was the only way I was going to find out the truth – and bring it to an end, I suppose, one way or another.

As I was driving into the West End, I remembered that I had met Ronnie at a hotel bar on the Haymarket about a year ago, so I parked my car and went to check it out. Sure enough, when I walked in there, they were in the corner.

'I knew I'd find you,' I said to Ronnie, with a weary smile – and then I looked at Katia. 'And I knew *you*'d be here.'

'Hey, Jo, have a drink!' He was acting totally normally, as if the situation wasn't remotely weird. So typically Ronnie.

I ordered a vodka and tonic. Katia was very coy, always directing everything she said to Ronnie. I tried asking her about what she did for a living, but she wouldn't tell me. I later found out that Ronnie had told Jamie on the plane to Kenya that he'd met a girl who worked in a 'lap-dancing' club and that they were having sex. Can you imagine telling that to your wife's son?

We'd had a few drinks in the bar and had gone outside for a fag break when I looked at my watch. It was well past midnight.

'Ronnie, I'm tired,' I said. 'Shall we go home?'

He took a long drag on his cigarette, then turned to me. 'Nah. I want to be with my baby,' he said. 'I'll leave it up to you to work out who that is.'

I felt like the air had been punched out of me. I couldn't believe what he had said. *I* had always been his baby! I just stood there, stunned, my eyes starting to pool with tears.

Then Katia piped up: 'Listen, do you mind if I just have a private word with Ronnie?'

I looked at her in disbelief. 'A private word with Ronnie?' I said, weakly. 'My husband?'

'Yeah.'

And I was standing there, thinking, *You've got to leave now, Jo. Just go. You've got your proof. Get out of here with whatever dignity you have left.* But I couldn't walk away because my husband, the man I had known and loved so completely for 30 years, was effectively telling me he didn't want me any more, and it was just a huge, horrible shock.

'Come on, Jo,' said Ronnie. 'Just go and stand over there a minute. Let me see what she wants.'

So, like an idiot, I did what he said. In a daze I turned and walked away, leaving the pair of them whispering together. It wasn't until I saw him put his arm around her – his *baby* – that something in me finally snapped.

'You know what?' I said. 'Enjoy your life, Ronnie. I'm going home.'

I ran back to my car, trying to hold it together, but as I got ready to drive away, my phone rang. It was Ronnie.

'Jo,' he said. 'Come back. Please. I'm at the front of the hotel.'

Despite everything, my heart leapt. I knew he wouldn't have been able to just throw away our lives together – we'd been through too much. As I drove round the block I started to think about how we could rebuild our marriage. Maybe we could go for counselling. Perhaps, in time, this would even make us stronger.

I pulled up outside the hotel, but instead of opening the door Ronnie motioned for me to put the window down. Then he leant in and said, 'You've been drinking – you should get a taxi.'

So that was it. That was why he wanted me to come back: not to tell me he'd made a huge mistake, that I was still his baby, and beg my forgiveness, but to caution me against drink-driving.

'Fuck you, Ronnie,' I said.

I slammed my foot down and drove away.

29

It was past one o' clock when I got home. Leah was on her honeymoon and Ty was out – I was all on my own. I went straight upstairs and lay on our bed, still dressed. I wasn't crying; I was numb. *Oh, my God, it's actually over …* I lay in the dark for three hours, turning the evening's events over endlessly in my head. Then at 4 a.m. I got back into my car and started driving to Essex. I remember going through the Dartford Tunnel just as the sun came up. When I was a few miles away from Southend, where my brother Paul and his wife, Sandra, live, I pulled over and called him – thankfully, he's an early riser.

'Paul, is it okay if I come and stay with you for a bit?'

'Of course. Just let me know when you'd like to come.'

'Um, how about in ten minutes' time?'

It wasn't until I got to Paul's front door that I started to cry – and the tears didn't stop for the next two weeks. I stayed with Paul and Sandra for a few days, just sitting in their spare room or wandering vacantly around the garden. My kids and the rest of my family rallied round and were a huge support. My mum was on the phone every day. Lize was so furious she sent Ronnie a text that began, 'Hello, Mr Paedo …' Funnily enough, he never replied.

When I got back to London, Ronnie had taken Katia to stay in Ireland. The thought of them in our beautiful house, sleeping in our bed, triggered more hysterical tears. I wrote Ronnie an email begging him to be discreet and he promised he would: I couldn't bear the prospect of it being splashed over the press. I still thought that perhaps it was just a fling and that he might come to his senses and realize that dating a girl who was 10 years younger than his own daughter didn't really have much of a future.

I hadn't been home for many days when our cleaner, Fatima, came and found me in the kitchen.

'Meessis Wood!' she said. 'Your friend, he is waiting in the living room.'

I walked into the living room to find a guy standing there. *My friend?* I'd never seen him before in my life.

'Hi, Jo, my name is Richard White. I'm from the *Sun*.'

Oh, fuck. But I knew I had to hold it together.

'I'm sorry to tell you this,' he went on, 'but a teenage girl named Ekaterina Ivanova is saying she's Ronnie's girlfriend. They're together at your place in Ireland.'

'Oh, I know all about that,' I said, breezily. 'She's his drinking buddy. They're just friends.'

'I think it's more than that.'

I later discovered that the press had found out because little Katia had been sharing everything on Facebook, boasting to her friends about her trip to Ireland with her new boyfriend, Ronnie Wood – even posting pictures of herself with one of our dogs. So much for being discreet.

As soon as the reporter left I phoned Ronnie. 'Oh, this is a mess,' he slurred. Then, after a long silence, 'Don't worry. It'll blow over.'

Two days later it was in all the papers: 'Rolling Stone Ronnie Wood is living with Russian bargirl less than a third of his age – who is bragging to her pals of how he has dumped his wife of twenty-three years.'

As soon as the story broke I was swamped by goodwill messages and offers of help from friends. Keith and Patti were one of the first on the phone to check if I was okay; Slash and Perla invited me to stay with them in Los Angeles; Bob Geldof called to tell me not to worry and that I deserved better. Not a word from Mick, and Charlie didn't make contact until a year later. 'Sorry I didn't call before,' he said. 'I was just waiting to see how things would pan out.' I suppose he'd thought I'd stand by Ronnie, just as I had done so many times in the past.

The next two weeks were complete and utter madness. The press had set up camp outside Holmwood so I escaped to Lize's house. I was chased down the motorway by reporters, but managed to shake them off; Leah was in the car, cheering me along as I swerved off down a slip road at high speed. 'Yeah, go on, Mum! You've lost them!'

Meanwhile Ronnie was trapped in Ireland, surrounded by paparazzi – although I later discovered Katia had been smuggled out before the story broke. Jesse went in to talk to his dad and then, with Damien Hirst's help, Ronnie was flown out and taken straight to the Lifeworks clinic near Weybridge for his seventh stint in rehab.

Ronnie stayed in the clinic for five weeks. During this time stories kept appearing in the papers: I'm convinced our phones were hacked, because details of private conversations leaked out and I certainly didn't say anything. I took comfort, though, from the incredible outpouring of warmth and support in the press. People would write comments like, 'He doesn't deserve you' and 'Jo, don't take him back. Stay strong.' It really helped me feel better about myself during a tough time.

It was a very different Ronnie who phoned me after a month in rehab and asked if I would join him for Family Week, when patients' loved ones come in to work through any issues. I took this as a sign that he wanted to make our relationship work – and he was so sweet to me on the phone – so I travelled to the clinic with cautiously high hopes.

I was given lots of forms to fill in before our group sessions and on one of them I wrote that I was hurt because Ronnie had betrayed me, but when this came out in discussion he looked confused. 'I don't think I betrayed you,' he said.

'You don't think that running off with another woman is betrayal?'

'No, not really.'

I went through five days of this, breaking down in front of strangers, trying to work through our problems, but it was apparent that Ronnie and I were on totally different wavelengths. In another meeting I mentioned how I had cried for two weeks when he left.

'Whatever for?' said Ronnie.

'Because you left me and I was devastated!' *Christ*, I thought, *what am I wasting my tears for?*

The thing is, although Ronnie could be utterly charming and brilliant company, he had quite a narcissistic streak. He had always seemed to find it hard to relate to other people's emotions. There was a time at Holmwood when Ty was in bits after splitting up with his girlfriend. We were sitting in the kitchen together and I had my arms around him, trying to comfort him, when Ronnie came in.

'Look at these new shoes I've just got from the shoot.' He grinned.

'Ronnie,' I said quietly. 'Ty is really upset …'

'Yeah, but check out my shoes! The shoot went so great – it all worked out so well!'

Suddenly Ty lost it – for the first and only time I can ever remember. He exploded in complete rage and screamed at his father, 'All you fucking care about is yourself!'

But Ronnie didn't even flinch. He just walked into the other room and started reading the paper, as if nothing had happened.

*　　*　　*

At the end of Family Week Ronnie and I went for lunch at a nearby pub. It had been a traumatic few days and I was still so confused and unsure of what the future held, yet at the same time I couldn't imagine life without him. But as we waited for our food to arrive, Ronnie told me he had decided he wanted to be with Katia. There were no apologies, no expressions of regret – he just came out with it, as if he was telling me it was going to rain at the weekend.

'So I've just done all this time with you in rehab for nothing?' I asked, in disbelief.

'Look, if it doesn't work out with Katia we can make another go of it,' he said. 'It'll be just like getting to know each other all over again!'

I started to cry, so we went outside and had a cigarette. I was trying hard to be brave, but I noticed my hand shaking as I held out my lighter.

He doesn't want me, I thought. *He's moved on.* Perhaps if I'd told Ronnie I'd wait for him while he got whatever it was out of his system we'd be together now, but when I drove away from the pub that afternoon I made a decision. Whatever happened in the future, I would never, ever go back to him.

30

Golden Prison
He lives in a golden prison
Surrounded by those who care
He lives in a golden prison
While people crowd out there
He draws out of his golden window
To the reality of life outside
He watches from his golden room
While inside he has to hide

He lives in his golden prison
And plays to a world so wide
Up there on his golden stage
He's free and full of pride
And when the golden show is over
He's ushered into a golden car
Back to his golden prison
Away from a world so far.

*   *   *

When you become famous you live your life in a bubble, completely separate from the rest of society and, over time, that bubble becomes increasingly secure and detached from real life. You go to a restaurant and have security sitting at the next table; you are whisked from airport to hotel in a blacked-out limo; at home you're hidden away behind high walls and solid gates. You've got everything you want and have an army of staff to ease your path through life. This might sound like a wonderful way to live – and in many ways, it is – but in return for all the luxury and ease you have to give up your freedom. Of course, unlike the boys in the band, I could easily step outside and nobody would have a clue who I was, so I was always far freer than they were, but Ronnie's life was completely inside that bubble so at the end of the day that was always where I would have to return.

After I got over the initial shock that my marriage really had ended, that I had lost the love of my life and my best friend, my biggest fear was of how I would cope with life in the outside world after 30 years in that golden prison. To say I was devastated was an understatement. My Stones support network literally vanished overnight: I was completely on my own. Not only that, but it was now plainly obvious to me that I'd largely put my own passions and interests aside to devote my life to Ronnie. As the summer days stretched ahead of me, silent and empty, I realized I would have to build myself a completely new life. I was going to have to fend for myself, just as I had done at 16. And that was the *really* scary bit …

* * *

After Ronnie left, I spent the rest of the summer sitting at home on my own. Most of my friends had gone on holiday and many asked me to join them, but I couldn't face leaving the house. I would wander from room to room, looking at pictures, photos and furniture – every item a testament to our life together – wondering how on earth we were going to disentangle it all. It wasn't like these were Jo's things and those were Ronnie's things: they were *ours*.

Those months were so hard. I'm not a depressive sort of person, but I was intensely unhappy. I felt utterly lost. For most of my adult life, I had been defined by my relationship with Ronnie and with the Stones. I had been part of them and protected by them. Now, not only was I losing my husband, I was effectively losing my identity. I had been 'Jo Wood, wife of Rolling Stone Ronnie Wood'; the thought of being known as 'Jo Wood, ex-wife of Rolling Stone Ronnie Wood' was just horrible. The only positive to come out of the whole awful mess was that I completely lost my appetite and dropped to a size eight. I might have had a broken heart, but I had a great arse. My state of mind was something like this: 'Wow, I'm getting so skinny! But, oh, Gawd, he's *goooooooone …*' (Cue more tears.)

I barely talked to Ronnie over those months and the kids didn't hear from him, either. It was like he'd disappeared off the face of the earth – except, of course, he hadn't, because in every newspaper I'd open there would be pictures of Ronnie and Katia walking on Primrose Hill, Ronnie and Katia having a coffee, Ronnie and Katia going to Tesco. *Do you have any idea how ridiculous you look with her, Ronnie?* I would think, sadly.

* * *

It was a sunny Sunday morning in late August and I was sitting up in bed reading a stack of Sunday papers. I was drinking my second espresso of the day, but hadn't had any breakfast. The heartbreak diet was still proving highly effective – I'd cooked myself a nice dinner last night but had managed to eat just one prawn. As usual, I had nothing planned for the day. Jamie had been on the phone the day before, clearly running out of patience with my low mood.

'Mum, you need to get it together,' he had said. 'You can't spend the rest of your life moping around at home.'

But how could he possibly understand what I was going through?

I was flicking through one of the supplements when a letter on the agony-aunt page caught my eye. It was from a reader who had been separated from her husband for five years, yet was still struggling to deal with the heartache. 'I miss him so much,' she had written. 'I can't even sleep on his side of the bed.'

Jesus, I thought. *That poor woman!* I glanced to the side of the bed where Ronnie used to sleep. I could almost see him lying there still, his black hair contrasting against the white of the pillow. I felt another wave of unhappiness begin to wash over me, but rather than surrender to it and let the tears flow again, I checked myself. I could either become that woman in the paper, pining away for her lost love, or I could pick myself up and get on with my life. And with that I moved straight over to Ronnie's side of the bed – *my side of the bed*, I thought, with the ghost of a smile.

Reading that letter proved a turning point for me. Having reclaimed the bed, I turned my attention to the rest of the house. Ronnie had covered the walls of our downstairs toilet with loads of scraps of paper – press cuttings, sketches, photos of himself – and the clutter drove me mad. That afternoon I ripped it all down. Standing in that little room, ankle-deep in the confetti of Ronnie's memories, I felt the stirrings of hope for the first time since he had left.

But although I was starting to tackle the outward evidence of our lives together, I knew I would need some extra help to sort out what was going on in my head. I'd never really been one for therapy, but I went to see a counsellor to talk through the split. Only for about a month, but it was long enough for me to accept what had happened and begin to move on. One of the best pieces of advice I took from our sessions was that, if I wanted to get over the split, I needed to concentrate on me.

'It's all about you now, Jo,' the counsellor had said.

At first, I didn't really understand what she meant. Concentrate on me? *Um … how?* Like many women with families, I'd got so used to putting everyone else first that I had forgotten how to focus on myself.

'Well, what do you enjoy doing?' the counsellor asked.

And that was when I hit upon the idea of getting fit – *really* fit. For the past few years, exercise had been an important part of my life. When we'd first moved to Holmwood I had started seeing a fabulous yoga teacher called Tina, who gently coaxed me into a regular yoga and meditation practice. I loved it so much I turned one of our spare bedrooms into a yoga room, where I could cut myself off from the hectic household for an hour or so.

Then, as I got fitter and wanted more of a challenge, I'd found a personal trainer, Mike, who would also come and work with me at home. During one of our first sessions I had been lying on the floor while Mike leant over me to manoeuvre my leg into a stretch, when Ronnie burst in through the door, blind drunk. 'Caught you!' he roared – and staggered out again. He clearly thought that Mike and I were working up a sweat by doing more than just a few sets of crunches, although the next day he'd forgotten about catching the two of us supposedly *in flagrante*.

So, when I found myself with all this spare time, the first thing I did was to step up my sessions with Mike. At first I really struggled with our workouts – not because I was especially unfit, but because when Mike put on music every single song seemed to be about love or breaking up, and my poor, raw emotions just couldn't cope. I eventually hit upon the solution of exercising to Brazilian music, of which I couldn't understand a word.

The workouts played a huge part in boosting my self-esteem in the wake of the split. As my energy levels soared and my body toned up, I started to feel more confident and positive about myself. To this day I still work out regularly, now with Jon Denoris – last year I even took up boxing with Dino when I was in Miami – and am now fitter than I was in my forties or even thirties.

Phase Two of Operation Me-time was to give myself a make-over. I didn't want to look like the woman who had been married to Ronnie any more. Inspired by a portrait of Brigitte Bardot I'd had on my wall for years, I tried styling my hair into a sixties sex-kitten bouffant. I didn't wash that man right out of my hair – I *backcombed* him out. I loved the way it looked and it went perfectly with the sooty, smoky eye makeup I always wore: I wasn't giving up my Mac eyeliner for anyone.

By now I was so skinny that none of my clothes fitted me so *obviously* I had to go out and buy a whole new wardrobe. As I have said, I had always loved vintage fashion and just so happened to have befriended a wonderful woman called Mairead Lewin, who was an antique-clothing dealer. As I wandered among the rails and rails of beautiful dresses in her Notting Hill home, I thought, *Who needs men when you've got fabulous clothes?*

On the advice of a friend, I also went to see a life coach, who shared several pieces of advice that proved invaluable. To start with, he taught me the importance of forgiveness. To forgive, this man told me, is to set yourself free, as in doing so you release yourself from all your anger and negativity. I can't say it happened overnight, but as I started to regain my confidence and feel better about myself I found I could let go of my anger towards Ronnie.

More importantly, the life coach showed me that, rather than being a helpless victim (which was how I'd been feeling about myself), I still had control of my own destiny. 'If you really want your husband back, I'm sure you can get him back,' he said to me. 'But you've got to think, Is that *truly* what I want? If not, then you have to make your own life.'

Well, that got me thinking. I was already well aware of how nice it was not to have someone shouting at me, not to have that constant twitchy feeling of anxiety in the pit of my stomach, not to spend hours cooking a meal, then watch it get pushed aside after two mouthfuls. When I realized that I'd never have to cover for Ronnie, make excuses for him or clear up after him ever again, it felt like a weight had been lifted from my shoulders. So when the life coach asked if I really, truly would want Ronnie back, I realized that perhaps I wouldn't. And that was when I thought: *Okay, I'm going to build myself a new life on my own.*

*   *   *

The first night out I had after the split – my first as a single woman in well over 30 years, was at the *GQ* Men of the Year Awards in September. Jerry Hall, who had been such a fantastic support since Ronnie left, invited me along as her date. I spent ages getting ready, furiously backcombing my hair and choosing a floral sixties dress that clung to my skinny 9-stone figure, yet still I felt very timid and uncertain as we pulled up outside the Royal Opera House. It was the first time since my early twenties that I had been invited to something as just Jo, rather than as Ronnie's wife Jo, and I had no idea of who this new person was – or, rather, I had no recollection of what she *used* to be like. Also, I didn't have a clue how people would respond to me now I didn't have my Rolling Stones gang – or my husband – to provide my identity.

But as I stepped onto the red carpet in front of the paparazzi, clinging to Jerry for support, there was an explosion of flashes.

'Hey, Jo, look over here!' *Snap-snap-snap.* 'Turn this way, Jo!' *Snap-snap-snap.*

And as I posed for the cameras, stunned and delighted by the warmth of everyone's response, I began to relax and enjoy myself. *Oh, yeah, I remember how to do this.* I felt like I was starting from where I'd left off all those years ago.

I had made a decision during the long, dark weeks that summer that I wouldn't have any alcohol until I felt strong, but that night I had a glass of champagne with Jerry. I was ready to get back out there and start rocking again.

* * *

Just before Christmas, Emily called with a request from the charity Save the Children for me to decorate an eco Christmas tree. The offer combined my two favourite things, children and anything eco, so I accepted at once.

I was very proud of the tree I created, which was sustainable (of course!) and covered with recycled decorations and threaded garlands of popcorn, but when the invitation arrived for the charity's dinner at the Natural History Museum I couldn't find anyone who would be free to come along as my plus-one. The idea of going by myself was terrifying – what if I didn't know any of the other guests? Who would I talk to? Who would I sit with at dinner? – but I couldn't just not turn up: I'd designed a tree for the event. I had no choice: I would have to go on my own.

On the evening of the dinner I sat in the car outside the Natural History Museum, watching the other guests walk up to the grand entrance. Some were in twos, others in larger groups, but I didn't spot anyone arriving solo. I wished more than ever that I had someone with me to hold my hand, but I was on my own now – tonight, and for all the other nights. I had to prove to myself that I could do it.

I checked my makeup in the rear-view mirror one last time. *Right, get out there, Jo …*

Trying to look more confident than I felt, I walked up the steps, gathering up my long forties floral dress so I didn't trip. (I figured the only thing worse than arriving on my own would be arriving on my own and falling flat on my face.) I hovered by the entrance and scanned the crowd, hoping to find a familiar face, but couldn't see anyone I knew. I had a sudden flashback to a party another lifetime ago when I'd been delighted to discover that I was in a roomful of strangers. Now, however, the prospect terrified me. But, just as I was wondering if I should creep out and go home, an immaculately dressed guy in his twenties who was standing nearby beckoned me over.

'Hi, Jo!' he said. 'My name's Michael, and this' – he gestured to an outrageously handsome man standing next to him – 'is David. Can we get you a glass of champagne?'

My knights in shining armour turned out to be Michael Evans, a flamboyant club promoter, and the supermodel, David Gandy. The pair of them took me under their wing for the rest of the night. Like me, David is from Essex, born in Billericay, so we hit it off instantly, while Michael has since become one of my loveliest friends. It was a fantastic night – and it reminded me of how much fun it can be meeting new people.

From that day on, I accepted every invitation that came my way. I hit the town, going to parties and after-parties and clubs until 4 or 5 a.m., often seven nights in a row. I was going to the proverbial opening of an envelope – and proud of it! I remember applying my makeup one evening, so tired that I was barely able to focus, and thinking, *I really should stay in tonight* … But off I went anyway. There are some really embarrassing paparazzi shots of me falling out of clubs around this time. On one particularly memorable night I went to Mahiki with Sarah Harding, then back to her house and played Nintendo Wii until the sun came up.

Leah and her husband Jack were living at Holmwood at this time, and one night I staggered in, long after they'd gone to bed, to find a terse email from my daughter:

> Mother, I really don't think you should be
> going out like this. Don't you realize that
> you're 53 years old – and a grandmother?

I knew Leah was just looking out for me, but I wrote back:

> What do you want me to do, darling? Get out
> and make some new friends? Or stay home on
> my own and do some knitting?

She went quiet after that.

*   *   *

I'd been far too busy finding myself to worry about finding a
man, but when Jerry suggested, in a very roundabout sort of way,
that perhaps I'd like to go out for a drink with a friend of hers,
I tentatively agreed. He was an actor, a really lovely guy, and we
had a few dates. It was so wonderful to be showered with compli-
ments and lavished with attention by a smart, handsome man.
We would sit and talk for hours about the world, culture, spiritu-
ality – everything. It made me realize how few conversations I'd
had in my marriage. And here was someone who was not only
talking to me about anything – from outer space to organic
farming – he was asking my opinions *and* listening to my replies!
We only saw each other for a few dates as it was far too soon for
me to get into another relationship, but it was such a huge help
in building myself up again and we're still friends.

I had been on my own for six months when my best friend
Lorraine and her husband Simon came over to London from the

States for a visit. We were driving to lunch one day when I realized we were passing near Ronnie's new flat and suggested we take a quick detour to have a look at the place. We pulled up outside the building and I sat in the car staring up at the window.

My husband is in there with a 19-year-old girl, I thought. *How weird is that?*

I waited for the familiar rush of sadness or anger, but it didn't come. All I felt was a sense of how surreal the situation was; that I had been with someone for all those years and now here he was, living in this unfamiliar place, leading a totally separate life. It was just … bizarre.

'You okay, Jo?' Lorraine was looking at me with concern.

'Yes,' I said, with a smile. 'I'm really fine.'

And I really was.

*　*　*

The first Christmas without Ronnie was strange. The hardest part was waking up in Holmwood on my own; all the kids had spent Christmas Eve with their own families, but Leah had put Polaroids around the house with little messages – 'Morning, Mummy!' 'Happy Christmas!' – and they joined me later for a big Christmas dinner.

A few days later, Jerry and I took all our kids on holiday to a beautiful little safari lodge in Kenya. Early one morning we set off through the bush to hike up a nearby mountain, and as I started to climb, feeling a little daunted by what was ahead, I suddenly remembered the date. It was 2 January – my wedding anniversary. *Right*, I thought. *If I can get to the top of this mountain, I can do anything.* With a burst of determination, I stormed up to the top, reaching the summit just as the sun rose, and as I stood there taking in the incredible views across the endless miles of African bush I felt utterly elated. *I can do anything …*

Later that holiday we flew to Manda Bay, one of my favourite beach spots in the world, and it was there that I had an idea for a project that I'm still involved with. I had mentioned to Leah's husband Jack that I'd been to this great place in London called the Double Club.

'Oh, yes. It's a pop-up nightclub,' he said.

I'd never heard the term before. 'Pop-up? What's that?'

As Jack started telling me about the explosion of pop-up clubs, restaurants, shops and galleries, I had a light-bulb moment. *I should turn Holmwood into a pop-up organic restaurant.* I could use the vegetables from my garden and eggs from my chickens. Arthur Potts Dawson, who had done such a great job with the food at the Harrington Club, could be the chef. I would talk to everyone who came about sustainable living and prove that an eco lifestyle could be luxurious. I was so excited that I couldn't wait to get back to London to get started. Jamie thought it was a terrible idea, but I went ahead and did it anyway.

The following summer I opened Mrs Paisley's Lashings at Holmwood for three weeks. The name was inspired by something I'd seen in a magazine: 'Mrs Marmite's Lover'. I loved getting the house ready, laying the tables with all my mismatched crockery, using jam jars for glasses and tin cans to hold the flower arrangements. As they enjoyed a pre-dinner cocktail, diners could watch Arthur walk to my vegetable garden and pick the food that they would be eating in a couple of hours. All the ingredients came from within a five-hour radius of London. As well as celebrities like Kate Moss, Heston Blumenthal, Noddy

Holder and Gary Kemp, I hosted people from the eco world and members of the public – it was open to everyone.

At first I think people just came to have a nose around the house, but as it became obvious that this wasn't a gimmick, word of mouth spread and they came for the food. I even had a couple from Mexico who had read about the restaurant online and flown over especially for dinner!

On the first three-week opening of Mrs Paisley's Lashings we had 25 people a night, but by the fourth and final three-week stint we had built that up to nearly 60. As I had proved to myself that morning on the mountain in Kenya, if you put your mind to it, you really can do anything.

31

I was so excited and nervous it felt like a whole flock of butterflies was fluttering in my stomach. I had been dreaming about this moment for weeks – and now it was finally here.

'Jo,' he said softly, as he took me in his arms. 'Look at me.'

I glanced up to find his eyes staring into mine with shocking intensity. Then, without warning, he pulled me to him with such force that I gasped. Our bodies were now pressed together so closely that I was aware of the rise and fall of his chest, the warmth of his skin. I just hoped he couldn't feel my heart, which was now galloping in anticipation.

Come on, Jo, try to focus ...

Somehow I managed to speak. 'Is my tummy supposed to be touching yours?'

'Yes, Jo,' he said.

'Are ... are my boobs meant to be pressed against your chest?' My voice came out as a whisper.

'Yes, Jo. That's one of the perks of my job.'

'Just go easy on me, please,' I muttered, as the music started. 'I've never done the tango before.'

He grinned at me. 'Go easy on you? Not a chance ...'

* * *

In February 2009 I got a call from the BBC asking if I wanted to be a contestant on *Strictly Come Dancing*. I had already been approached to appear on *I'm A Celebrity, Get Me Out of Here!* and *Celebrity Big Brother*, both of which I had turned down without a moment's hesitation. The idea of being stuck with a load of strangers, either in a jungle or a house, was highly unappealing. *Strictly Come Dancing*, though, was different. I'd always wanted to learn to dance properly. I was pretty good at hitting the floor in clubs, so I reckoned I might even have some natural talent, and I'd often watched the Stones on stage and imagined how fabulous it must feel to be up there entertaining everyone. But more than just a chance to unleash my inner show-off, it seemed like the perfect opportunity to do something in the public eye as my own person, not just as Ronnie's ex-wife. As a friend of mine kept reminding me: in the wake of a split, when one door closes, another opens – and now I felt ready to cha-cha-cha straight on through. After thinking it over for a few months, in the summer of 2009, while I was busy with Mrs Paisley's Lashings, I accepted the BBC's offer to appear in the next series of *Strictly*. My mother was *thrilled*.

* * *

It was a scorching late-summer day when I made my way to Television Centre in Shepherd's Bush for the first day of filming on *Strictly*. It was the show's big press launch, at which we contestants would be introduced to the world's media – and also to our professional partners. After a quick chat with the producers, I was led to a dressing room where I was told my partner would come to meet me. It would be the first moment either of us knew who we were paired with for the show. I sat there sweltering in the little windowless room (I was wearing a leather jacket but didn't want to take it off and ruin my carefully put-together look) and all the time I was thinking, *Please, please, don't let it be that guy, Brendan Cole.* I'd barely watched the show before, but I'd heard enough about his reputation – how he was an absolute slave driver with a terrible temper – to put me right off.

After a few anxious minutes a camera crew came in and positioned themselves to capture my reaction, and then the door opened and in walked … 'Oh, *hiiiii*, Brendan!'

As we chatted, I began to think that perhaps he wasn't so bad after all – little did I know what a good friend he would become.

* * *

The first dance I performed on the show was a group dance, the mambo, with the other celebrities. It was during our very first rehearsal that my fantasy of being revealed as a great undiscovered dancing talent vanished in a blur of forgotten steps and flailing arms. I was useless – although at that early stage, I couldn't have imagined exactly *how* useless – but I had such a laugh that I didn't really care. Besides, I felt sure I'd improve with some one-to-one tuition with Brendan.

I know the viewers like to think it's all bitchiness and diva tantrums backstage, but I got on brilliantly with everyone. There's such a warm and supportive atmosphere and all the other celebrities and professional dancers seemed to want me to do well – probably because they knew I wasn't going to be much competition! Among the contestants I grew particularly friendly with were Zoe Lucker, Natalie Cassidy and Ricky Whittle ... Well, in fact, most of them. As for the presenters, I'd known Tess Daly since she and her husband, Vernon Kay, used to come to the Harrington, so it was lovely to see her again, while Sir Bruce Forsyth was exactly the same off camera as he was on. I was thrilled one week when he told me I was his favourite, even though I think it was probably a sympathy vote.

Then there were the dresses. For a fashion junkie like myself, the show was absolute frock heaven! At the start of production I had a morning in the BBC costume department trying on racks of dresses so that the show's producers could work out what style I felt comfortable in and how much skin I was happy to expose. It was like the most fabulous dressing-up box ever. I was so excited by all the frills and feathers and flounces that I just said yes to everything.

With the group dance out of the way (pretty shakily in my case) my first solo dance with Brendan was the Tango. They had wanted the two of us to perform to a Rolling Stones track, but I said absolutely no way – the whole point of me going on the show was to leave all that behind – so in the end we settled on David Bowie's 'Let's Dance'. The music was the least of my worries, though: I couldn't get the hang of the dance at all. It wasn't just the steps and intensity of the rehearsals that I struggled with, I was totally unprepared for how close the tango requires you to be to your partner.

I've never been a very touchy-feely person, so to be pulled up hard against Brendan's body while his leg slid between mine was something I initially found very uncomfortable. You don't usually have that kind of physical intimacy with anyone but a lover, but this was Brendan whom I'd just met and was barely on air-kissing terms with. I would find myself pulling away, but Brendan would just pull me straight back in. It was very intense. I can totally understand why so many celebrities who appear on that show end up having an affair with their dance partner. If I'd been 20 years younger and Brendan had been single … Well, you can easily imagine it happening. On our series alone the boxer, Joe Calzaghe, got together with his partner, Kristina Rihanoff, and actress Ali Bastian with Brian Fortuna – and those were just the ones we found out about!

Despite my fears, I couldn't have asked for a better partner than Brendan. He was so good to me, despite my total lack of confidence and ability. It took me ages to pick up the steps and at one point I ended up in tears of sheer frustration, which, of course, the ever-present camera crew loved. I stormed out of the rehearsal room and they followed me, so I ran out to the car park – and they followed me there, too! (If they wanted tears, they'd picked the right person for the show. I cry at *Britain's Got Talent*.) Most of the time, though, Brendan and I had a brilliant laugh, and if it all got too much for me, he would just say, 'Come on, Jo-jo, let's go and get a coffee,' and we'd start afresh a bit later.

* * *

It was Saturday, and in a few hours' time Brendan and I would perform our tango for millions on live TV. Although the show didn't start until the evening, we contestants had to be there by about 10 a.m. so the team had enough time to get everyone ready. You'd be in Hair and Makeup quite early, which meant you'd be walking around in sweatpants and false eyelashes for most of the day.

There was no official rehearsal time on the Saturday, but Brendan and I stood in the corridor outside the studio frantically going through the tango steps. It was not going at all well.

'I can't do it, I can't do it, I can't do it,' I said, stamping my feet in frustration.

'Jo, yes, you can,' said Brendan, patiently. 'We've gone through this enough times, so when you get out there your feet will know what to do.'

Feeling far from reassured, I went and got into my dress, a gorgeous red and black lacy number, and tried to think positive thoughts, but then the show's theme music started and the nerves kicked in like you wouldn't believe. The other contestants seemed so calm, but they were used to performing in front of people as part of their day jobs, whether they were sportspeople, actors or presenters. I'd never done anything like this before. They would very sweetly try to empathize with me, saying, 'Gosh, I'm really nervous, too!' but I'd just think, *You have no idea …*

As the show went on, I sat backstage, staring at the board that lists each couple's name in the order we were scheduled to perform that night. *Oh, God, only three more couples to go … Only two more couples to go … Only one more couple to go –* and I still *can't remember the steps!*

My mouth was dry and I had butterflies like you wouldn't believe. I don't think I will ever experience nerves like that again.

Brendan kept saying to me, 'This is just excitement, Jo! You're *excited* about doing this!'

'No, Brendan,' I said. 'These really are nerves. Believe me.'

When it was our turn, I stepped out onto the dance-floor and got into the starting position with a terrified smile plastered across my face. I kept reminding myself of what Brendan had said, that I'd be able to do the steps without even thinking, but as the applause died down and the music started I found that my feet didn't have any more of a clue about what to do than the rest of me did. I was screwed. Poor Brendan ended up throwing me round the dance-floor. Afterwards he told me that he had looked down at my face at the very start and had known in that instant that I had forgotten the whole thing.

He gave me a huge hug when we finished, but the ordeal wasn't over yet. Now it was time for the judges' comments – and if anything, I was dreading that more than the performance. The idea of having to stand in front of the panel while they picked holes in my performance (and, let's be honest, there were a lot of holes to pick) was daunting to say the least.

Craig kicked things off and, as I feared, it wasn't good. 'You were a disaster, *daaaah*ling,' he said.

Alesha and Bruno were a bit more encouraging, saying they were sure I'd get better, and Len, especially, was lovely to me.

'The one good thing about you is that you have a go,' he said, cheerily. 'Have-a-go Jo!'

But despite the mixed reviews, as Bruce gave me a consolatory kiss and sent Brendan and me up the sparkly stairs to chat to Tess and get our scores, I felt weirdly elated. Okay, so I might not have remembered much of the dance, but at least I hadn't tripped over! I didn't even mind that the judges only gave us 18 out of 40. Brendan told me that it was better to be at the bottom or the top of the scoreboard: if you were in the middle people forgot you. So, from that perspective, it was better to be terrible than quite good! Perhaps the tango wasn't my dance anyway, and – as the public voted to keep me in – I vowed to do better next week.

After the show everyone went upstairs to the BBC bar for a drink, which was when Craig came over and said, 'Just remember, darling, it's all theatre.' It was his way of telling me that I shouldn't take his bitchy comments personally – and from then on I was never offended by his remarks, not even when he told me that the best part of my rhumba was when I was 'standing still'. I knew it was all pantomime and he was the wicked witch (although he might well have had a point).

I was stunned when Brendan and I were voted through to the next round, as I was convinced I would be out first. It gave my flagging confidence such a boost and made me determined to do a better job next week. In the early stages of the competition I still had high hopes that I'd make a miraculous turnaround and suddenly become this fantastic dancer. I really did try my hardest at every dance, and perhaps that was obvious because week after week the public kept voting Have-a-go Jo back in.

For the next six weeks my diary looked something like this: Monday was the first day of rehearsals and a bit of a high point of the week, as I would be excited about learning the new dance. Tuesday would usually end in tears, as I'd get home and start panicking because I couldn't remember any of the steps. On Wednesday I would finally start to get the hang of it and feel a surge of hope – *Perhaps I can do this after all!* Thursday was spent going over and over the steps, trying to perfect them (I never did). On Friday we had the dress rehearsal, and Saturday was the live show, when I would forget everything I'd learnt that week.

I never once got through a dance without making mistakes. Yet throughout the whole process, Brendan remained unwaveringly patient and upbeat. The two of us got on so well. He would occasionally get a bit frustrated with me: 'We've just been through that for 10 whole minutes and now you've forgotten!' but we never had any big rows. I didn't suffer from any aches or pains, either. It must have helped that I was fit when I started, as I was one of the only contestants who didn't have to see the show's doctor – and I was one of the oldest, as well!

I was so touched by all the support from the public during my time on *Strictly* – and from my family and friends who came to sit in the audience and cheer me on. The only one who didn't was Jamie: he said his nerves just couldn't cope. Although Ronnie and I still weren't really speaking at this stage, I know he was watching at home because he told the kids he was voting for me every week.

At the time I had become friends with Christopher Wicks, a fashion designer from Manchester who now lives in Los Angeles, and he was brilliant at giving me long-distance pep-talks when I got in from another disastrous rehearsal. 'Come on, babe, you can do this,' he'd say. 'I believe in you!' We used to talk all the time on the phone and now we see each other whenever he comes to town: he's one of those people I have such a laugh with.

My highest-scoring dance of the series was the Viennese waltz, with 23 out of 40. It was the only time I came off the dance-floor feeling I'd made quite a good job of it, but then Craig burst my bubble by telling me I'd waltzed like 'a jumping bush kanga-roo'. I found I was not the natural dancer I'd hoped, and dancing in a club, when all you've got to worry about is moving in time to the music, is very different from Ballroom or Latin where you've got to remember the steps, what to do with your arms, whether to carry your weight in your toes or your heels, and a million other things.

On week six Brendan and I danced the samba, which I'd hoped would be a high point after my Rio carnival experience, but on the night my timing went out of the window, and once your timing goes wrong, your feet go wrong, and it's all over. In Bruno's words, I 'dragged poor Brendan into samba hell'. I got just 14 out of 40, which was then the lowest score for that dance in the show's history. In the bottom two for the first time after the public vote, I was facing a dance-off with Jade Johnson, the Olympic track athlete, and there was no way in the world I was ever going to style that one out. I was going home. And as I walked down the corridor at the BBC on that last night, sad to go but elated that I'd come so far, I promptly tripped and fell flat on my face. *Phew*, I thought, as I picked myself up. *Thank God I didn't do that on telly.*

I was actually quite relieved to go. I knew it was going to get harder when the contestants had to learn two dances a week – I could still barely remember one. But I felt so proud to have been there for six weeks and – despite the nerves and the low scores – I had loved every sequin-sprinkled, fake-tanned moment of the whole *Strictly* experience.

32

When I was younger my life was completely focused on the world of fashion: the people I worked and partied with were models, photographers, designers and retailers. When I met Ronnie, fashion made way for rock 'n' roll; I gave up my career and drifted out of touch with many of my friends. When my marriage ended and I started again where I'd left off all those years ago, I decided to focus on my passion for fashion.

I'd always loved going to fashion shows, and was really pleased when I was invited to attend the London College of Fashion graduate show and check out the designers of the future: even more so when I arrived to discover I had been seated in the front row. I was looking around, soaking up the pre-show atmosphere and remembering my own catwalk days, when a very dapper gentleman came and sat down next to me.

'Jo?'

I turned to him. *Could it be ...?* 'Harold! How are you?'

I couldn't believe it. Talk about a blast from the past! It was Harold Tillman, former friend of my former husband Peter Greene, fashion entrepreneur and now chairman of the British Fashion Council. I'd barely seen him and his girlfriend – now wife – Stephanie, since we'd had those holidays in the South of France while I was married to Peter.

Harold and I went for a drink after the show, and met up a few days later for lunch at Cipriani. Harold was fabulous company and a fashion oracle, but it was wonderful for me to spend time with someone who had known me from my past. When I was talking to him I felt respected for who I was, rather than who I had been married to. Harold and his friends Marshall and Chris have become my buddies (again!) and I often meet up with them at fashion and charity events.

In many ways, my life seemed to be coming full circle. I started to do bits of modelling again, on the catwalk for Vivienne Westwood at London Fashion Week and in a Fashion for Relief charity show alongside Kate Moss and Naomi Campbell. Then in 2011 I was asked to style a fashion show at a vintage festival. I dressed the twelve models, each in three changes of outfit, entirely in clothes from my own vintage collection. Ozzie Clark, Biba, Jean Muir, Yves St Laurent – it was such a buzz to see all the gorgeous items I'd collected over the years on the catwalk.

It was at another fashion show, this time for organic and sustainable clothing, that I met Safia Minney, the founder of the Fairtrade fashion label, People Tree. Safia is hugely passionate about her cause and, as we were chatting, she asked if I would like to visit Bangladesh to see Fairtrade fashion in action.

'Yeah, that would be great!' I said, caught up in her enthusiasm. 'When are we going?'

It was only when I got home that I thought, *Where the bloody hell is Bangladesh?*

* * *

The slums of Dhaka are built high on bamboo stilts to keep them out of the floodwaters of the Ganges. A system of ladders and gangplanks links this sky-city of huts, some of which are built several storeys high. As I picked my way across a narrow plank between buildings, stretching to reach over a gap, all I could think of was the baby I had just seen crawling happily along the precarious pathway. The water was a few metres below us, although you couldn't see it beneath the gently bobbing blanket of rubbish, filth and sewage. What if the baby fell down there?

I had been in Dhaka for two days and was stunned by the conditions in the slums. The stink oozing up from the waters below was so overpowering that I got a headache within minutes of arriving. Seen through my Western eyes, there seemed to be disasters waiting to happen at every turn. Not just those terrifying gangways or the stacked-up corrugated-iron buildings, which looked poised to tumble like a dominoes at any moment, but I spotted numerous bits of makeshift hosepipe connected to the gas mains. In one house I was shown round there were something like 140 people living in a higgledy-piggledy network of rooms. They'd just kept building up and up, linking it all with a series of ladders. The biggest surprise, though, was just how immaculate the whole place was. Each room was swept spotlessly clean; the beds were made; everything was folded neatly. Despite the shocking poverty, the inhabitants were clearly house-proud.

The conditions in the slums were in acute contrast to those in Swallows, a development programme in a village six hours' drive out of Dhaka in north-west Bangladesh, where local workers produced clothing for People Tree. I've never been somewhere so far away from what you might call civilization – although

Swallows itself is the very definition of civilized. The village is largely run by women and is self-sufficient, with its own school, a crèche, learning programmes and an organic garden. It was such a fantastic, inspiring place.

I spent four days there, talking with the women, singing and dancing with the children, learning to make chapattis. They also showed me how they made poo sticks, which are basically sticks covered with dried cow dung that are used to light fires, but I passed up the chance to have a go at making some myself. During the trip we also travelled on a boat down the nearby Ganges, where we saw freshwater dolphins, and visited a local market. It was literally like stepping back in time to when Jesus was around: the warren of passageways was lit by lanterns; there were people in long robes; sacks of spices and bunches of herbs; old-fashioned scales on the stalls. It was an amazing trip, and one that opened my eyes to issues I'd known little about.

*   *   *

In the summer of 2010 I went to San Diego with Jamie and his family for a month's holiday. I met up with Lorraine and we spent a week together at a spa in Palm Springs called We Care – except they didn't really care at all, because they starved us and sent us out on hikes fuelled by nothing but fresh juices and colonic irrigation.

While I was in California I also went to visit my friend Doris La Frenais, wife of the legendary comedy writer Ian and a brilliant, crazy artist herself, who possibly had an even more hedonistic youth than I did. As a belated birthday present, Doris had booked me on a three-day course with a mystic and spiritual leader called Sadhguru. I was a little sceptical (not least because the course was at the Ritz-Carlton Hotel in Los Angeles – hardly your typical guru hangout) but off I went.

There were about fifty of us on the course, a mix of Americans, Europeans and Indians. Many were unhappy or had lost their way and were looking to Sadhguru for answers; others, like me, were just curious and open to new ideas. Sadhguru talked to us about how to live a good, positive life and led us in yoga and meditation practice. During one of the group sessions I stuck up my hand and said, 'Hey, Sadhguru, I'm pretty happy anyway, so what can all this do for me?' He talked about the importance of yoga and meditation and how, if you do it twice a day, it will bring you to a higher level of consciousness. His philosophy is all about living in the now, rather than dwelling on the past or worrying about the future, because you can do nothing to change what has happened or will happen. It was a great lesson for me. He was an inspiring figure and his charitable Isha Foundation was clearly doing fantastic work in tackling environmental issues in India.

When he spoke about a pilgrimage he was making to India and the sacred Mount Kailash in Tibet later that year, I put my name down for it straight away. *A pilgrimage!* It sounded just like the sort of thing you should be doing if you were trying to redis-cover yourself.

I roped in my right-hand woman, Emily, and off we went for a month. We started at Sadhguru's ashram in India, where we saw his community projects – including Project GreenHands, which has replanted millions of trees in Tamil Nadu – then trav-elled on to Nepal and Tibet. It was the most exhilarating, eye-opening journey of my life.

I knew it was going to be quite basic, but I had no idea quite *how* basic. We drove across miles and miles of Tibetan plain, which looks a lot like the surface of the moon but with herds of yak everywhere, and camped or stayed in local guesthouses along the way. When we got to Mount Kailash we hiked up as far as we could go and watched pilgrims making their way around the mountain, the most devout of them prostrating themselves on the ground and praying at every step. We were told it would take them over a month to circumnavigate the 50-kilometre track.

There were so many fabulous things about Tibet, but the toilets were definitely not one of them. I won't dwell on the gory details – suffice to say I could never face using them and always went outside behind a rock (there were no bushes at that alti-tude). And much as I love curry, by the end of the trip I was struggling to eat it three times a day. But a little discomfort was a small price to pay for the incredible sights we saw and the people we met, and it occurred to me that I would probably never have had such an amazing adventure had I still been married to Ronnie. The two of us had had adventures, but they were nearly always in five-star comfort. Nowadays I'd always take an adventure to some far-flung wilderness over lying on a perfectly manicured beach – although I do still enjoy that, too!

*   *   *

All this time, the divorce was dragging on and on. It wasn't Ronnie's fault, because anytime I had a problem I could pick up the phone and talk to him. I'd vowed to myself I wouldn't be bitter about the split, so the first Christmas after he'd left I'd invited him to Christmas Eve drinks and caviar with the family. (He turned up with Jimmy White in tow.) We'd been on speaking terms ever since – although it was always me who made the effort. The reason for the delays was lawyers.

Unsurprisingly, I found the process pretty bruising. I was utterly devastated when, as part of the settlement, I had to put my Organics company into liquidation. It was so precious to me, but there was no way I could afford to finance it without Ronnie as guarantor. I bought back my remaining stock, continued to sell it through my office and started hatching plans for a new company.

By January 2011, after months of negotiation, we were finally nearing an agreement in the divorce. I was on holiday in Miami with Lorraine when she asked what I was going to do with the money from the settlement. 'Have you thought about investing it in property?' she asked.

The very next day we went to look at apartments by the beach. I was so taken with one of them, in a seventies block by the seafront, that in a moment of madness I put in a crazy offer, never imagining it would be accepted. It was – and even though my divorce was yet to be finalized, I nervously started the process of buying an apartment.

I finally got the keys in April 2011, just two weeks after our divorce had been agreed. I might have lost a husband, but I had gained an apartment. The place was painted white throughout when I first saw it; it took me two manic weeks, with Lorraine's help, to transform it into a vintage gem. I was determined not to buy anything new for the place, apart from a bed and a TV; everything else we sourced from second-hand shops and junk-yards. With vintage wallpaper throughout – a brown-gold shell design in the main bedroom and a gorgeous pattern of dancing women in the spare room – I indulged all my interior-design fantasies and created a gorgeous retreat that was totally Jo.

33

I t is only now, with a few years' hindsight, that I realize there was nothing to be afraid of outside the golden prison. Nowadays I am completely in control of my life and free to do exactly what I want to do when I want to do it. I get respect for my own achievements. I'm not going to lie – I do miss being absolutely spoilt and receiving the sort of service where people bend over backwards for you. That *is* wonderful! But if you're constantly treated like a cosseted child, you can sometimes start to behave like one, too. In that respect, stepping outside the Rolling Stones was a huge growing-up process for me – and I think I have now grown into the person I was meant to be all along. And while I might not fly first class every time, these days, I'll take freedom and independence over a bit of extra leg-room any day.

As for my future – well, I'm just taking each day as it comes and enjoying my friends, children and grandchildren. I'd love to get my Organics business up and running again and am currently in talks about a new licensing deal, so watch this space. And hopefully Mrs Paisley's Lashings will be popping up again some-time soon. And I still want to save the planet and turn everyone organic! As for my love life, if the right man came along then of course I'd consider getting married again. Third time lucky, perhaps? But if he doesn't, I can honestly say I'm happy just the way I am.

I was looking back through my diaries while I was writing this book and found a note from my mum, slipped into the pages of 2002. 'Confucius say, "If you are not happy you must make yourself happy," it read. "'It is easier to wear a pair of slippers than try and carpet the whole world.'"

Looking back now, I can't imagine where my head was at when I first read that note. At the time I was struggling with Ronnie's alcoholism after he'd had yet another failed stint in rehab, and our dear friend Chuch had died from a heart attack. I was quite lost, but while I didn't realize it at the time, it had been clear to those closest to me. Things are very different, these days. Nowadays I am proudly wearing my slippers, day in and day out.

* * *

Ronnie and I rebuilt our friendship slowly. He rang to tell me he was having the most terrible arguments with Katia, and I spoke to him after he was arrested for fighting in the street with her, just to check he was okay. About a year after the split, I went to visit Jamie at his home in Cobham and was taking my grandson Charlie to the movies in nearby Esher when I saw Ronnie sitting in a restaurant window with a young girl. I knew he was renting a house in Surrey (well, it was more of a castle, really) but it was still a shock to see him sitting there. It was the first time I'd seen him in the flesh since he had left and I thought about walking past, but then I said to Charlie, 'Look, there's Granddad!' and we went in to see him. It was all very friendly: the girl was sweet, and Ronnie asked us to join them for a drink, but I told him we had to be getting home. I left the restaurant feeling a little shaken, but glad to have seen Ronnie – and certainly with no sense of regret that we were apart, or longing that we were still together.

These days Ronnie and I are friends and I'll happily pick up the phone to him. At the time of writing, he is happy with his latest girlfriend, Sally Humphreys, and has been sober for a year. (We actually met Sally years ago, when Ronnie had an exhibition of his artwork at Drury Lane and she was working at the theatre dressed as Moll Flanders.) Ronnie might have done some shitty things in the past, but when I think back on all those years we spent together, it's the many good times that I now focus on. It still feels a bit weird when I see him, though; I suppose it always will. He's just so instantly familiar to me that I look at him and think, *Gosh, I loved that man so much for so long, I know every hair on his head, every little thing about his face and hands …* But it's like it was another lifetime. I will always love Ronnie, but now it's with a feeling of warmth and familiarity. Anything more than that has faded.

Ronnie's never apologized for what happened either to me or the kids – I don't think he feels he has anything to apologize for – although he came close at the beginning of 2012. I was round at his house, dropping off some of his belongings, and he was talking about a new girl who was flying in to see him at the weekend.

'I still haven't found the one, Jo,' he said, wearily.

'You won't, Ronnie,' I said. 'You had her and you lost her a few years ago. It was me.'

He paused, took a drag on his cigarette. 'You live and learn,' he said, eventually.

* * *

313

I stood on the street looking up at the elegant Georgian house – *my house*, I thought with a smile. It was set back from the street behind an overgrown front garden, and now I climbed the stone steps that wove among the creeper-covered trees to the front door. With a shiver of excitement, I put my key in the lock for the first time as the house's new owner.

It was July 2011 and after years of living in the suburbs, I had found the home of my dreams among the fab restaurants and boutiques of London's leafy Primrose Hill. It had been love from the moment I'd first laid eyes on the place, although clearly it hadn't been redecorated since the seventies and was in need of a makeover. It looked sad and unloved, and the rooms were crammed with furniture and old books; the current owner had four lodgers so there were three kitchens, one on each floor. But it was a beautiful building with so much potential – and I do love a project. I'd put in an offer after that first viewing.

And now the house was mine and I was looking around it as its proud owner. I had builders starting work tomorrow – rewiring, replacing the roof, ripping out the kitchens – but I wanted to enjoy this moment, just me and my gorgeous new home. As I wandered from room to room, amazed at how much space there was now it was empty, I could see in my mind how I would transform the place: a big new kitchen in the basement, an organic vegetable patch in the back garden, vintage carpet on the stairs, antique lace at the front windows … It would be a huge amount of work, but I knew that I would have enormous fun doing it.

Eventually I reached the top floor and looked out of the window at the back of the house. The view across the rooftops took my breath away. There was the BT Tower, a central London landmark, so close I could almost touch it. *Gosh, I'm right back in the middle of London*, I thought happily. *Back where it all started for me.*

The sun was setting, spreading rosy-pink streaks across the sky, and as I gazed out, I thought back to the dreamy girl who had climbed up a conker tree one evening to stare at the sun setting over Canvey Island. And just as I had back then, I marvelled at the world spread out below me, in all its beauty and promise, and I thought, *I wonder what extraordinary adventure life has in store for me?*